Frank Tyson
Complete Cricket Coaching

ILLUSTRATED

Pelham Books

First published in Great Britain by
PELHAM BOOKS LTD
52 Bedford Square
London WC1B 3EF
1977

First published in Australia by
Thomas Nelson (Australia) Limited
19–39 Jeffcott Street West Melbourne 3003
89–97 Jones Street Ultimo NSW 2007
95 Currie Street Adelaide 5000
and in Brisbane Qld and Perth WA
1976

Hardback ISBN 0 7207 1002 2
Paperback ISBN 0 7207 1012 X

Printed photolitho in Great Britain by
Ebenezer Baylis & Son Ltd, The Trinity Press,
Worcester, and London and bound by
Dorstel Press Ltd, Harlow

Foreword

I was playing some of my early first-class games when I encountered the 'Typhoon' Tyson. He had already made his reputation as the fastest bowler in the land, and the scourge of Australians among whom he now lives. Thankfully we met on Northamptonshire's dead pitch, but still the small insects gnawed at my belly as he raced in to bowl.

Two memories have stuck – the sight of the top of his balding head, because he approached with an exaggerated slope forwards towards the prey, and the sudden view of the spikes in his left boot. The coil of his body before delivery used to be so violent and rapid you only caught the briefest glimpse of his face.

Facing Frank Tyson left no time to observe the hints of a text book – but the skills should have been incorporated into natural talent by then. Where his particular approach to a written guide impresses me is in the thoughtful breakdown of the arts which can serve both coaches and players on the practice ground.

Even the best Test cricketers find faults creeping into their play from time to time, so how much more does it happen to the occasional player. Understanding what you are trying to achieve is vital. This book analyses it.

As a practical assistance to coaches it is original in many ways. There is no reason at all why cricket taught the Frank Tyson way is going to be boring or fruitless on the playing field. It is as expert as you would expect from a man who has played at the top level and whose job it is to nurture the grassroots.

Tony Lewis

Contents

Introduction

This coaching manual is the result of two of the main influences in my life: my forty-year love of cricket and a sixteen-year interest in teaching. Since leaving the ranks of professional cricket, I was, until my appointment as Director of Coaching for the Victorian Cricket Association, a schoolmaster, and throughout my practical teaching life, I was continually aware of the progress being made in improving methods of passing on knowledge. Scarcely a year passed without better technical aids being made available to teachers. Philosophies changed, with more and more emphasis being placed upon individual differences in students and greater use being made of pupil-motivated learning situations such as the open classroom.

My coaching career was contemporaneous with my teaching employment. As a schoolmaster I was also responsible for the cricket education of teams in extra-curricular time. Those sides ranged in age and ability from thirteen-year-olds to young adults of eighteen.

In my dual capacity as coach and teacher, I became aware of a philosophical anomaly in the minds of schoolmasters who filled the same dual role as myself. In the classroom they were enlightened and progressive, faithfully creating pupil-oriented learning situations recommended by methodology textbooks. On the sports field, however, they were unoriginal, authoritarian and not at all concerned about creating a learning atmosphere comprehensible to the student. As coaches they spoke in a cult language of technical terms understood only by themselves. The student wanted to know how to block a ball; instead he was taught the forward defensive stroke. They taught sport as they themselves had been taught. It was a time-honoured repressive teaching technique which had been handed down from generation to generation of coaches. It had not changed in fifty years and it revealed just how little cricketers knew and thought about teaching their sport.

This book is unique in two respects: it instructs coaches of cricket how to teach the sport and it reduces the explanation of the technique of cricket to a level which is easily understood by the youngest of laymen. It is a cricket coaching book for the coaches, but it is also essentially pupil orientated so that any youngster can pick it up and read in simple terms how he should execute a cricketing skill.

The manual is based on modern teaching methods and a sound practical knowledge of cricketing skills. To update the practical skills I consulted Victorian and Australian players whose contributions I gratefully acknowledge. The revised teaching methods were evolved from the advice given by lecturers in Physical Education in tertiary colleges in Victoria and throughout Australia. Often the blending of theoretical and practical skills and their application to cricket is an unhappy marriage because of the suspicion which exists between the pragmatist and the theoretician. In this manual I hope that theory blends comfortably with practical interpretation and that neither aspect seeks to dominate the learning situation.

Each lesson in the manual deals with a single cricket skill. The coach's first aim is to interest and motivate his student. He therefore tries to make him see the reason behind each skill. The coach and student are told why the cricket skill is learned. This reason becomes all the more apparent if the student is involved in a game or group activity which demands the use of that skill. The activity should resemble the parent game, be slightly competitive and contain a degree of assessment of the skill. A catalogue and description of such activities are to be found in chapter 38. It is left to the judgement of the coach to decide how best to use such activities within the context of his lessons.

The next judgement exercised in performing a skill is to decide when it should be performed. This is a more complex judgement than why. Behind the decision are considerations such as the state of the pitch, the weather and the players' weaknesses as well as how well the performer observes those conditions and can produce the requisite skill to exploit them. Thus a batsman may know that he should play a hook against a rising ball outside the leg stump, but his individual response may be too slow for him to execute the stroke. When to employ a skill differs according to each individual's ability.

Having established the reason and the timing of a skill, the coach and player learn how to perform it. The section in the manual on the body mechanics of a skill is divided into two columns. The left-hand column describes the technical biomechanics in detail and in chronological sequence but not necessarily in their order of importance.

The right-hand column translates the complex technical description of the movements into simple terms easily understood by the student. These terms are related to everyday experiences. They are not necessarily comprehensive or exact. The first steps in teaching a skill aim at communicating the basics of a skill for later polishing by constant repetition and modification. The comparisons are only intended to make communication with the student easier. The coach should not feel restricted to the exact wording in the right-hand column and he may discover other movement comparisons closer to the skill. Since cricket skills involve consecutive and associated actions, many of the biomechanical movements described in the sections on how to perform a skill overlap.

Each skill is carefully illustrated with photographs or diagrams. Check lists for coaches and students set down the points of the skill to be emphasised in a suggested order of importance. The prime requirements of any hitting or throwing skill revolve around the target to be hit and the hitting or throwing instrument: the main points to be emphasised must be to keep the eyes steadily on the ball, the wicket, and the projected bounce of the ball and to present the hitting surface to the ball as effectively as possible. I have also included sections on faults and corrective techniques listing the most common errors occurring in various skills, and giving pointers on how to diagnose and correct them.

Frank Tyson
DIRECTOR OF COACHING
THE VICTORIAN CRICKET ASSOCIATION

Acknowledgements

The author, publisher and the Victorian Cricket Association gratefully acknowledge the following for their help in the preparation of this manual.

Wally Bright; Ray Crawford, Senior Lecturer, Preston Institute of Technology; Ken Davies, Lecturer, Physical Education Department, State College of Victoria at Geelong; Dr Colin Davey, Head of the Physical Education Department, State College of Victoria at Rusden; G. E. Dickins; The Hon. Brian Dixon, Victorian Minister for Youth, Sport and Recreation; Len Diett, Lecturer, Physical Education Department, Footscray Institute of Technology; John Edwards; Norm Emerson; Ron Gaunt; Lindsay Hassett MBE; Arthur Horneman; Ian Huntington; Ian Johnson MBE, Secretary, Melbourne Cricket Club; Ray Jordan; Albert Keddie, Director General, Victorian Department of Youth, Sport and Recreation; Bill Lawry; Dennis Lillee; Ernie McCormick; Len Maddocks; George Murray; Jim Mann; Arthur Marks; Dick Mason, Australian Broadcasting Corporation; Brian Nettleton, Senior Lecturer, Physical Education Department, University of Melbourne; Stan Nicholes; Jack Potter, Lecturer, Physical Education Department, State College of Victoria at Hawthorn; Dr Frank Pyke, Physical Education Department, University of Western Australia; Ian Redpath MBE; Dr Peter Reichenbach, Head of the Physical Education Department, Preston Institute of Technology; Paul Sheahan; Wendy Smith; Bill Smyth, Victorian Umpires' Adviser; Garry Sparke; Dick Telford, Lecturer, Preston Institute of Technology; George Tribe; Keith Walters; Jack Watters; The Sports Goods Federation of Victoria; the Victorian Department of Education; and W. K. Tickner, chairman, and M. Gray, J. Hallebone and B. Thomas of the VCA Coaching Committee.

Our special thanks for their help with the illustrations go to Paul Sheahan, Richie Robinson, Bill Smyth, Max Walker, to the students of Geelong Grammar and Dick Johnson, and to the students of Carey Grammar and David Lord.

The Laws of Cricket are reproduced by permission of the Marylebone Cricket Club. The diagrams on pages 10, 27, 53, 55, 59, 63 and 68 are taken from *Successful Cricket* by Greg Chappell published by Pelham.

1 The coach

The coach's primary goal is to improve the player's technical skill and, through this increased proficiency, to increase his enjoyment and ability to participate. So the coach requires, beyond a knowledge about the game, an ability to communicate both his knowledge and his enthusiasm for it. His functions could be summed up as:

to encourage the players to enjoy the game;
to give the players knowledge about the game;
to enable the players to win;
to improve the individual's performance.

Teaching styles of coaches may differ. Some coaches may be authoritarian (play the forward defensive shot as I show you); some may teach by setting tasks (bowl 8 balls short of a length outside off stump. See how well you do.). Some teach by partner involvement (one partner informs the other during a drill that he is playing across the line); some by individual programmes (each batsman plays 8 cover drives, then 8 leg glances). Some teach by guided discovery (ask the question: how would you deal with a bowler pitching short outside the off stump?); others by problem solving. These styles move from an authoritarian approach through to an individually centred teaching method. The coach has to decide which method best suits him and his students. The needs of his particular students may require any one of these approaches so the coach should also be adaptable and observant.

Cricketers enjoy the game for many different reasons. Some get physical satisfaction from it so the coach will need to make sure that even in the worst weather he provides an outlet for their energy. They may enjoy the activity for its own sake or the pleasure of feeling that they are performing well—that their co-ordination in a particular stroke is smooth, that they beat the ball to the boundary or that they produced an ounce of extra speed on a fast delivery—or they may simply enjoy being out in the fresh air. Some cricketers get mental satisfaction from the game. They may become fascinated by the complexities of the game or by its unpredictability or they may want to understand the mechanics of the ball's movements in the air or off the pitch. The coach will need to be able to stimulate their curiosity and to have an armoury of knowledge to answer their questions. Some cricketers like to have a sense of achievement, whether it is simply not to get out before tea or to get a record number of wickets. The coach should praise them when possible and try to prevent them becoming discouraged with themselves and with the game. Some cricketers play for the companionship being part of a team provides. Some cricketers want to be leaders; others are content to be part of a team. Some play because they are aggressive and want to beat their opponents or even hurt them. Their aggression may grow if they are in a frustrating position. Some players like to be independent. They may thrive in a formal competitive atmosphere whilst they may get very little out of a routine practice.

In every case the coach should understand why each of his students plays so that he can put them, as far as is practicable, in a situation where each will get most enjoyment out of the game. He should understand his own motives and avoid letting his own likes or dislikes affect his decisions. Much of the conflict in coaching comes from a lack of understanding between coach and pupil, a lack of knowledge that the coach has about himself or an inability to communicate because of personality differences or failure to understand the player's problems.

The coach will need to organise his teaching material and to have a clear idea of his long and short term aims. For example, in the short term, he may aim to teach the simple skill of the forward defensive stroke, but as a long term aim he should think of all the shots which might develop from it. He should also, of course, be willing to modify his approach according to his students' responses. Each lesson should fit an overall scheme of coaching. Beyond this he must be able to organise equipment, time-tables, practices and so on so that he makes the best use of his and his students' time.

This book advocates the introduction into cricket coaching of as much constructive learning and interaction and communication between students and coach as possible. Problems and policy should be discussed and a collective solution sought. Coaching is a two-way process between coach and student, student and student. The coach is in a communication/interaction situation with individuals and with groups. He should be able to adapt to any situation he finds himself in. One of the most effective methods of encouraging communication and interaction is the group activity. Players are grouped with their peers and friends and the competitive atmosphere of more formal teaching approaches which may discourage the less confident students is played down.

Communication is the key to success in coaching. The coach's statements should be to the point, simple, clear and well timed. He should avoid being too technical and always discuss a specific issue directly with the person for whom it is intended instead of giving the students a general instruction or leaving them to make their own inferences. Since communication is a two-way process, the cricketer must also communicate with his coach. The coach should always be willing to listen and be approachable and available. Ask if your students do not understand. Hold regular players' meetings for discussion between player and player. Ask the player how he thinks he is performing. Involve yourself with the side.

If the coach gives support, advice and opinion to a cricketer about his performance, this will encourage the cricketer to repeat and improve his performance. Encouragement and advice should be given immediately after the performance, and the cricketer should know exactly what is being praised or criticised.

A coach can also correct a bad performance with punishment. This method may work quickly to prevent bad performances but it does not get at the cause. If a punishment routine is to be successful, it should be used every time and no lapse overlooked, and it should increase in intensity. Two punishment laps of the oval for a fielding error will have no effect if the cricketer can do it easily. Punishment may give the coach a sense of power but it will also cause resentment. If the coach does punish a player, he should do so unemotionally, and demonstrate the correct performance to the cricketer. As a general principle the coach should minimise failure.

The coach helps the student to see information in its proper perspective. Within a well-designed coaching programme, he helps players plan their own activities and skills practices. He helps to cement relationships between the members of the side by sharing in discussions with the cricketers, planning well ahead and outlining his goals and aims, planning and giving reasons for his practice routines, emphasising quality not quantity in skills practice, initiating new practice ideas and refusing to interrupt practice activities.

The coach should always hold his position with the agreement and support of the players. His leadership will depend upon:

his own personality;
the needs, attitudes, problems and interests of his pupils;
the relationships between members of the team. (Can he afford to be a leader to some and a tyrant to others?);
the exact nature of the sport and the cricketers' tasks. (The batsmen will need individual leadership in skills, whilst fieldsmen will need a co-ordinator of their activities.);
the needs of the situation. (Each team will have particular needs to make it more productive—encouragement, instruction, discipline, etc.)

The coach's advice to his students must be constructive, unguarded and genuine. He should be sensitive to the cricketer's problems and give his advice unconditionally. He should respect the cricketer's confidence so that he will feel secure and free to come to him at any time.

To communicate how to perform a particular cricket skill, the coach should be able to say not only 'do as I say' but 'do as I show you what to do'. He needs to know the theory of the front foot drive, and to be able to demonstrate it for imitation by his students. Demonstration helps the learner identify the skill. It should be one of the first steps in teaching.

When demonstrating a cricket skill, always bear in mind that the demonstration should be at the level of the ability of the student. Young children can only learn a limited number of movements at a time and remember these movements for a limited time. With young students it is better to make one important point about a stroke, which may lead to other correct movements, than to risk confusing them with less important points or the more complicated movements.

Demonstrate the skill at normal speed, since this is how the shot or bowling action will be executed under match conditions. If you analyse the skill in slow motion at one stage, remember to finish the demonstration at normal speed. Give brief descriptive comments before and during the demonstration, but don't theorise about the stroke or action. Before you start decide what is the main point of the demonstration. This will determine the positions of the coach and the class. For instance, straight back lift and the proximity of the bat to pad is more easily seen with the coach and class facing one another. The length of a delivery is more easily seen with the class watching from a side-on position. Bear in mind considerations such as the ability of the students to hear and see the demonstration and the effect of outside conditions such as wind and sun.

Always repeat the demonstration until the student has absorbed the main points even when this means repeating the demonstration very many times. It is useful to tell the watchers to try the stroke or skill as soon as they are clear what to do.

Always encourage the student. Tell him what he is doing right. While you should not reinforce a wrong action by allowing it to go uncorrected, minimise the fault and underline the good aspects of the performance.

2 The elementary skills

A mastery of the elementary skills of hitting, stopping, throwing, catching is necessary to give students a grasp of the ball skills needed in the game. They provide an introduction to the more formal skills of batting, bowling, fielding and wicketkeeping. The left-hand column describes the technical skill; the right-hand column the same skill in simple terms.

Remember: Be balanced.
Watch the ball.

Hitting	
Just before the ball is delivered, swing the bat back. This back swing enables you to put power into your stroke.	You are Tony Greig waiting for Dennis Lillee to bowl; swing the bat back before he bowls and get ready to strike.
Watch the ball before delivery, during its flight and on to the hitting surface.	Keep your eyes on the ball. Push your head towards it so that your eyes are right behind the path of its flight.
In most cases your body should be side-on to the direction in which you will hit the ball.	Point your leading shoulder at the ball.
In most hitting skills transfer your weight either forward or back but in the direction in which you will hit the ball. At the same time you will make a corresponding foot movement.	Step into the ball. Lean into the ball.
In all hitting skills you will need to follow through in the direction of the hit.	Throw your hands after the ball.
Stopping	
When stopping a ball which has been struck or thrown along the ground, the fieldsman must watch the ball right up to the time that it comes to rest in his hands.	Glue your eyes to the ball at all times.
After the ball has been struck, move quickly into the path of the ball, placing your body behind the line along which the ball is travelling as a second line of defence.	Move towards the ball and put up the barricades behind it.
Place your hands close together with the fingers pointing towards the ground behind the line of the ball.	Cup your hands together, fingers pointing to 6 o'clock.
Allow the ball to come into your hands, watching it all the way. Let your hands give with the ball to absorb its force. Never grab at it.	Don't snatch. Imagine that you are stopping a rolling raw egg.
Catching	
When catching a ball which has been struck or thrown into the air, watch the ball at all times, right up to the time that it comes to rest in your hands. The most effective catching is done above and just below eye level.	Eyes glued to the ball.

After the ball has been struck into the air, position yourself quickly in line with the flight of the ball, head and eyes behind its path.

Get behind and underneath the ball.

Stretch your arms out comfortably to receive the ball. Above and at eye level the ball can be sighted through the fingers.

Arms stretch towards the ball—relax. Sight the ball through your fingers.

The palms of your hands should face the ball. Your fingers should point up, down or to the side but never towards the ball. Your hands should be cupped together and work in unison.

Point all your fingers at 12 or 6 or 3 or 9 o'clock but never at the ball.

Let your hands give with the ball to absorb the force.

Your hands should be a mattress for the ball.

Catching low balls requires a crouched and stationary position which can be likened to sitting on the edge of a chair watching a detective movie on TV. You must be comfortable, relaxed and your weight evenly distributed, but mentally alert. Catching from this position is generally carried out close to the ground with the fingers pointing downwards and to the side. Movement into the path of the ball is limited because of the crouched position.

Catches can generally be classified into the three categories: above eye level (high outfield catches); at eye level (mid-field skimmers); and below eye level (catches which travel only a short distance quickly).

Throwing

When throwing, always watch the target.

Glue your eyes to the target.

Hold the ball in your fingers and not the palm of the hands.

Finger the ball.

In the 'cocking' action of the throw, swing the throwing arm downwards, backwards and then upwards. Your body should be side-on to the target. Your throwing arm is in a 'cocked' position when it is level with your back shoulder and the elbow bent. Stretch your front arm towards the target. Your weight should be on the rear foot and your head and eyes steady.

Draw your gun like a cowboy, then pull back your bowstring as though you were a Red Indian.

In the throw your elbow leads the arm action. Extend your throwing arm as your throwing shoulder moves forward towards the target.

Throw your elbow at the target.

Follow through with your throwing shoulder towards the target as you transfer your weight from the back to the front foot. Your arm finishes fully extended in front of your eyes.

Relax and let your body follow through on the action.

Check list
Emphasise points in this order.

Hitting
Keep your eyes on the ball and push your head towards it so that your eyes are right behind its flight.
Point your leading shoulder at the ball.
Step into the ball. Lean into the ball.
Throw your hands after the ball.
You are Tony Greig waiting for Dennis Lillee to bowl; swing the bat back and get ready.

Stopping
Eyes glued to the ball at all times.
Move towards the ball and put up the barricades behind it.
Cup your hands together, fingers pointing to 6 o'clock.
Don't snatch. Imagine that you are stopping a rolling raw egg.

Catching
Eyes glued to the ball.
Move behind and underneath the ball.
Your hands should be a mattress for the ball.
Point all your fingers at 12 or 6 or 3 or 9 o'clock but never at the ball.
Arms stretch towards the ball. Relax. Sight the ball through your fingers.

Throwing
Eyes glued to the target.
Draw your gun like a cowboy, then pull back your bowstring as though you were a Red Indian.
Throw your elbow at the target.
Relax and let your body follow through on the action.
Finger the ball.

Remember: Be balanced.
Watch the ball.

3 The batting grip and stance

The aim of gripping a bat and standing in an orthodox way is so that you will be ready to receive the bowler's delivery in a relaxed, comfortable position with the best chance of making quick, correct movements. The stance helps you to make your strokes correctly and comfortably.

Get ready to receive the ball just before or as the bowler turns at the end of his run and moves in to deliver.

Remember: Watch the ball.
Be balanced.

How to grip the bat and stand to receive the ball

The guard

When the batsman arrives at the wicket, he asks the umpire for guard by holding his bat perpendicularly in front of the wicket which he is defending. The umpire aligns the bat with the middle stump at the bowler's end and the stump which the batsman asks for.

If you want 'leg stump' or 'one leg' guard hold your bat in front of the leg stump. For 'middle and leg' or 'two leg' hold your bat between middle and leg stumps. For 'middle' or 'centre' your bat should be in line with your own middle stump. You may ask for 'off stump' but this would be unusual. Mark the guard on the batting crease with your boot or bat. This is your block mark which will give you a guide as to where you should stand in relation to the stumps which your are defending. Your guard may vary according to the bowler's tactics. Thus if a bowler attacks your leg stump, you may ask for guard on the leg stump in order to play more shots on the off-side and away from the bowler's strong field placement on the leg-side.

The grip

Grip the bat handle with both hands together near the middle. The 'V's formed by the forefinger and thumb of each hand should be aligned with the spine of the bat and also point up their respective arms at the shoulder. Hold the bat firmly but not tightly. Note that if your hands are too far apart on the handle they will not work together. If you grip the bat too low on the handle, you will not be able to drive and may scoop the ball into the air for a catch.

Place the bat on the ground in front of you, with the face of the bat downwards. Now imagine that it is an axe or a mallet and pick it up as though you were going to chop wood or hammer a tent peg. Your bat is your best friend. Grip it as though you were shaking hands with it.

Leg stump

Middle and leg stump

Centre stump

The stance

Wait for the bowler in a still, comfortable style with your front shoulder pointing up the wicket and towards the bowler's wicket. Your chest should face point. Your weight should be evenly distributed between your front and back feet, which are usually each side of the batting crease. Hold your head upright, motionless and turned towards the bowler. Look up the wicket at the bowler, with the eyes steady and level.

Grip the bat correctly, with the bottom of the bat resting in the block mark either behind or alongside the feet, and the handle leaning, with the hands, on the top of the front thigh or pad.

Imagine that you are a boxer like Mohammed Ali waiting for your opponent to attack. You are ready to move quickly, forward or back. Your chin is tucked behind your leading shoulder. Boxing like cricket is a side-on game. Watch your opponent very closely so that you do not miss any of his movements.

The bat is a very important stage prop but not a pit prop. Don't lean on it like a walking stick. Stand up and relax so that if you took your hands off the bat it would lean against your front leg.

Coaches often emphasise that the batsman's feet should be slightly apart, one each side of the popping crease, toes in a straight line and directed towards point. Knees should be slightly bent, and stance upright but relaxed rather than stiff. The main consideration, however, is an equal distribution of weight and comfort.

Check list

Emphasise points in this order.

Place the bat on the ground in front of you, with the face of the bat down. Now imagine that it is an axe or mallet, and pick it up as though you were going to chop wood or hammer a tent peg. Your bat is your best friend. Grip it as though you were shaking hands with it.
Imagine that you are a boxer like Mohammed Ali waiting for your opponent to attack. You are ready to move quickly, forward or back. You are relaxed like a panther. Your chin is tucked behind your leading shoulder. Watch your opponent very closely so that you do not miss any of his movements.
The bat is a very important stage prop, but not a pit prop. Don't lean on it like a walking stick. Stand up and relax so that if you took your hands off the bat it would lean against your front leg.

Remember: Watch the ball.
Be balanced.

4 The forward defensive shot

The forward defensive stroke is played to defend the wicket, without giving a catch, against a good length ball which bounces in line with or just outside the line of the stumps. This delivery is termed 'a good length ball' because it makes the batsman unsure whether to play forward or back. The ball bounces just outside the reach of the batsman stepping and stretching forward from his crease.

To build an innings you must be at the wicket to score runs. If you are out, you cannot contribute to the score. The basis of a good innings is therefore a sound defence. A defensive stroke can be adapted more quickly to an attacking shot than the reverse. Set yourself limited and attainable goals as stepping stones to larger scores. When you first go to the wicket aim at a goal of, say, twenty runs—then aim to add a further twenty runs to this ambition and so on.

Remember: Watch the ball.
Be balanced.

How to play a forward defensive stroke	Simplified hints
Back lift Lift your bat in its preparatory back swing as the bowler is about to deliver the ball. The back lift should be in line with the middle and off stumps. Control the bat with your top hand. A straight back lift ensures that these straight-batted shots are played with a greater chance of success.	Just before the bowler bowls, imagine that the wicketkeeper has tied a piece of string to the bottom of your bat and is pulling it back towards him.
Foot movement As the ball bounces on a spot just outside your reach, put your front foot forward towards and alongside the line of the ball and as close as possible to its bounce. Transfer your weight to your front foot with your front toe pointing to extra cover. This is the movement which takes the head and eyes behind the line of the ball.	As the ball bounces, stride towards it as though you were trying to step or kick alongside it.
Head and eyes As you push your front foot towards the bounce of the ball, move your head and eyes towards the spot where the ball will bounce. The position of the head and eyes towards the line of the ball is the prime requisite of any hitting skill.	Smell the ball.
Weight transference and body position In transferring your weight to the front foot, point your front shoulder towards the line of the ball. Your front elbow should be bent and pointing in the same direction. Bend your front knee slightly to maintain balance and point it towards a position just inside the line of the ball.	Lean into the ball with your front shoulder, side and elbow. Imagine that you are about to start kneeling alongside the ball and bend your front knee.

Bat swing and follow through

As the bat swings down from the top of the back lift, keep it perpendicular. Your bent front elbow will bring the bat alongside your front leg or pad leaving no gap between the two for the ball to pass through. The bat contacts the ball level with the instep of the front foot.

Almost brush the pad with the bat and try to play the ball alongside your front foot.

Check list

Emphasise points in this order.

Smell the ball.
As the ball bounces, stride towards it as though you were trying to step or kick alongside the ball.
Lean into the ball with your front shoulder, side and elbow. Imagine that you are about to start kneeling alongside the ball and bend your front knee.
Push or grind the ball into the ground.
Almost brush the pad with the bat and try to play the ball alongside your front foot.
Just before the bowler bowls, imagine that the wicketkeeper has tied a piece of string to the bottom of your bat and is pulling it back towards him.
Imagine that your back foot is pegged behind the popping crease.

Remember: Watch the ball.
Be balanced.

5 The front foot drive

The front foot drive is played to punish an overpitched ball, that is, a bad ball which does not bounce or bounces within reach of the batsman as he steps forward from the batting crease. At the same time hitting an overpitched delivery has to be carried out in the safest way. The front foot drive is played to an overpitched delivery or full toss which is in line with or outside the line of the stumps. The overpitched delivery which bounces within reach of the batsman as he steps forward is called a half volley.

The first movements for the front foot drive are identical with those for the forward defensive shot.

Remember: Watch the ball.
Be balanced.

How to play the front foot (off) drive	Simplified hints
Back lift Lift the bat in its preparatory back swing as the bowler is about to deliver the ball. Your back lift should be in line with the middle and off stumps and, since you will hit this shot hard, is higher than in the forward defensive shot. The top hand controls the bat.	Just before the bowler bowls, imagine that your bat is made of metal and the wicketkeeper has a strong magnet. He draws your bat way back and high.
Foot movement As the ball arrives full toss, or bounces within reach, move your front foot towards the line of the ball and alongside the bounce or the ball on the full, transferring your weight to the front foot. Your toe should point to extra cover. Strike the ball when it is level with the instep of your front foot. Your weight should be over the ball on contact so that you can control the shot.	As the ball arrives on the full or bounces within reach, stride towards it as though you were trying to step or kick alongside it.
Head and eyes As you push your front foot towards the line of the ball, move your head and eyes over the point of contact between bat and ball.	Smell the ball as you hit it. Look at the spot beneath your eyes where the ball has been, and imagine that there is a weight on your head.
Weight transference and body position Your front shoulder should point towards the line of the ball. Your front elbow should be bent and pointing in the same direction. Bend your front knee slightly for balance. It should also point alongside the line of the ball.	Lean into the ball with your front shoulder, side and elbow. Imagine that you are about to start to kneel alongside the ball and bend your front knee.
Bat swing and follow through By this stage you will have swung the bat down from the top of the back lift. It should be perpendicular. Your bent front elbow will enable you to swing it close to the front pad, leaving no gap between the bat and pad. Tuck your rear elbow into your side on the downswing. This will ensure a straight downswing so that you will swing the bat on the same line as the approaching ball.	Try to hit the ball alongside the front foot and as close to it as possible. Almost brush your front pad with your bat as you strike the ball.

Your bent front elbow and front shoulder will push the top of the bat blade ahead of the bottom at the point of contact with the ball.

Hit first with the top hand, then underneath the top hand with the bottom.

Follow through on the stroke. Swing your arms in the direction of the shot. Let your bat travel through and high after the point of contact, finishing over your front shoulder which points in the direction of the stroke. Your weight is now travelling beyond the front foot. Keep your head down with your eyes still on the ball. A straight follow through will indicate that you have swung the bat through in a straight plane. The follow through shows that your weight has been transferred and that the stroke has power and timing.

Throw your hands after the ball and in the direction of the stroke with the bottom hand hitting beneath the top.

Make sure your back foot stays grounded behind the front foot.

Imagine there is a weight on your back foot keeping it behind the front.

Check list
Emphasise points in this order.

Try to smell the ball as you hit it. Look at the spot beneath your eyes where the ball has been and imagine there is a weight on your head. Your eyes must be above and behind the line of the ball upon contact.
As the ball arrives on the full or bounces within reach, stride towards it as though you were trying to step or kick alongside it.
Lean into the ball with your front shoulder, side and elbow.
Imagine that you are about to start to kneel alongside the ball and bend your front knee.
Try to hit the ball alongside the front foot and as close to it as possible. Almost brush your front pad with your bat as you strike the ball.
Just before the bowler bowls, imagine that your bat is made of metal and the wicketkeeper has a strong magnet. He draws your bat way back and high.
Hit first with the top hand and then underneath the top hand with the bottom.
Imagine that there is a weight on your back foot keeping it behind the front foot.
Throw your hands after the ball and in the direction of the stroke with the bottom hand hitting beneath the top.

**Remember: Watch the ball.
Be balanced.**

6 Variations on the front foot drive

The front foot cover drive

Play the cover drive to punish an off-side overpitched ball, that is, when an overpitched delivery bounces within reach or arrives on the full toss wide of the stumps on the off-side.

The first movements of the cover drive are identical to those of the front foot drive described in chapter 5, but the movement of the front foot, the head and eyes and the front shoulder, elbow and knee will be more towards the cover position and the ball will be struck far squarer towards cover. The toe of your front foot should point towards cover point. This shot can be risky since the direction of the stroke is across the line of the ball in an off-side direction.

The front foot straight drive

The straight drive is a front foot drive which returns a straight overpitched ball back past the bowler. It is played when an overpitched delivery bounces within reach of the batsman or arrives on the full toss in line with the stumps.

The straight drive is like the front foot drive, except that the movement of the front foot, head and eyes and the front shoulder, elbow and knee will be back towards the bowler. The toe of your front foot will still point towards mid-off. This shot can be used to loft the ball back over the bowler's head if you strike the ball with the bottom of the bat ahead of the top at the point of contact.

The front foot on-drive

The on-drive is played to punish an overpitched ball bouncing around the line of leg stump through the area between mid-wicket and the bowler. It is played to an overpitched delivery bouncing within reach of the batsman or arriving on the full toss in line with or just outside the leg stump.

The on-drive is identical to the front foot drive, except that the front foot, head and eyes, and the front shoulder, elbow and knee will move more towards the mid-wicket-mid-on area and the ball will be struck in that area. Your front hip and foot have to adopt a far more open position, so that they do not obstruct the stroke. Your toe should now point towards mid-on and your chest should be square-on to the bowler. The right hand plays a more important part in this drive than in the others, providing the power at the end of the stroke to swing the ball away on the leg-side.

Moving out to drive (on, off, straight and cover drive)

The batsman moves out to drive in order to make a slow good length ball into a delivery which can be punished. In this way he can dictate terms to the bowler and seize the initiative. He may move out to resolve uncertainty in his mind about the length of the ball and the problems of flight. Thus he can be sure of reaching the ball on the half volley or full toss before it can turn off the wicket or even bounce.

It is possible to move out when the flight of the ball allows enough time to move out of your crease to meet it on the half volley or full toss. Moving out of the crease means you must take one, two or three paces down the wicket before you can go through the movements of the drive. First, take a long step down the wicket with your front foot. Your head should be steady, eyes on the ball and your front shoulder pointing at the line of the ball. Then draw your back foot up to and behind the front in a sideways, skipping, crab-like motion and transfer your weight to the back foot once more. Now move the front foot forward towards and alongside the bounce of the ball and

The front foot cover drive

The front foot straight drive

The front foot on-drive

continue the movements of the forward drive. The movement out of the crease should be definite and pronounced—once out of your ground you can be stumped by a centimetre or a metre—degree is of no importance once the decision has been taken.

Moving out to drive

Initial front foot movement pronounced, front shoulder towards line of ball. Head and eyes steady.

Rear foot drawn to and behind front foot in sideways skipping motion.

Contact. Ball struck alongside front instep. Hands thrown at ball with bottom hand hitting after top.

Follow through. Weight on front foot. Bat finishes above front shoulder.

7 The leg glance off the front foot

The leg glance off the front foot is played in order to deflect a good length or over-pitched ball when it bounces on or outside the line of the leg stump going further down the leg-side in the direction of fine leg.

Remember: Watch the ball.
Be balanced.

How to play the leg glance off the front foot

Back lift
Lift your bat in its preparatory back swing as the bowler is about to deliver the ball. Your back lift should be in line with the middle and off stumps and controlled by the top hand.

Foot movement
As the ball bounces just outside leg stump or on the leg stump going further down the on-side and on a good length or over pitched, move your front foot alongside and outside the line of the ball and as close as possible to its bounce. Your front toe should point to mid-on with your weight on the front foot.

Head and eyes
As you push your front foot towards the bounce of the ball, move your head and eyes to a position as close as possible over the bounce of the ball and behind its line.

Weight transference and body position
In transferring the weight to the front foot, your front shoulder should point towards and outside the line of the ball. Your front elbow should be bent and pointing in the same direction. Your hips should be square-on to the bowler and the front knee bent slightly to maintain balance and also pointing towards a line outside that of the ball.

Bat swing and follow through
By this stage you will have swung the bat down from the top of the back lift. The blade should be perpendicular and, as your front elbow is bent, it will pass alongside the front pad leaving no gap. The bat will contact the ball just in front of your front foot. It is important to swing the bat along the line of the ball as this gives a better chance of contact. Too many players try to leg glance playing towards mid-wicket, and across the line of the ball.

At the point of contact your bent front elbow and front shoulder push the top of the blade ahead of the bottom. With your top hand turn the blade from a full-face position to the ball to a full-face position towards mid-wicket.

Simplified hints

Just before the bowler bowls imagine that the wicketkeeper has tied a piece of string to the bottom of your bat and is pulling it towards him.

As the ball bounces, stride towards it as though you were trying to step or kick alongside and outside it.

Sniff the ball.

Lean into the ball with front shoulder, side and elbow. Imagine that you are about to begin kneeling alongside the ball and bend your front knee towards a spot just outside its line.

Swing the bat towards the ball almost brushing alongside the front pad. Let the speed of the ball do the work—just help it on its way to fine leg.

Push the ball into the ground, just helping it on its way down the leg-side.

Check list
Emphasise points in this order.

Sniff the ball.
Push the ball into the ground, just helping it on its way down the leg-side.
Swing the bat *towards* the ball, almost brushing alongside the front pad. Let the speed of the ball do the work—just help it on its way to fine leg.
Lean into the ball with your front shoulder, side and elbow. Imagine that you are about to begin kneeling alongside the ball and bend your front knee towards a spot just outside its line.
As the ball bounces, stride towards it as though you were trying to step or kick alongside and outside it.
Just before the bowler bowls, imagine that the wicketkeeper has tied a piece of string to the bottom of your bat and is pulling it towards him.
Imagine that, like Ranjitsinjhi, you have your back foot pegged to the ground. The England Test player, Prince Ranjitsinjhi, who played 15 tests against Australia between 1896 and 1902, scoring two centuries, was a renowned player of the leg glance. It was reputed that he learned it by having his back foot pegged down so that he could not back away.

Remember: Watch the ball.
Be balanced.

8 The sweep

The sweep is played to punish an overpitched delivery which bounces or arrives on the full toss outside the line of the leg stump at slow pace. The overpitched delivery could be a full toss or half volley and it is struck in the direction of square leg.

Remember: Watch the ball.
Be balanced.

How to play the sweep

Back lift

Just before the bowler releases the ball lift the bat back in its preparatory back swing. The back lift should be straight in a line above middle and off stumps and controlled by the top hand. Make sure your back lift is high since this stroke requires power. At the end of the back lift your bottom hand should take control, swinging the bat slightly behind your shoulder ready to execute a crossbat stroke parallel to the ground.

Foot movement

As the ball arrives on the full pitch or half volley, move your front foot towards and inside its line. Bend your front knee with the toe pointing towards mid-off until your back knee touches the ground with your rear toe resting on the ground behind the batting crease. Your weight should be evenly distributed between front foot and back knee.

Head and eyes

Before the foot movement move your head and eyes towards and inside the line of flight of the ball and as close as possible over its bounce. Keep your eyes fixed on the ball and your head steady and low behind the bounce as your rear knee makes contact with the ground.

Bat swing

After you have positioned your feet, begin the down-swing. Keep your front elbow tucked into your side and your leading shoulder above your bent front knee as your bottom hand takes control. Swing the bat horizontally in a scything motion from outside off stump to the leg-side almost brushing the ground until it makes contact with the ball level with and to the leg-side of your front foot. At the point of contact with the ball, your bottom hand rolls above the top, turning the face of the bat towards the ground, thus keeping the ball down.

Simplified hints

Imagine that you are swinging a golf club with a short flat back swing.

Try to step alongside and just inside the line of the ball. Kneel just inside the line as though you were being knighted.

Sniff just inside the line of the ball.

Imagine that you are scything down some grass at ground level. As you kneel on your rear knee, the grass is just outside the line of your bent front knee. Roll your wrists over the ball.

Check list
Emphasise points in this order.

Sniff just inside the line of the ball.
Imagine that you are scything down some grass at ground level. As you kneel on your rear knee, the grass is just outside the line of your bent front knee.
Roll your wrists over the ball.
Try to step alongside and just inside the line of the ball. Kneel just inside the line as though you were being knighted.
Imagine that you are swinging a golf club with a short flat back swing. Let the scythe go through towards square leg as you pivot on your knee and leg. Look at the spot where the ball was.

Remember: Watch the ball.
Be balanced.

9 Correction of faults in front foot shots

It is virtually impossible to describe every error. They will vary according to the problems of each player. The following faults are the commonest.

Uncertainty about the length of the delivery and consequent unsureness about whether to play forward

This can only be cured by experience in situations which demand the decision to play forward. A batsman can be helped to resolve his uncertainty by:

(a) Drawing a line approximately $1\frac{1}{2}$ metres (4′) in front of the batting crease. Play forward at any delivery which bounces on the nearer side of the line.

(b) The coach cues the batsman by holding up a flash card stating 'play forward' or by calling out each time a delivery bounces in the appropriate spot. The drawback of cues is that they may distract the batsman.

(c) Using a bowling machine or accurate bowler who pitches the ball consistently on a full length appropriate to the front foot shot.

Playing across the line of the ball

Playing across the line of a ball means that the batsman does not swing the bat along the same plane as the ball. The fault can be caused by a variety of factors. If the back lift is incorrect and towards third slip, the resultant shot could be towards mid-on and across the line of the ball. If your front shoulder falls away too soon towards the leg-side, and the bottom hand controls the swing of the bat, your hips will open and your front foot move towards mid-on. The stroke will be made in the same direction and across the line of a straight ball. This early opening movement is correct when the batsman is playing front foot strokes at balls outside the leg stump.

If you always place your front foot down the wicket in line with middle stump irrespective of the direction of the ball, you will have to reach across and around your front pad to play a delivery on leg stump. This will mean that the swing of your bat will not be at the ball but towards mid-wicket.

If you overbalance because you have not bent your front knee, your back leg will swing in an arc around your front leg. The path of the bat will be controlled by the bottom hand and consequently will be towards the leg-side and across the line of flight of the ball. If you allow your bottom hand to control the shot, you will tend to hit harder with your more naturally strong hand towards the leg-side and across the line of flight of the ball.

Playing across the line of the ball can be caused by the very origins of the shot, the batsman's grip and stance. If your stance is too open or 'chest-on', there is a very good possibility that your back lift will be towards third slip and the following stroke across the line of the ball. In this case try to bring your front shoulder towards the bowler, bearing in mind that the stance should always remain comfortable. Some players achieve good results with open stances, but in their case their back lift will be straight despite their openness. If you allow the Vs formed by the thumb and forefinger of each hand and pointing down the back of the bat blade to face point instead of the wicket-keeper, there is a very good chance that the back lift will be towards point.

If the bottom hand holds the bat too close to the blade and a long way from the top hand, this is an indication that the bottom hand is controlling the strokes.

The stance and grip can be corrected. A good exercise to ensure the straight back lift is to practise in front of a mirror, lifting the bat with the top hand only.

The early falling away of the front shoulder is attributed by many coaches to the early opening of the front foot and hip in the execution of the stroke—a correct procedure in the case of the front foot leg-side strokes. Your front foot should not be pointing down the wicket but towards extra cover for all strokes except the front foot leg-side shots. If you lock your front toe towards extra cover, this will prevent the front shoulder falling away. 'Show the bowler the number on your back.' Lean into the stroke with your front shoulder, knee and side.

Playing forward automatically in line with middle stump is a common fault. If the coach throws or even drops balls from a short distance on different lines in relation to the stumps, the batsman will have to reach for the deliveries which are wide on the off-side and open his front foot when playing at balls in line with the leg stump.

In executing the front foot leg glance the bat should swing directly at the line of flight of the ball, with the front foot and hips opening with the front shoulder. The ball is deflected to fine leg not by the swing of the bat but by the turn of the wrists at the point of contact.

If you overbalance in playing the front foot strokes you are probably very stiff in your movements. Relax, bend your front knee and lean into your front foot strokes. You will always play across the line of the stroke unless, in the front foot shots, your back foot stays behind your front foot. Even when you move down the wicket to drive, keep in a side-on position. Your foot movement will be governed by the fact that your front foot moves first, with the back foot coming up to it or behind it before the front moves off again further down the wicket. The whole movement is like a series of sideways skips.

If your bottom hand dominates the stroke, try to practise the front foot shots holding the bat with the top hand only. The bottom hand contributes power to the front foot drives at the end of the stroke, hitting late and underneath the top hand. 'Throw your hands after the ball.'

Failing to play close enough to the bounce of the ball with the front foot
This fault originates in a batsman's uncertainty about whether to play forward or back, thus he plays halfway or shuffles across his crease. On good wickets where the ball does not deviate off the wicket after bouncing, if you position yourself behind the ball's line of flight you may escape; but when the ball turns or seams off the pitch and you don't move to the bounce, you give the ball more time to deviate and will be at a disadvantage.

The fault is hard to eliminate. The logic of moving to the pitch of the ball is obvious. In defence the ball is stifled before it can deviate too much; in attack your body weight is moved over the bounce of the ball and the stroke is hit along the ground. The coach should feed the batsman balls either by placing, dropping or throwing them on a spot which he must reach by placing his front foot forward and alongside the bounce of the ball. The 'ball in the sock' activity could also be used. Hang a ball in a sock a couple of centimetres from the ground and practise placing your front foot alongside it and striking the ball.

Scooping the ball into the air
This fault is caused by an inclination to play too strongly with the bottom hand. Thus the top of the bat is behind the bottom of the blade at the point of contact. It can also be caused if you mistime the ball, or do not have your head and eyes over the point of contact with the ball.

The top hand must dominate in the front foot shots; the bottom hand plays a late role of power in the drives. In defensive strokes the bottom hand relaxes its grip on the bat handle at the point of contact with the ball. In drives the bottom hand hits after and underneath the top as they are both thrown at the ball. A forward defensive shot should have no follow through which might cause you to scoop the ball into the air through mistiming the ball. Remember too not to throw your head back. This may create an illusion of power but it lessens your chances of hitting the ball because you take your eyes off it.

Not playing close enough to the pad
This fault can be caused by an incorrect swing of the bat due to the faulty back lift or the dominance of the bottom hand. It can also be caused if your front foot is not close enough to the bounce of the ball.

All the contributory causes have already been dealt with and remedies suggested. Try almost to brush your pad in front foot strokes and hit the ball alongside your instep. If you bend your front elbow and point it at the line of the ball, this will keep the bat perpendicular and bring it closer to the front pad.

10 The back foot defensive shot

The back defensive stroke is played to defend the wicket against a ball which bounces short of a length and in line with or just outside the line of the stumps, and in such a way as to prevent the batsman being dismissed. A ball which is short of a length is a delivery which bounces in front of the batsman and out of reach when he steps or extends forwards from the batting crease. It is short enough to make the batsman decide that he has to play back, but not short enough to be a long hop or half-pitcher (a bad, short ball which allows the batsman a long time in which to hit it).

Remember: Watch the ball.
Be balanced.

How to play the back defensive shot

Back lift

As the bowler is about to deliver the ball, lift your bat back in its preparatory back swing. Your back lift should be straight and in line with middle and off stumps. Your top hand should govern this action.

Foot movement

As soon as you decide that the ball will bounce short of a length, move your back foot into the stumps and across towards the off-side, bringing your body and legs into a position just inside the line of the ball. Now draw your front foot towards your back. This foot movement will take you right back close to the stumps to give you extra time in which to sight the ball. The toes of your back foot should point towards point. Your front foot will act as a balancing agent with the toes resting lightly on the ground.

Simplified hints

Just before the bowler bowls, imagine that the wicketkeeper has tied a piece of string to the bottom of your bat and is pulling it back towards him.

Now first slip has joined in the act and pulls your back leg towards him with a piece of string. Try to keep your front foot on the ground and your chest towards point.
If you want extra time to watch the ball, step back and gain an extra metre which the ball has to cover.

Head and eyes
In moving back to the stumps, bring your head and eyes into a position directly behind the line of the ball and slightly to the off-side of the back leg. Keep your head steady and alongside the leading shoulder. Your eyes should be level and fixed on the ball.

Your head and eyes must be behind the ball if you want to see what it is going to do. Sniff the ball.

Weight transference and body position
Your weight should be firmly on the back foot with the front foot acting as a counterbalance. The leading shoulder, side and bent front elbow should point in the direction of the ball's flight. Your chest faces the general direction of point and you should be side-on to the bowler.

Plant yourself on the back foot. Point your front shoulder, elbow and hip at the line of the ball. Side-on!

Bat swing and follow through
From the top of the back lift, bring the bat down as you bend your front elbow and tuck your rear elbow into your side. This will bring the bat down in perpendicular fashion almost brushing the top side of the back pad. With your front shoulder, elbow and top hand on the bat, push the top of the blade ahead of the bottom. Slacken the grip of the bottom hand at point of contact and stop the follow through level with the rear pad and at point of contact with the ball.

Imagine that a crane hook is hooked in the crook of your front elbow and hoists it high as you try to brush your back pad with the bat. Grind the ball into the ground. Don't leave the garden gate open between bat and pad.

Check list
Emphasise points in this order.

You must have your head and eyes behind the line of the ball if you want to see what it is going to do. Sniff the ball.
Imagine that a crane hook is hooked into the crook of your front elbow and hoists it high as you try almost to brush your back pad with the bat. Try to grind the ball into the ground. Don't leave the garden gate open between bat and pad.
Now first slip has joined in the act and pulls your back leg towards him with a piece of string. Try to keep your front foot on the ground and your chest towards point.
Plant yourself on the back foot. Point your front shoulder, elbow and hip at the line of the ball.
Just before the bowler bowls, imagine that the wicketkeeper has tied a piece of string to the bottom of your bat and pulls it back towards him.

Remember: Watch the ball.
Be balanced.

11 The back foot drive

The back foot drive is played to punish a ball which bounces very short of a length, generally just outside the line of the stumps, in such a way as to prevent a batsman being dismissed. This stroke should only be made to balls pitching in line with the stumps if they are short enough, and you are well set.

It is played when the ball bounces short of a length, just outside the line of the stumps or sometimes in line with the stumps. The ball could be a long hop or a half-pitcher (a bad, short ball which gives you a long time in which to hit it).

Remember: Watch the ball.
Be balanced.

How to execute the back foot (off) drive

Back lift

As the bowler is about to deliver the ball, lift the bat back in its preparatory back swing. The back lift is straight and in line with the middle and off stumps. Your top hand controls this action. The back lift for a back foot drive is higher than for the defensive back foot stroke.

Foot movement

When you have decided that the ball will bounce short of a length, move your back foot back to the stumps towards the off-side, bringing your legs and body into a position just inside the line of the ball. Pull your front foot back to your rear foot. The foot movement will take you close to the stumps, giving you more time to sight the ball. The toes of your back foot should usually point towards point. Your front foot will act as a balancing agent with the toes resting lightly on the ground.

Head and eyes

In moving back to the stumps, bring your head and eyes into position directly behind the line of the ball and slightly to the off-side of the back leg. Keep your head steady and alongside the leading shoulder. Your eyes should be level and fixed on the ball.

Weight transference and body position

Your weight is firmly on the back foot with the front foot acting as a counterbalance. Your leading shoulder, side and front elbow should point towards the ball's flight. Your chest should face the general direction of point and you should be side-on to the bowler.

Bat swing and follow through

From the top of the back lift, bring the bat down as your front elbow bends and the rear elbow is tucked into the side. This brings the bat into the perpendicular as it almost brushes the side of the back pad. Your

Simplified hints

Just before the bowler bowls, imagine that the wicketkeeper has tied a piece of string to the bottom of your bat and pulls it back and high towards him.

Now first slip has joined the act and is pulling your back leg towards him with a piece of string. Try to keep your front foot on the ground and your chest towards point.

You must have your head and eyes behind the ball if you want to see what it is doing. Smell the ball.

Plant yourself on the back foot. Point your front shoulder, elbow and hip at the line of the ball. Side-on.

Imagine that you are rocking a baby in the crook of your arm vigorously and pointing it at the ball. Swing your bent front elbow and your shoulders at the ball.

front shoulder, elbow and top hand on the bat push the top of the blade ahead of the bottom of the point of contact with the ball. In the follow through the bottom hand and back shoulder push the bat through giving power to the stroke and carrying the bat high above your head.

Don't leave the garden gate open between the bat and pad.
In the follow through, throw your hands after the ball. Hit under your top hand with your bottom hand.

Check list
Emphasise points in this order.

You must have your head and eyes behind the ball if you want to see what it is doing. Smell the ball.
Imagine that you are rocking a baby in the crook of your arm vigorously and pointing it at the ball.
Swing your bent front elbow and your shoulders at the ball. Don't leave the garden gate open between the bat and pad.
In the follow through, throw your hands after the ball. Hit under your top hand with your bottom hand.

Now first slip has joined the act and is pulling your back leg towards him with a piece of string. Try to keep your front foot on the ground and your chest towards point. If you want extra time to watch the ball, step back and gain an extra metre in which to see it.
Plant yourself on the back foot. Point your front shoulder, elbow and hip at the line of the ball.
Just before the bowler bowls, imagine that the wicketkeeper has tied a piece of string to the bottom of your bat and pulls it back towards him.

Remember: Watch the ball.
Be balanced.

12 Variations on the back foot drive

The back foot cover drive

The back foot cover drive is played to hit a ball bouncing short of a length on the off-side of the wicket through the cover area, without risk of dismissal. It is played when a short pitched delivery bounces outside the batsman's reach if he steps or stretches forward from the batting crease. It is well wide of the off stump.

To hit a back foot cover drive move as if you were hitting the back foot drive described in chapter 11, except that the movements of your back foot, head and eyes and the front shoulder will be more towards the off-side. The movement of your front foot to the rear foot will bring that foot and the front shoulder to the off-side of the rear foot and shoulder. This shot incurs greater risk since the direction of the stroke is across the line of the ball in an off-side direction.

The back foot straight drive

The back foot straight drive is played in order to hit a short, straight ball back past the bowler without risk of dismissal. It is played when a short pitched delivery bounces outside the reach of the batsman if he steps or stretches forward from the batting crease. The ball is in line with the stumps.

To hit the back foot straight drive follow the movements of the back foot drive, except that your back foot, head and eyes move towards middle stump and front shoulder should point straight back towards the bowler. The movement of your front foot to the rear foot will bring it and the front shoulder into direct line with both the back foot and shoulder. Your front shoulder will point up the wicket, just inside the line of the ball. Strike the ball back past the bowler either to the off- or leg-side.

This shot can be used to loft the ball back over the bowler's head if you move the bottom of the bat at point of contact with the ball ahead of the top of the blade.

The back foot on-drive

The back foot on-drive is played in order to hit a short delivery bouncing on or outside the line of leg stump through the area between mid-wicket and the bowler without risk of dismissal. It is played when a short delivery bounces outside the batsman's reach if he steps or stretches forward from the batting crease. The ball is on or outside the line of leg stump.

For the back foot on-drive follow the movements of the back foot drive, except that your back foot should move back nearer leg stump and your front shoulder, elbow and hip fall away to the leg-side and point in the direction of the stroke. As your front foot moves back near the back foot it passes to its leg-side and rests on the ground roughly level with the back foot with your toes resting lightly on the ground and acting as a counterbalance. In the back foot on-drive make sure your front foot and side are removed from the striking area towards the leg-side, or they may obstruct the stroke. Your chest should face the bowler. The bottom hand plays a far more important part in this drive than in the others as it provides the power in all leg-side shots.

The back foot cover drive

The back foot straight drive

The back foot on-drive

13 The leg glance off the back foot

The leg glance off the back foot is played in order to deflect the ball which is short of a length and bounces on or outside the line of the leg stump and is going further down the leg-side towards fine leg, in such a way as to prevent the batsman being dismissed. It is played when a ball short of a length bounces on or outside the line of the leg stump and is directed further down the leg-side.

Remember: Watch the ball.
Be balanced.

How to play the leg glance off the back foot

Back lift

As the bowler is about to deliver the ball lift your bat in its preparatory back swing. The back lift is in line with the middle and off stumps and governed by the top hand.

Foot movement

As the ball bounces short of a length and just outside or on the leg stump going further down the leg-side, move your back foot well back to a position just inside the line of the ball. The toes of your back foot should point down the wicket or slightly to the off-side. Move your front foot back alongside the rear heel resting it lightly on the ground.

Head and eyes

In moving back towards your stumps, bring your head and eyes into a position just inside the line of flight of the ball and slightly to the off-side of the back leg. Your head should be steady and tucked alongside the leading shoulder. Keep your eyes level and fixed on the ball.

Weight transference and body position

Your weight should be firmly on the back foot with the front foot acting as a counterbalance. Your leading shoulder, side and bent front elbow should point at the line of the ball. Since this is a leg-side stroke your chest is in a more open position pointing approximately at mid-off.

Bat swing and follow through

From the top of the back lift, bring the bat down as you bend your front elbow and tuck your rear elbow into your side. This will keep the bat perpendicular almost brushing the back pad. Swing the bat towards the line of the ball. Your front shoulder, elbow and top hand on the bat push the top of the blade ahead of the bottom at the point of contact. As the bat makes contact with the ball just in front of your back pad, turn the face of the bat towards mid-wicket with your top wrist. Slight follow through with the wrist turn will take the bat towards mid-wicket.

Simplified hints

Just before the bowler bowls, imagine that your bat is metal and the wicket-keeper has a strong magnet and pulls the bottom of your bat towards him.

Imagine that your back leg is attached by a strong spring to the bottom of the leg stump and as you lift your back foot it shoots back towards the wicket. Stand on the back foot with your front foot pointed like a ballet dancer, keeping your balance.

Sniff the ball.

Make your back foot a pedestal. Point your front side and elbow at the ball.

Swing your bat like a pendulum at the ball, flicking it away with your wrists at the last minute. Help the ball on its way to fine leg.

Check list
Emphasise points in this order.

Sniff the ball.
Swing your bat like a pendulum at the ball, flicking it away with your wrists at the last minute. Help the ball on its way to fine leg.
Imagine that your back leg is attached by a strong spring to the bottom of the leg stump and as you lift your back foot it shoots back towards the wicket. Stand on the back foot with your front foot pointed like a ballet dancer, keeping your balance.
Make your back foot a pedestal. Point your front side and elbow at the ball.
Just before the bowler bowls, imagine that your bat is metal and the wicketkeeper has a strong magnet and pulls the bottom of your bat towards him.

Remember: Watch the ball.
Be balanced.

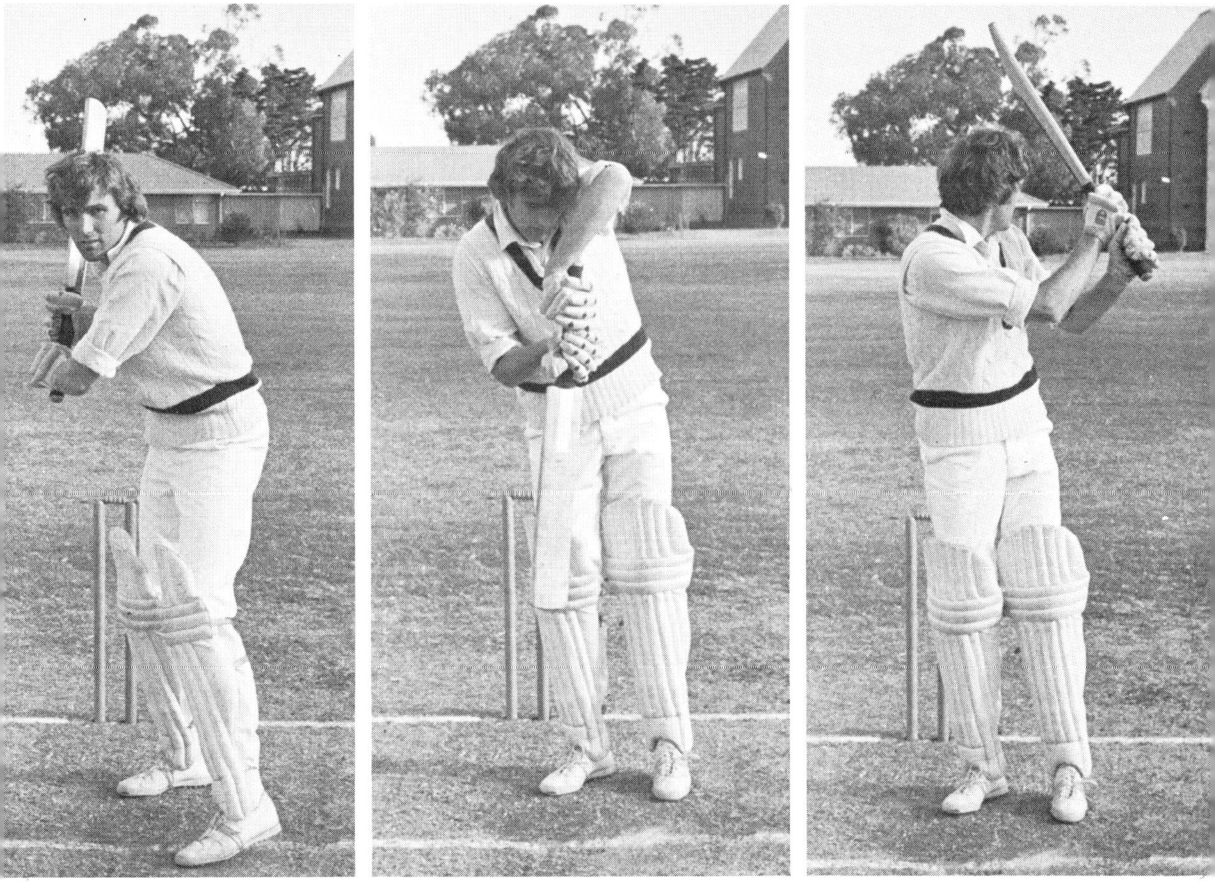

14 Correction of faults in back foot shots

It is virtually impossible to describe every fault and difficulty. The following are some of the most frequent.

Uncertainty about the length of the delivery and consequent unsureness about whether to play back

This can only be cured by experience in situations which demand the decision to play back. A batsman can be helped in resolving his uncertainty by the same methods as in the front foot shots but he should play back to any ball which pitches on the far side of a line drawn $1\frac{1}{2}$ metres (4′) in front of the batting crease. Flash cards or verbal cues can be used to instruct him to play back. In practice the coach should provide deliveries for the batsman which are consistently short of a length and in the desired direction suitable for the required stroke.

Playing across the line of the ball

As in the front foot strokes this fault can be produced by a variety of factors. An incorrect back lift towards third slip will produce a stroke towards mid-on or mid-wicket and across the line of a straight delivery except in the case of a leg-side stroke.

If your bottom hand assumes control of the stroke, it may cause you to hit harder with your more naturally strong hand towards the leg-side and across the line of flight of a straight ball.

If you move too far across the wicket to the off-side, you will tend to play the straight delivery squarer on the leg-side and will be hitting across the line of flight.

The commonest error which causes a batsman to hit across the line of flight when playing back, however, is a tendency to play in a chest-on position with your chest, and not your front shoulder, pointing at the bowler. This position causes your back lift to be towards point and, unless the swing of the bat is corrected, you will try to strike the ball towards mid-wicket and consequently across the line of flight of the delivery.

As in the front foot strokes, check your stance and grip when you execute the back foot straight-bat shots. The same process of diagnosis and correction applies in the case of both types of stroke. The parallel between the front foot and back foot straight-bat faults also applies when your bottom hand dominates the stroke and the same corrective procedures should be adopted.

If you play across the line of the ball because you move too far across the wicket to the off-side, remember to concentrate on keeping your head and eyes behind the line of the ball in order to detect its movement. Your back leg should be just inside the ball's line of flight. If you move too far across to the off-side you won't be able to pick up the movement of the ball, and you will be unable to use off-side strokes. Coaches could try placing a stump behind the batsman and in line with the middle and off stumps, so that if he moves too far back and across towards the off-side, he will kick it.

The chest-on fault is caused by pivoting on the back foot towards the leg-side. Make sure that the toes of your back foot point towards point. The chest-on position will make you play across the line of the flight of the ball. The bat also duplicates the defensive role of the body since the bat placed in front of the pad defends a lesser area than when the bat is placed alongside the pad. This is a difficult fault to correct but the most effective way to correct it is to insist that the batsman's front shoulder points at the line of the ball throughout the stroke.

Failing to play far enough back
This fault originates in the batsman's uncertainty about whether to play forward or back. Thus he plays all his shots standing on the batting crease. On good wickets where the ball does not deviate off the wicket after bouncing, you may be able to position yourself safely behind the line of flight of the ball; but on pitches on which the ball seams or turns you will be at a disadvantage since you will be depriving yourself of the extra metre in which to see the ball. By going right back to the stumps you gain the advantage of an extra metre or a fraction of a second more to see the ball.

The coach can feed short balls to the batsman by throwing from a short distance and insisting upon a decisive movement backwards from the batsman.

Scooping the ball into the air
As in the case of the front foot strokes, this fault is largely due to the batsman's inclination to play too strongly with the bottom hand at the point of contact. This causes the top of the bat blade to be behind the bottom on contact. The fault can also be caused by mistiming or by not having the eyes behind the ball's line of flight.

The corrective techniques of the front foot shots also apply to the back foot strokes.

Not playing close enough to the pad
This fault can be caused by the back foot not moving far enough into the stumps and into a position just inside the line of flight of the ball. When this occurs and the bat strikes at the ball, a gap through which the ball can pass appears between bat and pad. It may also be caused by a back lift towards third slip or the dominance of the bottom hand in the stroke or if you follow a delivery which moves away towards the off-side in the air and then cuts back off the pitch.

Watch that your bottom hand does not dominate the stroke and check your grip and stance. The front elbow plays a large role in keeping the bat close to the rear pad. The more the elbow is bent and the more it is pointed at the ball, the more perpendicular your bat will be and the closer it will pass to the pad. Try not to chase wide balls with a straight bat. At all times try almost to brush your back pad with the bat.

Backing away from the line of the ball
This is the commonest fault amongst young players and stems from fear of the hard ball. It creates numbers of problems. If you back away your head and eyes won't be behind the line of the ball and you won't be able to see its movement. You will be leaving the stumps exposed and a gap between bat and pad. Sometimes the player backs away so much that he cannot even reach the ball from his position on the leg-side.

The irony of this fault is that, in backing away from the ball, you will probably incur a far greater risk of injury than if you moved into line behind it. When you are behind the line of flight you will be able to sight the ball and take last minute evasive action if necessary. If you back away, the ball often follows without your knowing it. Obviously you should move into line with the ball and watch it closely if you are to strike it. You should also be in a position to defend the stumps and reach the ball.

To check this fault the coach could place a stump behind the player and to his leg-side so that if he retreats he kicks the stump and is aware of his error.

15 The square cut

A square cut is played in order to punish a delivery which is short pitched and very wide of the off stump. The ball should be at least 30 centimetres (1′) wide of the off stump. The ball has to be struck past point on the ground with the least risk of dismissal.

A square cut is played when a short ball, a long hop or half-pitcher from the bowler bounces at least 30 centimetres (1′) outside the batsman's off stump. A long hop or half-pitcher is regarded as a bad ball. It bounces very short, well outside the reach of the batsman if he plays forward by stepping or reaching from his crease. Because the ball is so short, the batsman has a lot of time to play his shot. Don't try the stroke against the ball which bounces above waist height, since this ball is difficult to hit downwards.

Remember: Watch the ball.
Be balanced.

How to play a square cut	Simplified hints
Back lift Just before the bowler delivers the ball, lift the bat back in the early stages with the top hand, over the middle and off stumps. At the end of the back swing your bottom hand takes control pulling the bat behind the rear shoulder ready to execute a cross-bat shot.	Swing the bat back as though you were swinging a golf club.
Foot movement As the back lift is executed, move your back foot back and across the stumps to a position just in front of or outside off stump. The toes of your back foot should point towards point. Your weight should be on the back foot, leaving your front foot resting on the ground, level with the popping crease, to act as a balance.	Lunge with your back foot, as though you were trying to hit first slip over the head with your bat.
Head and eyes Move your head and eyes as you transfer your weight, to a position just above the bent back knee to ensure the bat meets ball at arm's length. Hold your head steady and keep your eyes on the ball. In previous strokes the head and eyes have been behind the point of contact with the ball. In the square cut, if the head and eyes are too close to the line of the ball, the stroke will be cramped; if they are too far away you won't hit the ball with the centre of the blade or you may not even be able to reach it.	Sight the ball along your arm as though your arm were a rifle and your back shoulder was the sight.
Bat swing and body position Swing the bat horizontally from behind the back shoulder. Straighten your arms and strike the ball downwards in the middle of the bat, with both arms straightened out at a point level with the back hip.	Point to the ball with both arms fully extended, indicating that it should be on its way downwards through the point area. Imagine you have a scythe in your

Let the ball do the work rather than hitting it hard. At the point of contact roll your bottom hand on the bat over the top hand thus hitting the ball into the ground.

Follow through
In the follow through bring the bat down and across the front of your body at arm's length, finishing over the front shoulder. The face of the bat should point downwards and your eyes should still be fixed on the point of contact with the ball.

hands—or an axe—and you are chopping down some grass—or a tree—at hip level.

Your axe has missed its mark. Let it swing through.

Check list
Emphasise points in this order.

Sight the ball along your arm as though your arm were a rifle and your back shoulder was the sights.
Point to the ball with both arms fully extended, indicating that it should be on its way downwards through the point area.
Lunge with your back foot, as though you were trying to hit first slip over the head with your bat.
Your axe has missed its mark. Let it swing through.
Swing your bat as though you were swinging a golf club.

Remember: Watch the ball.
Be balanced.

16 The late cut

The late cut is played in order to punish a ball bouncing short of a length just outside or wide of the off stump, with the least risk of dismissal. Strike the ball along the ground in the area between gully and the wicketkeeper and between the fieldsmen.

The late cut is played when a ball bounces short of a length and just outside or wide of off stump. A ball which is short of a length is a delivery which bounces in front of the batsman and out of reach when he steps or stretches forward from the batting crease. The ball must be wide enough to allow room for the stroke, and not involve any danger of the batsman being bowled or hitting the ball in the air.

Remember: Watch the ball.
Be balanced.

How to play the late cut	**Simplified hints**
Back lift Just before the bowler delivers the ball, lift the bat first with the top hand, over the middle and off stumps. Then allow your bottom hand to take control at the end of the back swing, pulling the bat slightly behind the rear shoulder, ready to execute a cross-bat shot.	Swing the bat back as though you were swinging a golf club in a short, flat arc.
Foot movement As the back lift is executed, move your back foot back and across the stumps to a position just in front of or outside the off stump. The toes of your back foot should point slightly behind point and your weight should be on your back foot. Bend your rear knee slightly leaving your front foot towards mid-on or mid-wicket with the toes resting lightly on the ground to maintain balance.	Lunge with your back foot, as though you were trying to hit first slip over the head with the bat.
Head and eyes Move your head and eyes to the off-side above the rear knee and just inside and above the point of contact with the ball. Keep your head steady and your eyes on the ball. At the point of contact look towards the direction of the stroke and along your arm.	Sight the ball along your arm as though it were a rifle and your rear shoulder the rifle sight.
Weight transference and body position Your weight should be on the back foot from the first foot movement. Your rear shoulder, hip and leg should point in the direction of the shot and your front side, shoulder and leg should be angled towards mid-wicket or mid-on. Your weight should be above the shot. Don't crouch too much.	Imagine that you are going to pat the ground vigorously just in front of slips with your bat.
Bat swing and follow through From behind the rear shoulder, swing the bat from the horizontal downwards on top of the ball. The follow through takes it down on to the ground with the arms extended. Control the stroke with your bottom hand.	Point down to the ball with both the arms extended, indicating that it should be on its way through the slips.

Check list
Emphasise points in this order.

Sight the ball along your arm as though it were a rifle and behind your rear shoulder as though the back shoulder was the rifle sight.
Point down to the ball with both arms extended, indicating that it should be on its way through the slips.
Lunge with your back foot, as though you were trying to hit first slip over the head with the bat.
Swing the bat back as though you were swinging a golf club in a short, flat back swing.

Remember: Watch the ball.
Be balanced.

17 The pull

Play the pull stroke in order to punish a long hop or half-pitcher which bounces in line with the stumps or just outside off or leg stump and to hit it into the area between square leg and the bowler. The stroke must be carried out in such a way as to prevent the batsman's dismissal. It may also be used against a full toss in line with the stumps or outside leg stump.

It is played when a long hop or half-pitcher from the bowler bounces either in line with the stumps or just outside off or leg stump and rises above stump height to the level of the batsman's midriff. A long hop or half-pitcher is a bad ball. It pitches very short and outside the reach of the batsman playing forward by stepping or reaching from his crease. The shortness of the ball means that the batsman has a lot of time to play his shot. This stroke should only be played when the batsman has been at the crease for some time and is accustomed to the pace of the wicket, the light, the bowling, etc.

Remember: Watch the ball.
Be balanced.

How to play the pull stroke	Simplified hints
Back lift As the bowler is about to deliver the ball, lift the bat back in a flat arc, in the early stages with your top hand then, at the end of the back swing, let your bottom hand take control pulling the bat behind your rear shoulder ready to execute a cross-bat stroke.	Swing the bat back as though you were playing baseball and were about to hit a home run.
Foot movement As you lift the bat back, move the back foot back and across to the off-side to a position close to the stumps or bowling crease. The toes of your back foot take your weight and point towards mid-off or the bowler. Swing the front foot back in an arc until it is level with the back foot and ground it lightly with the toes pointing towards mid-on.	Step back and face the bowler with your feet astride. Weight on the back toes.
Head and eyes Move your head and eyes until they are slightly to the off-side of the ball or in line. Keep them steady and your eyes on the ball.	Look at the ball as if you were trying to line it up with the mid-on fieldsman.
Bat swing As you begin to swing the bat from behind your rear shoulder, straighten your arms, swinging the bat horizontally in front of your body at midriff height. Make contact with the ball at arm's length on the leg-side, in front, and sometimes on the off-side of your body. Uncock your wrists at the last moment to roll the bat over the ball and keep it down.	Imagine that you are scything the tops off some tall flowers with a walking stick held in both hands.

Weight transference and follow through

At the beginning of the stroke move your weight on to the toes of the back foot. As you begin to swing the bat, transfer your weight slightly on to the front foot, which is now on the leg-side of the stumps. Thus your weight adds power to your stroke. The follow through should be full causing your body to pivot on the toes of the back foot. Your original front foot is now behind the back foot and your back towards the off-side. Finish with the bat over your original front shoulder, which is now closer to the stumps.

Retreat to a position to hit the ball and then advance to attack the enemy. Pivot with the stroke on the toes of the back foot.

Check list

Emphasise points in this order.

Watch the ball as if you were trying to line it up with the mid-on fieldsman.
Imagine that you are scything the tops off some tall flowers with a walking stick.
Step back and face the bowler with your feet astride.

Retreat to a position to hit the ball and then advance to hit the enemy. Pivot with the stroke on the toes of the back foot.
Swing the bat back as though you were playing baseball and were about to hit a home run.

Remember: Watch the ball.
Be balanced.

18 The hook

The hook stroke is played in order to punish a ball which pitches very short of a length in line with, or outside, the leg stump and rises above the height of the batsman's waist. The ball should be hit between square and fine leg in such a way as to prevent the batsman's dismissal. The difference between the pull and the hook shot is that the pull drags the ball off its original course into the area between square leg and mid-on. The hook merely helps the ball on its way into the area between fine leg and square leg.

The hook is played when a ball bounces very short of a length in line with the stumps or outside leg stump and rises above the height of the batsman's waist. The stroke is generally made against a fast bowler's 'bouncer' or 'bumper', a very short ball directed just over the stumps or in line with the batsman's body and continuing on an upward path when it arrives at the batsman's crease. The stroke can be played against a ball which has bounced as high as the batsman's head provided it is steered downwards into the ground. Above that height, control of the stroke is lessened. You should only play the hook when you have been at the crease for some time.

Remember: Watch the ball.
Be balanced.

How to play the hook stroke	**Simplified hints**
Back lift As the bowler is about to deliver the ball, lift the bat back in a flat arc, in the early stages by the top hand, then at the end of the back swing, let the bottom hand take control, pulling the bat behind the rear shoulder, ready to execute a cross-bat stroke.	Swing the bat back as though you were Babe Ruth ready to hit a home run at baseball.
Foot movement As you lift the bat back, move the back foot back and across towards the off-side and to a position close to the stumps or bowling crease. Take the weight on the toes of your back foot which should point towards mid-off or the bowler as they act as a pivot. Swing your front foot back in an arc past the back foot, continuing towards the leg stump, and behind the back foot.	Step back and face the bowler with your feet astride. Weight on the back toes and pivot.
Head and eyes Move your head and eyes with the feet until they are slightly to the off-side of the ball, but keep them steady and your eyes fixed on the ball.	Sniff the ball from a position in which the ball is coming over your front shoulder, now pointing to square leg.
Bat swing As you begin to swing the bat from behind the rear shoulder, straighten your arms slightly, swinging the bat horizontally in front of your body. Make contact with the ball at arm's length and on the leg-side of your body, level with the shoulders. Roll your wrists at the last moment to keep the ball down.	Imagine that you are chopping down a tree, which is slightly on the leg-side alongside your front shoulder. You are chopping it down at shoulder level.

Weight transference and follow through
At the beginning of the stroke move your weight on to the toes of your back foot which acts as a pivot for the shot. Your front foot should swing in an arc from the batting crease to a position in line with or outside and very close to leg stump, then in front of the stumps to complete a semicircle, finishing outside the off stump. Carry the shoulders and bat in a horizontal circular movement, finishing up with the bat over your original front shoulder and your rear shoulder pointing to square leg.

Imagine that you are an ice-skater about to perform a spin on the back foot, with your arms extended and together in front of your chest.

Check list
Emphasise points in this order.

Sniff the ball from a position in which the ball is coming over your front shoulder.
Imagine that you are chopping down a tree, which is slightly on the leg-side alongside your front shoulder. You are chopping it down at shoulder level.
Step back and face the bowler with your feet astride. Weight on the back toes.
Imagine that you are an ice-skater about to perform a spin on the back foot, with your arms extended and together in front of your chest.
Swing the bat back as though you were Babe Ruth ready to hit a home run at baseball.

Remember: Watch the ball.
Be balanced.

19 Correction of faults in cross-bat shots

The cut

The following are some of the commonest errors.

Crouching when cutting

This is a common fault in executing the cut. Crouching may give you the impression of cutting correctly, but it merely increases the probability that you will hit underneath the ball and edge it into the slips.

Stand up when you are cutting and hit the ball down into the ground so as not to provide chances to the fieldsmen behind the wicket on the off-side.

Not hitting down on the ball

Some batsmen try to cut the ball without paying enough attention to the need to keep it on the ground. Usually these strokes are attempted with a flat bat and with too much power.

To play the cut successfully the ball should be guided rather than hit by the batsman. The bowler provides some 100 km.ph (60 mph) if he is fast-medium. Use this power and guide the ball into the desired area with a minimum of risk. Steer the ball into the ground by rolling the wrists over it and hitting downwards.

Coaches can teach these last two points by feeding the ball to the batsman practising the stroke. From a short distance pitch the ball to the batsman short of a length and wide of the off stump.

Hitting the ball high on the bat

This is generally caused when the batsman tries to cut a ball which is too close to the line of the off stump. The back foot off-drive might be a more effective stroke for such a ball.

Some people do play the cut by drawing away to the leg-side and giving themselves room to play the shot. This is dangerous and should only be attempted by good batsmen when well set. You must have room to play the cut to move your back leg back and across towards the off-side and to strike the ball at arm's length.

Again the coach should set up a simulated practice situation by throwing the ball from a short distance.

The pull

Backing away to leg

The pull can be executed against a ball which pitches short and outside the off stump, short and in line with the stumps, or short and outside the leg stump. Backing away or retreating outside the leg stump merely creates a situation in which it seems to the batsman that he is dragging the ball from outside the off stump to mid-wicket. When the batsman retreats to square leg, he exposes his stumps and increases his chances of being bowled if the ball keeps low.

The movement of the back foot backwards and towards the off-side is most important. Keep your eyes and head behind the ball or just to its off-side.

Simulated match situations for the pull should be provided in the nets.

Attempting to pull the wrong ball
This probably leads to most of the dismissals when a batsman tries to pull. Don't try the shot against balls which are not short enough and which don't rise above stump high. Because the stroke is possible even against straight balls this produces a great danger of being bowled.

The coach can only seek to remedy this fault through experience and this again means that he must simulate conditions in a net situation to practise the pull.

Lofting the pull stroke
In the pull the ball is dragged from its original direction towards the area of mid-wicket. This requires great bat power and the use of the flat-batted technique. The body lends its power by moving first on to the back foot in line with or just inside the line of the ball and then on to the front foot as the stroke is executed.

Irrespective of the bat power used in the stroke never forget that at the point of contact you must roll the face of the bat over the ball to keep it down.

The hook

Not moving inside the line of the ball
This is a dangerous fault, since if you don't move inside the line of an intended hook the ball may strike your body and face. The fault is generally caused by the batsman's failure to move far enough back and to the off-side in his first movement. In young players it may also be caused by fear of the ball.

Your first movement in the hook should be pronounced. Move back and across to the off-side and on to the toes of the back foot quickly and firmly. Pivot on the toes of the rear foot. Always keep your head to the off-side of the ball.

The coach can establish practice situations in the nets to execute the shot, throwing or pitching short balls, with the knowledge and consent of the batsman, at first consistently and then sporadically as in a match situation. Many players do not like to practise the hook in the nets because of the risk of injury. If the stroke is to be mastered, however, it must be practised.

Hooking upwards as a catch to deep fine leg
This is a common fault. The hook should be hit backward of square leg. The shot helps the ball on its way rather than forcing it away. Often a ball bounces too high to be hooked effectively since the stroke cannot be kept on the ground. It is better to ignore these deliveries. You must roll your wrists over the ball as contact is made.

The coach should emphasise the guiding nature of the stroke. Again produce practice situations so the batsman can practise the shot.

The batsman's strokes

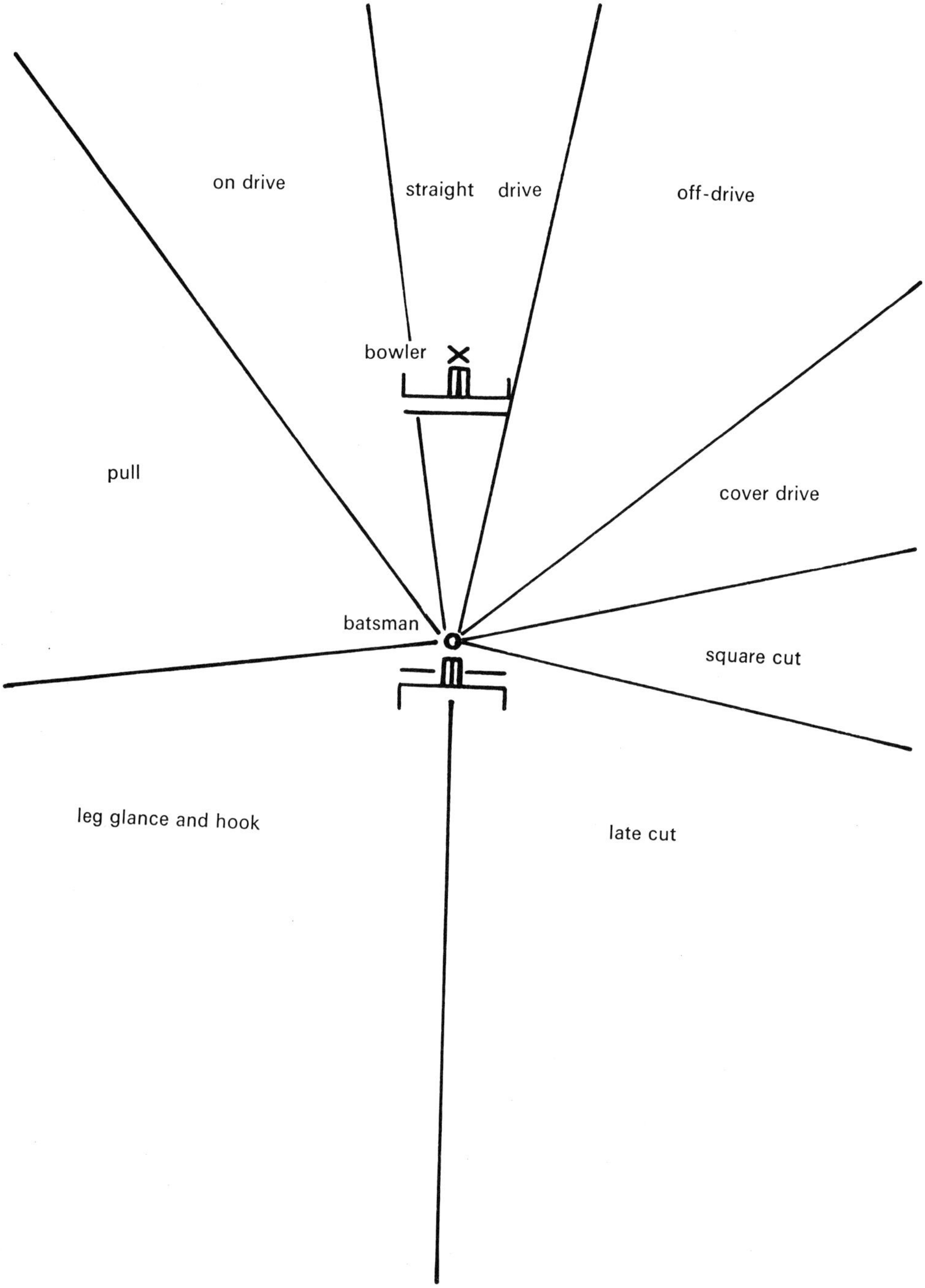

20 Running between the wickets

The batsman should learn to run well between the wickets in order to score the maximum number of runs and to eliminate the unnecessary 'run-out' method of dismissal. With correct placement of shots and good running between the wickets the batsman can cause changes in bowling tactics and field settings.

Remember: Be balanced.
Watch the ball and the fieldsman.

How to run well between the wickets	Simplified hints
Know the bowler's tactics, the field and your partner The batsman should acquire a knowledge of the bowler's intentions, e.g. whether he is concentrating on the off stump short of a length. This will enable you to know where your best chance of runs lie. Watch where the field is placed and note their positions before taking strike. Pinpoint the good, mobile, strong throwing fieldsmen and take no risks with them. Learn the right and left-handed throwers. You would normally be able to run a single to cover's left hand but *not* if he is left-handed. You should also know your partner: whether he is a fast or slow runner, hesitant or reliable. Most good partnerships are based on trust and understanding.	Know what you are up against in the field and at the bowling crease. Where are the strengths and the left and right-handed power throwers? Understand your partner.
The call The call is short for immediate response and loud and clear for understanding. There are three calls: 'yes', 'no' and 'wait'. Beware of calls which may be misheard such as 'go'. 'Wait' is used only when there is some doubt that the ball will pass the fieldsmen.	Yes, no and wait—thou shalt have no other loud and clear commandments but these.
Call immediately every ball has been struck and after each run call again to indicate the possibility of an additional run. You can call as you and your partner cross in mid-wicket to make your intentions about the next run clear.	You will say them every ball, and after every run. Don't forget the asides as you pass.
If there is any doubt, the call should always be 'no'. An extra run is not worth a wicket. Always call 'no' for a misfield when it is impossible to judge the recovery power of the fieldsman.	If in doubt, never go out.
The batsman who has the clearer sight of the ball should always call. For strokes in front of the wicket, the striker usually has the clearer view and calls. For those strokes travelling behind the wicket, it generally is the non-striker who calls. This may vary in certain instances, for example, striker hooking the ball fine past leg slip may see the fieldsman miss the ball and block the view of the non-striker. In this instance the striker calls for the run.	Those who see shall receive the call.
The batsman who is running to the 'danger-end'—that is, to the stumps to which the ball is being returned on the completion of two, three, four or five runs, etc., always has the final say.	Danger—man running to get home.

The caller must always guarantee his partner a safe passage, otherwise trust and understanding between them disappear. The non-caller must always obey a caller whom he trusts.

He who does not trust and who hesitates is lost.

Backing up

Backing up must never be regarded as a means of 'stealing' a start in a run. It is merely a 'moving barrier' start by the batsman as the ball is in the air and before it is struck (approx. $\frac{1}{2}$-1 second). The non-striking batsman walks up with the bowler in the last few strides of his run-up. The non-striker is on the opposite side of the wicket to the bowler, watching his hand, advancing sideways, chest-on to the bowler and trailing his bat in his rear hand. If you are backing up always keep some part of your bat or body behind the batting crease until *after* the bowler has released the ball. While the ball is in the air, take two or three steps down the pitch until the ball is struck and the call for runs made or until it is missed. From this position you can go through for a run or quickly regain your crease.
If the batsman tries to steal a start before the bowler releases the ball, it is within the Laws of Cricket for the bowler to run the batsman out without prior warning.

Thou shalt not steal, but that does not prevent you borrowing a few yards after the bowler has let go of the ball.

The run

After calling, with the non-striker backing-up, run the first and subsequent runs as quickly as possible. Never slow down until all possibility of further runs has been eliminated and you are completing an obviously finite number of runs. Remember there could be overthrows. In completing the final run ground your bat a metre in front of the popping crease and slide it in at arm's length. Thus you can extend the reach of your body.
Never run too far beyond the wicket in case of overthrows.

Run the first and subsequent runs as though you were winning the game with them. Only relax when all hope of winning has gone. Slide!—as though your bat was a baseball player making first base. Your bat is an earthling. You must never go too far.

The turn

In your haste to gain extra runs you often neglect the turn, forgetting that a correct turn can save time and distance wasted running around in a circle. Running between the wickets, watch the ball and the fieldsman chasing it. Transfer the bat into the hand opposite to the ball. Stop for a fraction of a second at the end of the run in a side-on position with your chest and head facing the ball. At full stretch reach out, grounding your bat lightly behind the batting crease, before calling for another run, receiving the agreement of your partner and embarking on the additional run. Both feet are out of the batting crease. Your back foot is ready to push off on the next run and your leading leg points down the wicket.

Remember the time-saving in a swimmer's tumble-turn. Watch the fieldsman and the ball as you do a feet astride armstretch to ground your bat behind the batting crease—call and run again.

A good shot hit hard does not automatically mean a run. Quick singles result largely from placement of the stroke and touch, that is, if you place the ball gently short of the fieldsmen and into vacant spaces in the field. Understanding between the partners is essential. This understanding will only come from batting and practising together.

The batsmen must think between the wickets. 'When in doubt, never run out' should be the golden rule. The remedy of faults in running between the wickets depends largely on their correct diagnosis. The following are the most frequent errors:

Failure to understand the weaknesses and strengths of one's partner.
Failure to detect the strengths and weaknesses of the opposing fieldsmen.
Failure to analyse the tactics of the opposition.
Failure to call correctly, clearly and immediately.
Failure to back up at the bowler's end.
Failure to slide the bat home on the final and dangerous run.
Failure to turn correctly.
Failure to keep one's eyes on the ball in the field.
Failure to guarantee a safe run to the man making for the danger end.
Risking a run from a misfield which is not clearly sighted.
Backing up too early before the ball has left the bowler's hand.
Failure to take the first runs quickly.

Check list
Emphasise points in this order.

Yes, no and wait—thou shalt have no other loud and clear commandments but these.
Say them every ball, and after every run. Don't forget the asides as you pass.
If in doubt, never go out.
Those who see shall receive the call.
Danger—man running to get home.
He who does not trust and who hesitates is lost.

Run the first and subsequent runs as though you were winning the game with them. Only relax when all hope of winning has gone.
Slide—as though your bat was a baseball player making first base. Your bat is an earthling.
You must never go too far.

Remember the time-saving involved in a swimmer's tumble-turn. Watch the fieldsman and the ball as you do a feet-astride armstretch to ground your bat behind the batting crease—call and run again.

Thou shalt not steal, but that does not prevent you borrowing a few yards after the bowler has let go of the ball.
Know what you are up against in the field and at the bowling crease. Where are the strengths and the left- and right-handed throwers? Understand your partner.

Remember: Watch the ball and the fieldsmen.
Be balanced.

Backing up

Slide

21 Bowling: the run-up

The bowler runs up before delivery in order to add the impetus of forward movement to the weight of his body behind the ball in the delivery stride. The run-up contributes 20 per cent to a bowler's speed and correspondingly increases a slow bowler's spinning capacity. It also helps the bowler's balance in the forward movement in bowling. The run-up must be atuned to the speed of the slow or fast bowler's action. If his approach is too fast he may 'run-through' his bowling action, without time to gather himself. If it is too slow he may stop in his delivery stride and have to bowl entirely off the strength of his action, tiring himself unnecessarily and placing strain on his body because of the lack of follow through. If the bowler stops at the moment of delivery, he will have to gauge exactly how much strength he will have to put into each ball. Too much will result in a full toss; too little in a long hop.

Consistent body impetus at the moment of delivery will pitch the ball on a consistent length. Length and line are essential qualities of a bowler's action, but they ought to be the result of a good run-up and body action. The length of a run-up depends on each individual's action. It should not be too long and tiring, but carried out with correct acceleration and deceleration within the minimum space. The run-up also provides the basic rhythm of the bowler's action. Thus some bowlers approach in rhythmic groups of three strides—others of four or five. The ideal approach incorporates the minimum number of these units compatible with correct acceleration and deceleration and the best balanced speed at the crease. The bowler's run-up may be straight or at various angles towards the mid-off position. The more oblique his approach, the easier it will be for him to turn into his action in the delivery stride.

Remember: Be balanced.
Watch where the ball will bounce.

How to use the run-up

The length and rhythm

Establish the length, angle, and rhythm of the individual's approach by practice runs from a given starting point. Many coaches feel the run begins on the foot opposite the bowling arm. Start slowly, accelerate to the best speed for you, and decelerate just before the action. Once you have established the length and rhythm of your run up, measure it before each bowling spell in a consistent manner by steady pacing. This length may vary fractionally according to the suppleness of your body.

Simplified hints

Practise running up from a point and when you feel like bowling, bowl. Complete your action and follow through. Now measure your run in level strides.

Acceleration

Measure out your run-up and place your marker. Begin your approach slowly from that point. Gain some momentum with a few rhythmic strides, then accelerate. It may be helpful to make a second mark from which acceleration begins. Keep increasing your pace until a few paces before the bowling action begins—these paces are probably the last rhythmic group of strides in the bowler's approach.

Imagine that you are a car in your run-up and you move into first gear then into second and third.

Deceleration

Until recently it was thought that the bowler held the fastest pace possible together with balance, over the last few paces of his run. In fact, however, he slows down before the delivery stride as he moves into his action. As you move your front arm upwards and forwards towards fine leg, begin to jump on to your back foot in the bowling stride with the toes of this foot pointing towards the bowler's stumps. Your back foot should be parallel to the bowling crease. It is impossible to execute this sideways action running at full pace.

Slow up and gather yourself as though you are about to do a feet-astride jump facing the umpire at the bowler's end.

Follow through

The follow through is the shock absorber of the action and the run-up. It is a slow deceleration which places as little strain on your body as possible. Your follow through must, however, be long enough to absorb the shock of the action and run-up: two or three paces, for a slow bowler and four or five for a faster bowler. It must be straight for at least one pace if your action was correct; and it must then carry you quickly to the side if you are to avoid running on the wicket and the 'danger area', 1.2 metres (4′) in front of the popping or batting crease and 30 cm (1′) either side of middle stump.

Run after the ball. It's difficult to bowl a ball in one direction whilst stopping or running in another direction.

The run-up skill should be mastered until it is automatic. Intense practice is needed. Under the front foot no-ball rule, 'no ball' is called when the bowler's front foot completely clears the rear edge of the batting crease either in the air or on the ground. Since it is impossible for a bowler to watch his front foot whilst delivering the ball, coaches should try to cure the no-ball fault by concentrating on achieving a correct position for the rear foot behind the bowling crease and, according to the length of the delivery stride, keep the bowler's foot behind the popping crease. If need be, place a marker behind the bowling crease at the bowler's end so that the bowler will jump into his delivery stride with his rear foot level with that marker. The no-ball is an unnecessary fault.

Check list

Emphasise points in this order.

You are a car; move into first gear; then into second and third.

Slow up and gather yourself as though you were about to do a feet-astride jump facing the umpire at the bowler's end.

Run after the ball. It's difficult to bowl a ball in one direction whilst stopping or running in another.

Practise running up from a point and when you feel like bowling, bowl. Now measure your run in level strides.

1 Slow start

2 Accelerate

3 Gather yourself

4 Jump into the delivery stride

22 The basic action

An orthodox, side-on action will help the bowler to bowl consistently straight on a desired line, with the best chance of obtaining a good length, greatest speed, swing, spin and flight.

The effort expended in bowling slow should be almost as much as that expended in bowling fast. The body action should be just as strong and the bowling arm speed almost as fast. In slow bowling, however, the weight of the body flows around the side of the ball rather than remaining behind the ball as in fast bowling. The slow bowler who bowls with a strong body action is therefore able to spin the ball more since the weight of his body adds to the strength of his fingers.

Note: These directions are for a bowler delivering with his bowling arm over the top of the wicket.

Remember: Be balanced.
Watch where the ball will bounce.

How to bowl the basic action

The bowling stride

According to your rhythm, slow up in your approach two or three strides before the bowling crease. Move in to the bowling stride by jumping on to your back foot, which is the foot on the same side as your bowling arm. The toes of your rear foot point to the stumps at the bowler's end and the foot is parallel to the bowling crease and behind it. This will draw your body round into a side-on position with your chest facing the bowler's stumps. The bowling stride then becomes a sideways step towards the batsman with your front hip and leading side of the front leg pointing down the pitch, initially slightly towards the batsman's body or fine leg. Your head should be upright and steady, and your eyes fixed on where the ball will bounce.

Front arm and trunk movement

As you spring on to the rear foot, raise your front arm high, pointing your front shoulder towards fine leg. Look behind your front arm and over your front shoulder at the batsman. Now use your front arm as a lever to rock or push your front side back. Your head and eyes should be steady, your back slightly arched, and your weight on the back foot. Lift your front foot clear of the ground with the knee slightly bent. From this position, throw your front arm and shoulder forwards and upwards in the desired direction of the delivery. This will release the tension on the front side and transfer your weight from the back to the front foot.

Simplified hints

Gather yourself and jump on to the back foot as though you were going to do a feet-astride jump facing the umpire (or stumps). Watch where the ball should bounce.

Reach for the sky with your front arm and then imagine that you are a young tree (or ruler) being bent backwards ready to spring back into position and catapult the ball forwards. Stare at the batsman over your front shoulder.
Imagine that you are going through a door and you suddenly reach up with your front arm to touch the top of the frame. Look at the batsman behind your front arm and bend backwards like a young tree in a high wind.
You are serving at tennis, with a ball instead of a racquet in your back hand and your back arm straight. Throw an imaginary ball up with your front hand.

The bowling arm

As you raise your front arm, move your back or bowling arm with it so that both hands are high and fairly close together, in front of the front shoulder. As you throw your front arm forwards and upwards, begin a circular motion with your bowling arm, keeping it straight, alongside your chest, downwards, backwards and then upwards until it is high, straight and alongside your head. This is the area of the point of release.

Your bowling arm is the sail on a windmill. Raise it with your front arm and swing it right round. Brush your ear.

Front foot position

As you step down the pitch towards the batsman, transfer your weight from back to front foot; your toes should point towards fine leg. The swing of the bowling arm from behind your body to the front will cause your hips to rotate. When the front foot lands on the ground (with some part of it behind the popping or batting crease), your front leg and toes should point almost straight down the pitch or slightly towards fine leg. Brace this leg as your weight passes over it. Try to keep the movement of your front leg and foot towards fine leg as long as possible.

Throw your front foot down the wicket towards the batsman, as though you wanted to tread on his toes. Keep it going in that direction for as long as possible. Stamp your front foot down, and stand up straight. Brace your knee. Try to bowl across the front leg.

Follow through

In the follow through throw your bowling arm downwards then backwards as close as possible to the outside of your front leg. Your bowling arm and shoulder swing from behind to in front of the body, across and alongside and outside the front knee. Bend your back to allow the bowling hand to come as close to the ground as possible in front of your body. Swing your rear leg as close as possible past the front with the knee bent. Follow through for at least one stride directly behind the line of the ball before running off the wicket. Relax in the follow through and absorb the shock of the bowling action by continuing for three or four strides.

Almost brush alongside the outside of the front leg with the front arm. Try to reach for the ground alongside the little toe of your front foot with your bowling hand. Run after the ball. You can't bowl in one direction and run in another.

The basic bowling action is suited to the bowling of outswing, off spin, off cutters, and leg spinners.

The outswinger is a ball which curves or swings in the air from the leg-side to the off before it bounces. It is generally bowled at medium or fast pace.

The off spinner is a ball which turns in from the off-side after it bounces because of the spin imparted by the bowler. Generally this ball will swing away before it spins back. It is bowled at slow speed.

The off cutter is a ball which turns in from the off-side after it bounces because of the cut imparted by the bowler. The difference between cut and spin is that spin is largely imparted by both the wrist and finger movement of the bowler, whereas cut is largely obtained by the wrist action dragging the fingers down the side of the ball. The ball is usually bowled at medium pace.

The leg spinner is a ball which turns from the leg-side after it bounces because of the spin imparted by rotation of the wrist and fingers. It is bowled at slow speed.

Check list
Emphasise points in this order.

Reach for the sky with your front arm and then imagine that you are a young tree (or ruler) being bent backwards ready to spring back into position and catapult the ball forwards. Stare at the batsman over your front shoulder.
Imagine that you are going through a door and you suddenly reach up with your front arm to touch the top of the frame. Look at the batsman behind your front arm and bend backwards like a young tree in a high wind.
Throw your front arm forwards and upwards towards where you want to pitch the ball.
You are serving at tennis with a ball in your back hand and your back arm straight. Throw an imaginary ball up with your front arm.

Throw your front foot down the wicket towards the batsman, as though you wanted to tread on his toes. Keep it going in that direction for as long as possible.

Stamp your front foot down, and stand up straight. Brace your knee.

Your bowling arm is the sail on a windmill. Raise it with your front arm and swing it right around. Almost brush your ear.
Almost brush the outside of the front leg with the front arm. Try to reach for the ground alongside the little toe of your front foot with your bowling hand.
Run after the ball. You can't bowl in one direction and run in another.

Gather yourself and jump on to the back foot as though you were going to do a feet-astride jump facing the umpire. Watch where the ball should bounce.

Remember: Be balanced.
Watch where the ball will bounce.

23 The outswinger

An outswinger is bowled to make the ball curve or swing away from leg to off in the air before it bounces. It is bowled when a batsman shows a weakness against the ball which moves away from leg to off. This is indicated when the batsman tries to play the ball on the leg-side and consequently hits across the line of the ball which is curving in the opposite direction. Such a batsman hits the ball with most of the power in his bottom hand and tends to have his chest facing the bowler when he hits it. He may also follow the ball outside the off stump. The outswinger should be bowled when a wind coming from the leg-side will move the ball in the air from leg to off. The ideal winds for this movement are those which come from deep fine leg and mid-on. Humid, overcast conditions also help to curve the outswinger as does a head wind, though the latter situation reduces the pace of the bowler. The new ball, because of its shine and pronounced seam, helps the bowler to swing the ball more.

Remember: Be balanced.
Watch where the ball will bounce.

How to bowl an outswinger

The action
The basic bowling action is ideal for the outswinger since it imparts a body action which 'drags' the ball from leg to off. (This applies to right-handed bowlers bowling to right-handed batsmen or left-handed bowlers bowling to left-handed batsmen.)

The grip
Hold the ball with the seam running vertically and pointing at the moment of release towards first slip. The forefinger and second finger grip the ball at the top, one finger on each side of the seam. The side of your thumb should be on the seam at the bottom. Hold the ball well out of the palm and by the top joints of the fingers and thumb. Your third and little fingers are placed down the side of the ball. If there is a shiny side of the ball, place that side on the side opposite the direction of the desired swing.

The release
At the moment of release point the index and second fingers in the direction in which you want the ball to go. Allow your hand to come slightly around the outside of the ball pushing it towards the slips.

Simplified hints

Hold the ball in the three prongs of the first two fingers and the side of the thumb with the seam between the first two fingers pointing vertically towards the slips.

Steer the seam towards first slip as though you were steering the rudder of a ship.

The path of the outswinger

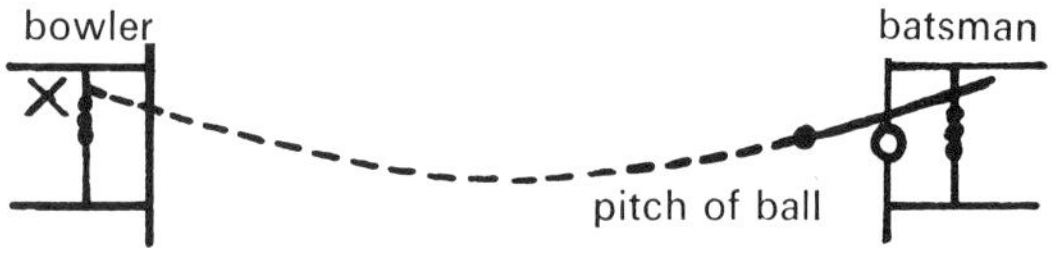

Check list
Emphasise points in this order.

At the moment of release, point the index and second fingers in the direction in which you want the ball to go, as though you were steering the ball with the rudder of the seam. Use your hand to steer the ship, coming slightly around the outside of the ball and pushing it towards the slips.
The basic bowling action.
Hold the ball in the three prongs of the first two fingers and side of the thumb, with the seam between the first two fingers and pointing vertically towards slips.

Remember: Be balanced.
Watch where the ball will bounce.

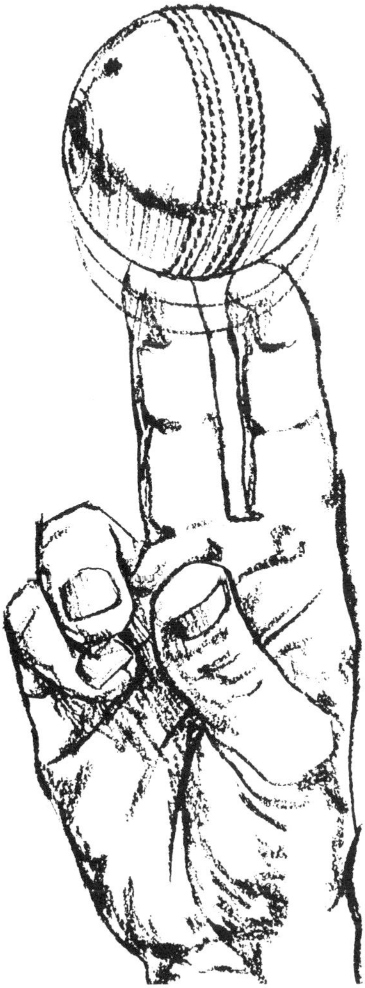

24 The off cutter

The off cutter is a delivery which turns *after* it bounces from off to leg, at medium to medium-fast pace. Sometimes the off cutter will swing away from the bat before it cuts back in because the off cutter is delivered with an outswinger body action.

An off cutter is bowled when a batsman is weak against the ball which turns into him from the off after it bounces. The batsman may not play closc cnough to his pads with the bat leaving a gap through which the ball can pass. If he does not grind the ball into the ground, he will play an off cutter into the air as a catch to close fieldsmen on the leg-side.

The off cutter is used when pitch and climatic conditions suit it. A dry pitch which 'dusts' or crumbles helps the ball turn, as does a wet wicket. Since the cutter is bowled at medium pace with wrist and finger 'cut' down the side of the ball, the ball turns quickly even on the slowest wickets. It also tends to lift suddenly.

A breeze blowing from the leg-side helps the off cutter since it blows the ball away to the off in the air, before it turns back in the opposite direction.

Remember: Be balanced.
Watch where the ball will bounce.

How to bowl an off cutter

The action
The basic action is ideal for the off cutter.

The grip
Hold the ball with the top joints of your fingers around the seam and well out of your palm. Grip the ball with your index and second fingers at the top at 11 and at 12 o'clock with your thumb at twenty to the hour and your third finger at twenty past. Your grip should be firm and with tension between your first, second and third fingers.

The release
Release the ball at the top of the bowling action. At the moment of release angle the seam in a line between cover and backward square leg. Drag your index and second fingers and wrist sharply downwards and forwards in the direction of backward square leg. Your rear shoulder and body action in the follow through will add to the cutting action by coming down the right-hand or leg-side of the ball.

Simplified hints

Grip the ball around the seam with the index and second fingers on top of it at 11 and 12 o'clock and pointing down the wicket. The thumb is at twenty to the hour and the third finger at twenty past.

At the moment of release, stand up tall and wind the ball and seam as though they were a clock key, with your wrist in the direction of backward square leg. Point with your index and second fingers and drag them downwards and forwards on the leg-side of the ball.

The path of the off cutter

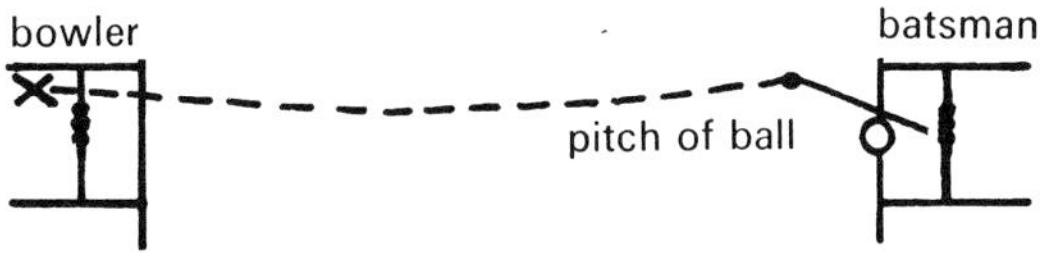

Check list
Emphasise points in this order.

At the moment of release, stand up tall and wind the ball and seam as though they were a clock key, with your wrist in the direction of backward square leg. Point with your index and second fingers and drag them downwards and forwards on leg-side of the ball.
The basic bowling action.
Grip the ball around the seam with the index and second fingers on top of it at 11 o'clock and 12 o'clock and pointing down the wicket. The thumb is at twenty to the hour and the third finger at twenty past.

Remember: Be balanced.
Watch where the ball will bounce.

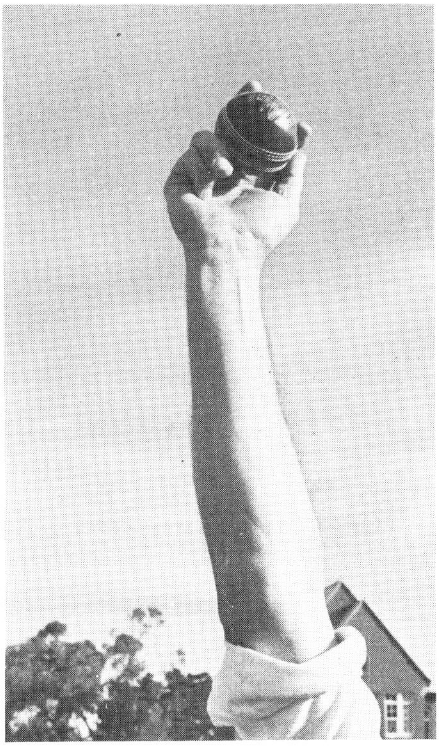

25 The off spinner and its variations

An off spinner is a delivery which turns at slow pace after it bounces from off to leg, and because of flight creates uncertainty in the batsman's mind about whether to play forward or back. Because the outswinger action is used the ball may curve away in the air before it spins back.

It is bowled to a batsman who shows he is weak against the ball which turns from the off into him after it bounces. He may not play close enough to his pads with his bat and leave a gap through which the ball can pass. He may also hesitate in deciding whether to play forward or back to the flighted off spinner, which is generally bowled at slow speed and may drop in the air producing a catch. Another weakness is when the batsman does not 'grind the ball into the ground' which causes him to play an off spinner in the air as a catch to close fieldsmen on the leg-side.

The off spinner is also used on a dry pitch which 'dusts' or crumbles helping the ball turn, or on a wet wicket. The speed with which the ball turns is determined by the dustiness or wetness of the pitch. The greater the dustiness of the pitch, the quicker the turn of the ball. This also occurs on a sticky wicket when a wet wicket is drying. A breeze blowing from the leg-side also helps the off spinner since it blows the ball away to the off in the air—curving it away before it turns back. A head wind makes the off spinner drop in the air and makes the batsman uncertain about whether to play forward or back.

Remember: Be balanced.
Watch where the ball will bounce.

How to bowl an off spinner	Simplified hints
The action The basic action is suitable for the off spinner. In the delivery stride accentuate the movement of your front foot to the leg-side, by pointing your front toe towards fine leg. Bowl against your front leg and swivel on your front toe. This will increase the amount of 'drift' towards the off-side in the air and the degree of spin.	Try to place the front foot in front of the stumps and swivel on it.
The grip Hold the ball by the top joints of your index and either the second or third finger around the seam, well out of the palm. Your index finger should be bent and you should exert tension between the top joints of the two fingers gripping the ball. Rest your thumb and little finger lightly on the seam.	Grip the ball around the seam with the top joints of the fingers, as though a tight elastic band has been placed around the tops of the fingers and thumb. Squeeze the ball between the index and second or third fingers until it hurts.
The release Release the ball at the top of the bowling action, early for more flight and late for a quicker delivery. At the moment of release the seam should be angled in a line between cover and backward square leg. Give the ball spin by pushing the index finger and wrist sharply towards backward square leg, and over the ball.	As you release the ball turn the wrist and fingers as though you were winding a clock with the seam in the direction of backward square leg.

Check list
Emphasise points in this order.

As you release the ball turn the wrist and fingers as though you were winding a clock with the seam in the direction of backward square leg.
Try to place the front foot in front of the stumps and swivel on it.
The basic bowling action.
Grip the ball around the seam with the top joints of the fingers, as though a tight elastic band has been placed around the tops of the fingers and thumb. Squeeze the ball between the index and second or third fingers until it hurts.

Remember: Be balanced.
Watch where the ball will bounce.

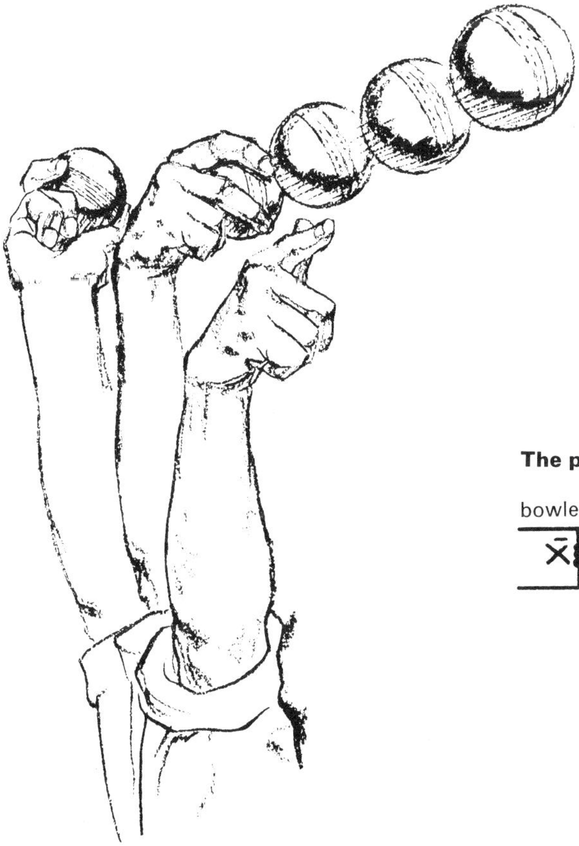

The path of the off spinner

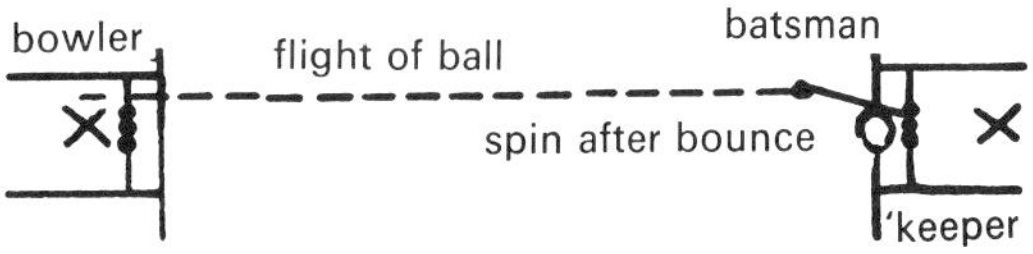

The left-handed orthodox leg spinner
The left-handed orthodox spinner has the same delivery as the off spinner but is bowled by a left-armed bowler. The left-handed leg spinner is a delivery which turns after it bounces from leg to off.

It is bowled in the same climatic and pitch conditions as the off spinner. The ideal breeze would be one which blows from off to leg and floats the ball in that direction before it turns in the opposite one. The right-handed batsman would display the same hesitancy against flight, but his technical weakness would be to play across the line of the ball towards the leg-side against the direction of the spin. He would hit with the bottom hand in control and have his chest facing the bowler in playing the ball. He could also be inclined to follow the ball which spins away outside the off stump.

All the details of the action, grip and release for an off spinner apply equally to the left-handed leg spinner bowling with finger rather than over-the-wrist spin.

How to vary off spin bowling
The batsman can become accustomed to dealing with the off spinner's delivery unless the bowler can vary his delivery. He can do this either by varying the flight of the ball or by sending down a ball which does not turn.

The drifting delivery
The drifting delivery is a ball which is disguised as an off spinner but does not spin. It 'goes with the arm', away towards the slips. The batsman plays for the turning ball and as a result edges the ball drifting away in the air as a catch to the slips.

Bowl the drifting delivery when the batsman plays inside the line and as though every ball is going to turn, or when he plays with the bottom hand in control and his chest facing you and consequently across the line of the ball. The wicket may be good and the wind suitable and from the leg-side.

Point the seam of the ball down the wicket towards first slip and grip the ball loosely on the smooth surface rather than the seam. Deliver the ball from close to the stumps and on delivery drop the arm slightly and slide the hand under and around the leg-side of the ball. Swivel on the front foot.

The overspun off spinner
An overspun off spinner is a delivery with a certain amount of over or forward spin. This makes the ball drop quickly in the air and lift so that the batsman will misjudge the flight of the ball and fail to reach the bounce, consequently lofting his shots for catches in front of the wicket.

The overspun off spinner should be bowled when the batsman is not judging the flight of the ball well and is either hesitant or rash in using footwork to reach the bounce of the ball.

Grip the ball as for the normal off spinner, but in spinning the ball angle the seam vertically towards fine rather than square leg. 'The clock is wound' by pushing the index finger and seam towards fine leg and over the top of the ball. The moment of delivery occurs just before the delivery arm reaches the top of the action.

drifting delivery

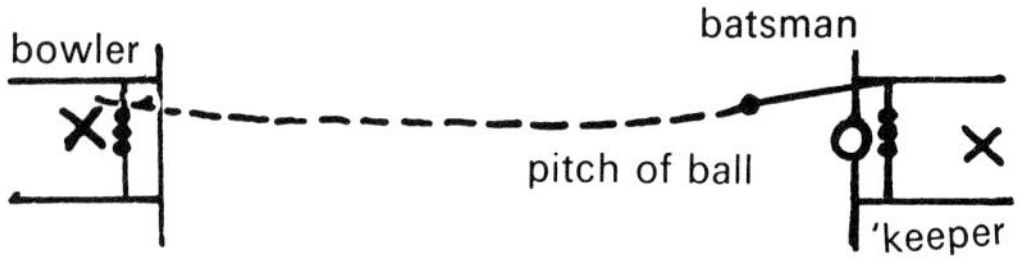

overspun off spinner

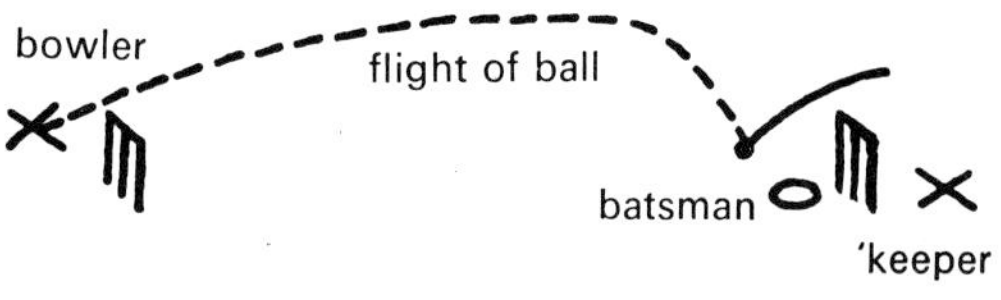

Check list
Emphasise points in this order.

The drifting off spinner
As you release the ball, slide your hand underneath it.
Point the seam in the direction of the slips as you release the ball.
The basic bowling action.
Grip the ball loosely on the smooth surface.

The overspun off spinner
As you release the ball, wind the seam forward towards the batsman letting go just a little early.
The basic bowling action.
Grip the ball around the seam with the top joints of the fingers as though a tight elastic band has been placed around the tops of the fingers and thumb. Squeeze the ball between the top knuckles of the third and index fingers.

The drifting delivery

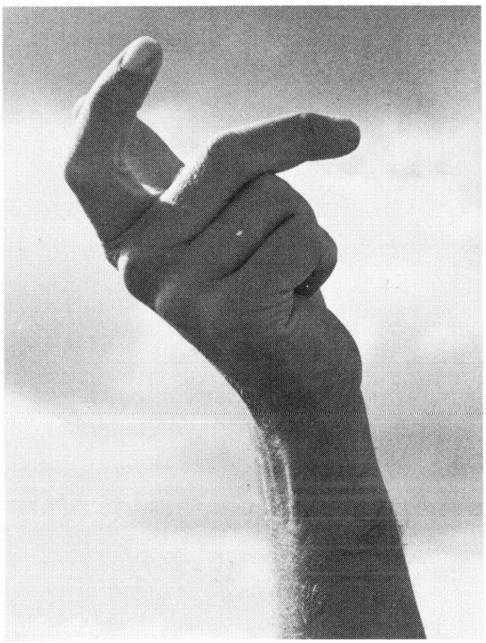

The overspun off spinner

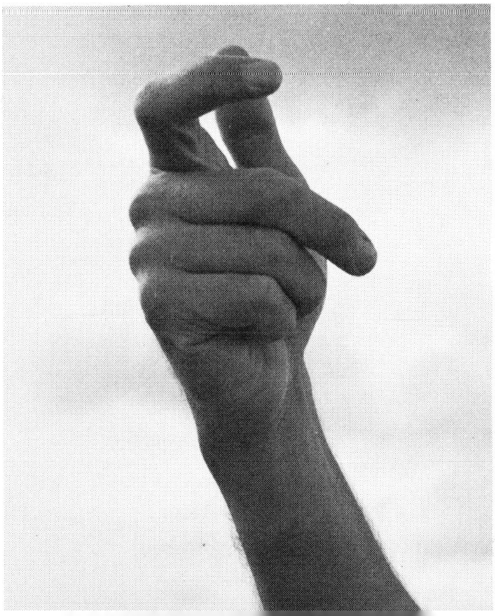

26 The right-handed wrist spun leg spinner and its variations

A right-handed leg spinner is a delivery which turns even on good wickets from leg to off. Its flight makes the batsman uncertain about whether to play forward or back. It is bowled when a batsman shows he is weak against a ball which turns away from his leg to off after it bounces. He may play across the line of the ball towards the leg-side and against the direction of the spin. He may hit with the bottom hand in control and his chest facing the bowler in playing the ball. He may also follow the ball which spins away outside the off stump. Or he may not grind the ball into the ground—a fault which causes him to play a leg spinner into the air as a catch to close fieldsmen on the off-side.

The leg spinner is also used when a good hard wicket enables the ball to turn slightly and makes it bounce. A dry pitch which 'dusts' or crumbles slightly enables the leg spin bowler to turn the ball a long way, quickly. A wet pitch helps the ball turn slowly and without much lift unless the pitch is drying.

A breeze blowing from the off-side helps the leg spinner since it floats the ball in from that direction before turning back from leg. A head wind will make the leg spinner drop in the air, increasing the flight of the ball and making the batsman uncertain about whether to play forward or back.

Remember: Be balanced.
Watch where the ball will bounce.

How to bowl a right-handed leg spinner	Simplified hints
The action In general the basic action is well suited to leg spin. The side-on position, the high delivery arm and bowling against the front leg place weight behind the delivery, impart more spin and make the ball turn quickly.	
The grip Hold the ball with the top joints of your index and third fingers, around the seam, well out of the palm. Your thumb and second and little fingers should rest on the seam with the tension between the top joints of the index and third fingers.	Grip the ball around the seam with the top joints of the fingers, as though a tight elastic band has been placed around the tops of the fingers and thumb. Squeeze the ball between the knuckles of the third and index fingers.
The release Release the ball at the top of the bowling action, earlier for more flight and later for a quicker delivery. At the moment of delivery angle the seam between gully and mid-wicket. In the delivery bend the hand inwards towards the inside of your wrist and then rotate it down and outwards until your wrist is straight and your palm faces the leg-side. Spin is imparted when you push the third finger and the wrist towards gully and over the ball.	As you release the ball turn the wrist and fingers of the bowling hand as though you are swimming the Australian crawl—only flick your wrist right over in an 11 o'clock direction. Spin the seam towards gully with the third finger.

Check list
Emphasise points in this order.

As you release the ball turn the wrist and fingers of the bowling hand, as though you were swimming the Australian crawl—only flick your wrist right over in an 11 o'clock direction.
Spin the seam towards gully with the third finger.
The basic bowling action.
Grip the ball around the seam with the top joints of the fingers, as though a tight elastic band has been placed around the tops of the fingers and thumb. Squeeze the ball between the top knuckles of the third and index fingers.

Remember: Be balanced.
Watch where the ball will bounce.

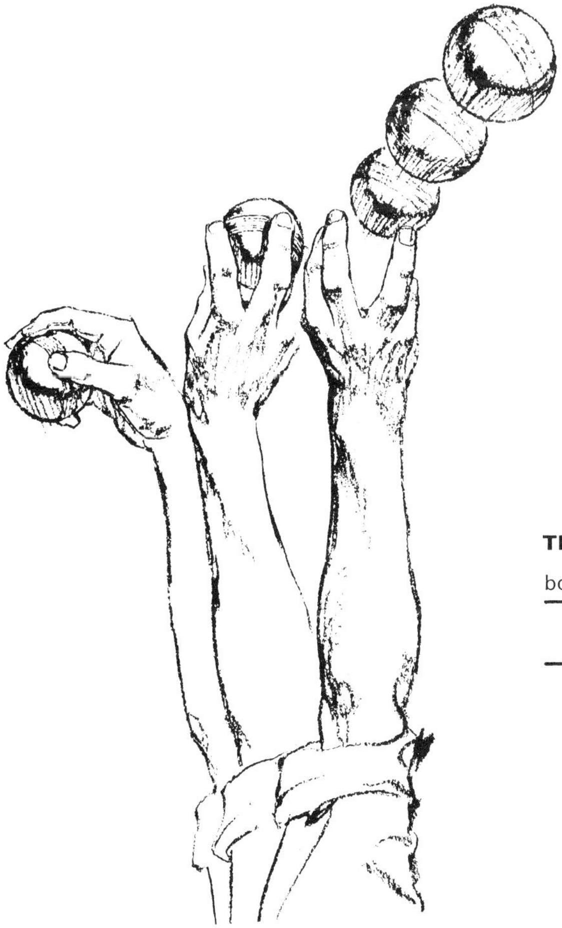

The path of the right-handed leg spinner

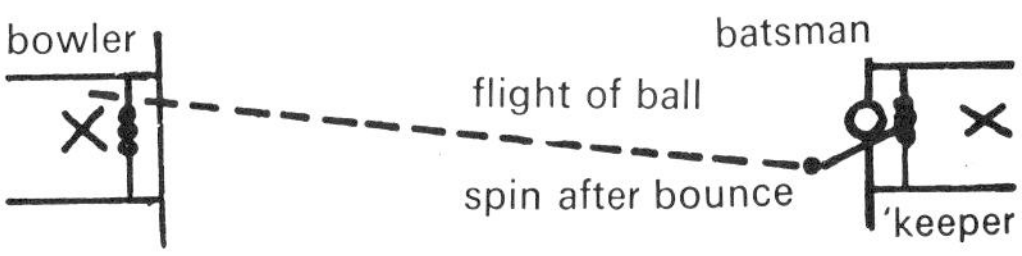

How to vary right-handed wrist spinning leg breaks

The 'wrong-'un'

The batsman may become accustomed to a ball which regularly bounces and spins from the leg-side. This delivery can be varied by the 'googly', 'wrong-'un' or 'bosie', all of which are used to describe a disguised ball which looks like a right-handed wrist-spinning leg spinner but turns after it bounces the opposite way, that is, into the batsman from the off.

A 'wrong-'un' is bowled to puzzle the batsman who is unable to detect which way the ball will spin from the action and wrist movement of the bowler. It is a good ball to exploit a batsman who does not play with his bat close to his pad. The flight of a delivery which turns after it bounces from off to leg, with a leg spinner's action, will make the batsman uncertain about whether to play forward or back. It can also be used against a batsman who does not grind the ball into the ground—he may play the 'wrong-'un' into the air as a catch to the close fieldsmen on the leg-side.

The 'wrong-'un' should be used when climatic and pitch conditions suit it. A good hard wicket provides turn and bounce. A dry pitch which 'dusts' or crumbles provides quick, pronounced turn and bounce. A wet wicket provides wide but slow turn unless the pitch is drying.

A breeze blowing from the off-side helps the 'wrong-'un' float in from outside the off stump and spin the same way. A head wind helps the 'wrong-'un' drop in the air and poses problems of flight for the batsman. The ideal wind for it comes from deep third man.

The 'wrong-'un' is bowled with a body action similar to that of the inswinger in delivery stride and arm and trunk action. This will be described in the next chapter. Your head should look in front of, not behind, your front elbow, your front leg should be thrust towards the batsman's off stump down the pitch, and your chest and hips should be in an open position facing the batsman. Follow through down the centre of the chest, with the bowling hand, shoulder and arm swinging in a line drawn between the legs. Grip the ball as if you were bowling a leg spinner, but spin the ball over the top and behind your third finger. At the moment of release accentuate the overarm 'Australian crawl' action of your bowling arm and wrist so much that the elbow points upwards and the back of your hand faces the ground. Spin the ball out of the back of your hand, and rotate the seam towards backward square leg.

The wrist spun top spinner

The wrist spun top spinner spins forward towards the batsman and turns neither from leg nor off but bounces slightly higher. It is bowled when a batsman picks up the direction of the spin of a wrist spinner easily and expects every ball to turn.

The basic bowling action is used. The grip is identical to that of the leg spinner, but at the moment of release point the back of your bowling hand down the wicket at the batsman with your elbow facing the rear. Spin the ball over the top of your third finger with the seam pointing down the wicket and not towards gully.

wrong-'un

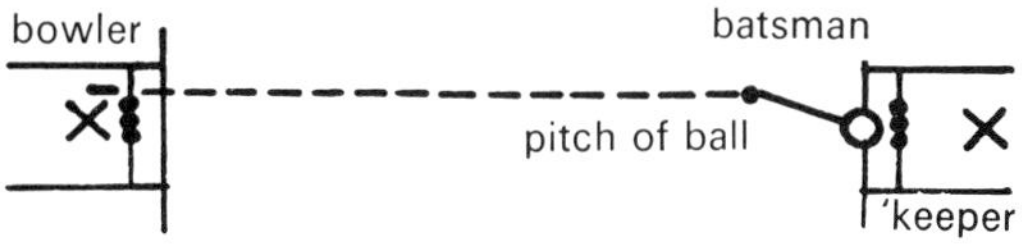

top spinner

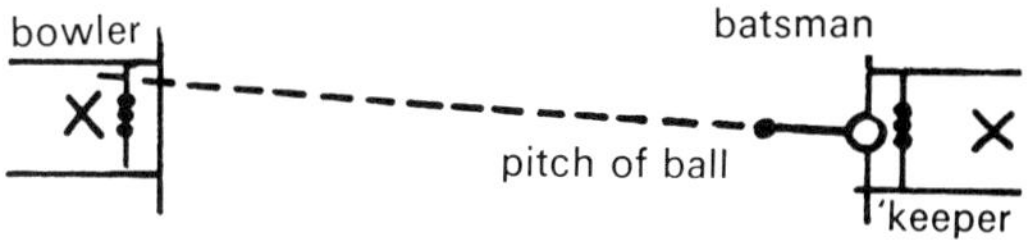

Check list
Emphasise points in this order.

The 'wrong-'un'
At the moment of release imagine that you are swimming the Australian crawl and trying to turn your bowling wrist over so far that the palm and the thumb point down the pitch. Drop your bowling shoulder a little and imagine that you are producing the ball from the back trouser pocket.
The inswing bowling action.
Grip the ball around the seam with the top joints of the fingers, as though a tight elastic band has been placed around the tops of the fingers and thumb. Squeeze the ball between the top knuckles of the third and index fingers.

The top spinner
As you let go of the ball, imagine that you are throwing the back of the hand downwards towards the batsman, and rotating the seam vertically towards him. Push the third finger over the top of the hand towards the batsman.
The basic bowling action.
Grip the ball around the seam with the top joints of the fingers, as though a tight elastic band has been placed around the tops of the fingers and thumb. Squeeze the ball between the top knuckles of the third and index fingers.

Remember: Be balanced.
Watch where the ball will bounce.

The 'wrong 'un'

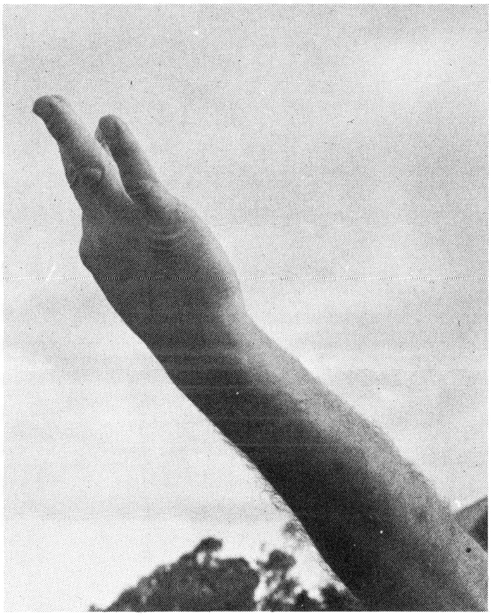

The wrist spun top spinner

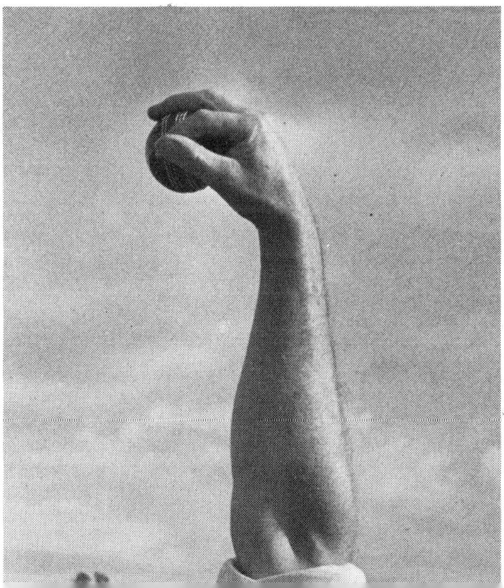

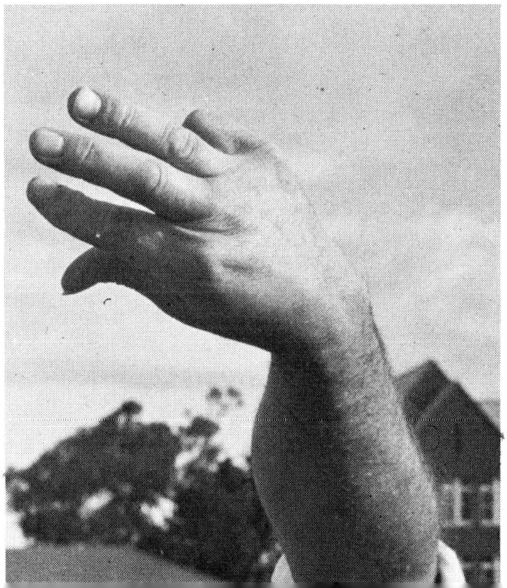

27 The inswinger

An inswinger is a delivery which swings or curves in the air from off to leg before it bounces. It is a medium-paced or fast delivery. An inswinger is bowled when a batsman is weak against a ball which swings into him from the off before it bounces. He may not play close enough to his pads with his bat. He may fail to 'grind the ball into the ground' and play the inswinger into the air as a catch to close fieldsmen on the leg-side.

The inswinger should also be used when there is a breeze blowing from the off-side which will curve the ball in from that direction. The ideal breeze is from deep third man or mid-off. A head wind will increase the swing of the ball but decreases the speed of the ball.

Remember: Be balanced.
Watch where the ball will bounce.

How to bowl an inswinger

Delivery stride

As you approach the bowling crease, gather yourself by jumping and placing your weight on to your back foot which is on the same side of the body as your bowling arm. The toes of your rear foot should be roughly parallel to the bowling crease and point towards the stumps. The rear foot should not be as parallel to the bowling crease as in the basic action. The toes point more towards mid wicket. Move your front foot in a line straight down the wicket not towards fine leg as in the basic action.

Front arm and trunk

As you jump on to your rear foot, reach upwards with your front arm, turning your body so that your front shoulder and hip point down the wicket and at the batsman. Your chest should be towards mid-on, your head upright and steady, and your eyes fixed on the spot on which you intend to bounce the ball. Look at this spot from a point in front of your front shoulder and not behind as in the basic action. Your front arm acts as a lever pushing your trunk back, stretching the front side, and lifting your front foot clear of the ground. From this position throw your front arm and shoulder forward and upwards towards a point just outside the batsman's off stump, transferring your weight on to your front foot. Rotate your hips and open them early in the action, bringing your chest to face the batsman.

The front foot

Step your front foot down the wicket transferring your weight on to it and landing so that some part of your foot is behind the rear edge of the batting or popping crease. Your toes should point towards the batsman. Straighten your front knee and brace it as your body passes over it.

Simplified hints

After gathering yourself ready to bowl, spring on to the back foot as though you you were jumping with your feet astride facing a spot just in front of the stumps at the bowling end.

Reach for the sky with your front arm, looking inside your elbow. Push your front arm backwards as though it were a young tree bending in the wind, or a ruler bent back ready to catapult the ball forwards. Look along the inside of your elbow at where you want to bounce the ball.
Imagine you are serving at tennis with a ball instead of a racquet in your rear hand. Throw an imaginary ball up with the front arm and, with a straight rear arm, slice the ball into the receiver.

Stamp your front foot down in the direction of the batsman and stand up on it tall.

The bowling arm

Raise your bowling arm at the beginning of the action with your front arm and in front of your body. Keeping your bowling arm straight swing it downwards, backwards and then upwards almost brushing the side of your head at the top of the delivery and the moment of releasing the ball. You should be upright at this stage striving for maximum height.

Your bowling arm is a windmill. Whirl it around and finish by brushing the inside of your back leg.

Follow through

After releasing the ball, swing your bowling arm and shoulder slightly across your body and downwards finishing on a line between your legs. As your bowling arm swings downwards as near the ground as possible, bend your back. Your front arm should precede the bowling arm, swinging backwards to brush the outside of the front knee and finish high behind your back. After taking one step straight down the wicket after the bowling stride, swing off the pitch towards cover for a further three or four steps in your follow through.

Throw your front arm, bowling arm and front shoulder in the direction of first slip, pushing the ball into the batsman. Run after the ball and in the same direction. Try to touch the ground inside the big toe of your front foot in the follow through.

The grip

Hold the ball by the two joints of your index and second fingers and the flat of your thumb well out of the palm. The seam should point vertically towards fine leg. Your index and second fingers should be slightly across, on each side and on top of the seam, slightly apart and pointing down the pitch. Your thumb should hold the seam underneath the ball with your third and little fingers positioned alongside the ball.

The seam of the ball is the rudder.

The release

At the moment of release the seam of the ball should point to fine leg and your hand should pass down the side of the ball pushing it in to the right-handed batsman. Your arm should be high. If there is a shiny side to the ball place it on the opposite side of the ball to the desired swing.

As you let go steer and push the ball into the batsman, standing tall and using the seam as the rudder.

The path of the inswinger

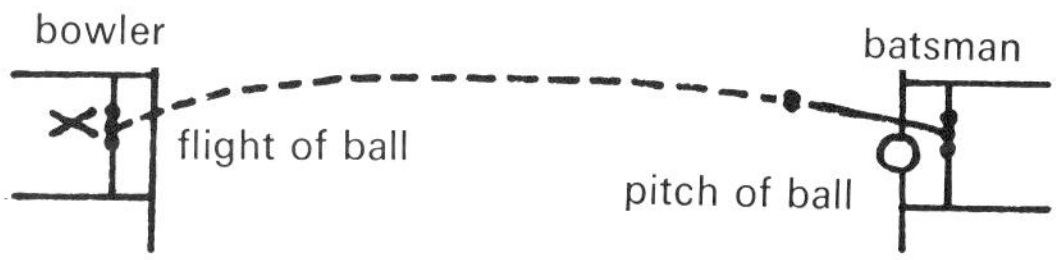

Check list
Emphasise points in this order.

Reach for the sky with your front arm, looking inside your elbow. Push your front arm backwards as though it were a young tree bending in the wind, or a ruler bent back ready to catapult the ball forwards.
Imagine you are passing through a door when you reach up suddenly to grasp the lintel with your front arm. Bend like a ruler catapult. Look along the inside of your elbow at where you want to bounce the ball.
Imagine you are serving at tennis with a ball instead of a racquet in your rear hand. Throw an imaginary ball up with the front arm and, with a straight rear arm, slice the ball into the receiver.
Your bowling arm is a windmill. Whirl it around and finish by brushing your back leg.
Throw your front arm, bowling arm and front shoulder in the direction of first slip, pushing the ball into the batsman. Run after the ball and in the same direction.
Try to touch the ground in front of you in the follow through.
Stamp your front foot down in the direction of the batsman, and stand up on it tall.
After gathering yourself ready to bowl, spring on to the back foot as though you were jumping with your feet astride facing a spot just in front of the stumps at the bowling end.
The seam of the ball is the rudder. As you let go, steer the ball in the direction you want, into the batsman and towards fine leg.
As you let go steer and push the ball into the batsman, standing tall and using the seam as the rudder.

Remember: Be balanced.
Watch where the ball will bounce.

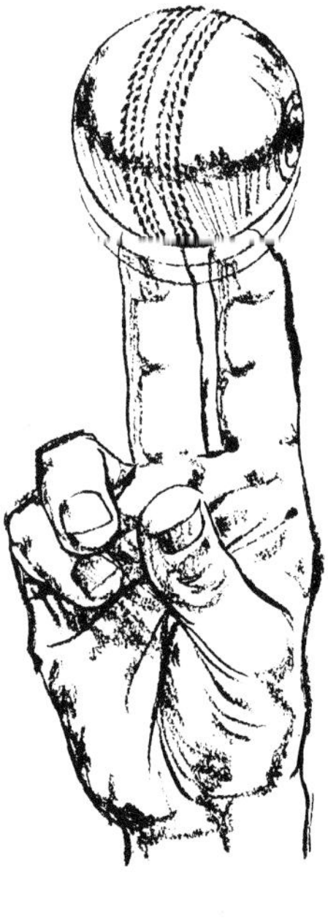

28 The leg cutter

The leg cutter is a delivery which turns after it bounces from leg to off at medium to medium-fast pace. Because the inswinger action is used the ball will sometimes swing in before cutting away. It is bowled when a batsman is weak against a ball which turns quickly from leg to off after it bounces. He may not position his eyes and bat behind the line of the ball, but play inside its line. He may be inclined to follow the path of the ball outside the off stump producing a catch to the off-side, as he would if he did not grind the ball into the ground.

The leg cutter is used when the pitch and climatic conditions suit it. A dry, 'crumbling' or 'dusting' pitch enables the ball to turn quickly, as does a sticky wicket. Since the cutter is bowled at medium or medium-fast pace with the wrists and fingers cutting down the side of the ball, it turns quickly on even the slowest of wickets. It also tends to lift suddenly.

The breeze blowing from the off-side helps the leg cutter since it blows the ball into the stumps before cutting it away in the opposite direction.

Remember: Be balanced.
Watch where the ball will bounce.

How to bowl a leg cutter

The action
The inswinger action is ideal for the leg cutter.

The grip
Hold the ball around the seam well out of the palm with the top joints of your index and second and third fingers. Your index and second fingers should be on top of the ball at 11 o'clock and 1 o'clock with the thumb at twenty to the hour and the third finger at twenty past. Your grip should be firm with tension between the index, second and third fingers.

The release
Release the ball at the top of the bowling action. At the moment of release angle the seam between mid-wicket and backward point. Cut is imparted by drawing the index, second, third fingers and wrist sharply downwards in the direction of backward point. Your second finger is the main 'cutting' agent and your rear shoulder and body action in the delivery swing will add to the cutting action by coming down on the off-side of the ball.

Simplified hints

Grip the ball around the seam with the index and second fingers on top of it at 11 and 1 o'clock, pointing down the wicket and well spaced. The thumb is at twenty to the hour and the third finger at twenty past.

At the moment of release stand up to your full height and turn your wrist and fingers as though you were turning a door knob sharply towards backward point. Point with your index, second and third fingers towards the batsman and drag them downwards on the off-side of the ball.

The path of the leg cutter

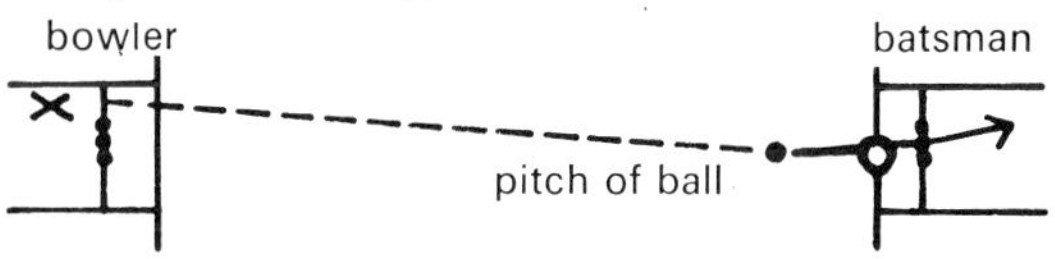

Check list
Emphasise points in this order.

At the moment of release stand up to your full height and turn your wrist and fingers as though you were turning a door knob sharply towards backward point. Point with your index, second and third fingers towards the batsman and drag them downwards on the off-side of the ball.
The inswing bowling action.
Grip the ball around the seam with the index and second fingers on top of it at 11 and 1 o'clock, pointing down the wicket and well spaced. The thumb is at twenty to the hour and the third finger at twenty past.

Remember: Be balanced.
Watch where the ball will bounce.

29 Bowling tactics

Variety is one of the most important weapons of a bowler. The bowler should confront the batsman with changing problems to which he must adapt in the half-second or second of the ball's flight. Varying the deliveries has dangers, however, since few bowlers have complete mastery of every type of delivery. To try the complete range causes inaccuracy and consequent punishment. Each bowler should therefore cultivate a regular or 'stock' ball over which he has a high degree of control and vary his attack in a limited way around that delivery. Variety can be achieved by several simple methods.

The use of the bowling crease
The bowling crease is 2.64 metres (8′ 8″) long between the return creases. The bowler can attack the batsman bowling over or around the wicket from any spot on the crease. He can therefore vary his angle of attack greatly and by varying his spin and swing produce a wide range of different balls. An outswinger bowled close to the bowling stumps and aimed at the batsman's leg stump could produce an edged catch to the slips. A similar ball delivered wide on the return crease and aimed at the batsman's leg stump would probably hit the wicket. Bowling around the wicket increases the angle away from the batsman but diminishes the chances of an lbw decision for under this law the ball which bounces in line with the stumps must turn back into them to eventually hit them.

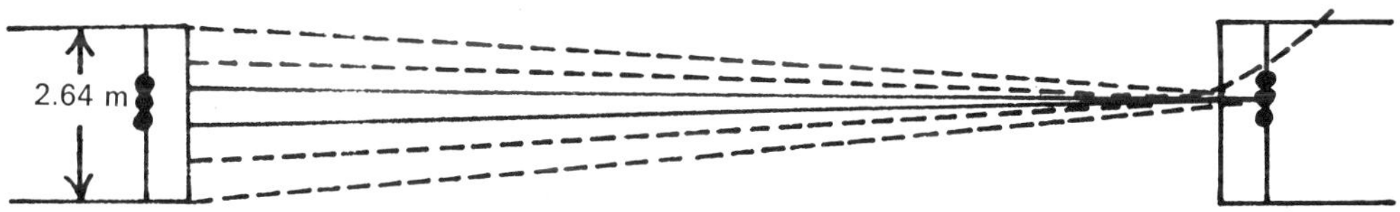

Change in pace
The bowler varies his pace to make the batsman play early or late. For this to be achieved the difference in pace need not be great but it must not be seen by the batsman. The speed of your run-up must be the same, the position of your body unchanged and the speed of your bowling arm constant.

Vary your pace only occasionally to prevent the batsman being constantly on his guard. Variations in pace are generally achieved by removing some part of the weight of the action or hand from behind the ball. The 'Demon' Australian bowler Spofforth used to bowl a 'half-ball' in which he held only half of the ball with half of his hand, thus cutting down the side of the ball. Other fast and medium bowlers send down off spinners or cutters: deliveries in which the hand draws down the side of the ball. Individual bowlers achieve spectacular success by their own unique methods and coaches should encourage this.

Variation in flight

The flight of the ball can be changed by varying the speed of the delivery or by increasing or decreasing the amount of top or side spin. The spin bowler can deliver a quicker ball by increasing the speed of his action and flattening his flight. He can 'lob' a slower ball by means of a slower arm action and earlier point of delivery. More difficult for the batsman to see is the ball which is spun forward harder than normal. This makes the ball 'loop' in the air like an overspun table tennis shot and drop suddenly before bouncing high off the pitch. The wrist-spun top spinner, and the overspun off spinner achieve this end. The side-spun off spinner or 'drifter' makes the ball float towards the slips with the arm, whilst the under-spun leg spinner or 'flipper' (a specialist and difficult ball flicked out of the hand between thumb and fingers) makes the ball skid through quickly off the pitch.

Varying the flight of the ball makes the batsman uncertain about whether to play forward or back and makes him loft his stroke because he has not reached the bounce of the ball. When to vary the ball's flight depends on the batsman's uncertainty or rashness in playing or moving forward, and on the bowler's mastery of the ball.

Length and line in bowling

Bowling on a good length and line is a great virtue in a bowler. A good length and line means that the batsman is continually uncertain about whether to play forward or back and is forced to defend. In the past these two qualities have always been placed before the virtues of speed, swing, cut and spin but this has meant that the coach, by making his students concentrate on length and line, restrained their natural abilities to bowl with exceptional speed, swing, cut or spin. The coach's job is to increase and improve on natural abilities, not restrain them. Length and line can be taught by practising the basic action. Place them second in coaching priorities to speed, swing, cut and spin.

30 Correction of bowling faults

The following are some of the most frequent faults in bowling.

An irregular run-up leading to no-ball faults

The run-up should be an automatic part of the bowling skill. Practise until it is mechanical and until your feet land in the same spot each time that you approach the wicket. Practise the run-up without going through the action of bowling. It should be consistent in total length and length of stride, rhythmic and smooth. Start slowly, then accelerate and decelerate before delivery. Your follow through should be long enough and straight for the first stride after delivery.

Hesitancy in the run-up occurs when a bowler realises that he is not at the correct distance from the bowling wicket a few steps before the delivery stride. A coach can help him establish a natural run-up by suggesting that he runs away from the bowling wicket and gathers himself when he feels ready to bowl. Then measure the natural run in paced, even strides so that a consistent length is established.

The run-up should not be too long. If you angle your approach slightly from mid-off you will be able to turn more easily into your delivery stride. The coach can cue the bowler from a position at mid-off level with the middle of his approach, with such phrases as, 'a slow start, accelerate, gather yourself'.

Too fast a run-up will mean that you may 'run through' your action without having time to gather yourself. Too slow and too short an approach will curtail your follow through and place a great strain on your body during and just after the delivery stride.

The bowler's front arm is too low

This fault will reduce the use you can make of your body in the delivery stride. If your arm is too low you won't be able to 'rock back' in your action and this will lessen pace and spin. It may also lead to your action being low and consequently producing little bounce from the pitch.

The fault stems from a lazy action. Your front arm acts as a lever for the explosive quality of the action and also as a 'signpost' controlling the direction of delivery. 'Reach for the sky' or 'reach up as though you were throwing up a ball to serve at tennis and were then bending backwards like a tree in a high wind'.

The bowler's action is too open

If you bowl chest-on rather than with your shoulder pointing to the batsman, this may be due to one of several faults. If your run-up is too fast you won't be able to turn properly into your action and your back foot won't be parallel to the bowling crease and will point down the pitch. If you fail to look behind the front arm and over the front shoulder the same problem will arise. But note that the inswinger demands a certain degree of openness in the action. Your action may be too open because you throw your front foot forward in the direction of slip and not towards fine leg.

The open position is a dangerous one since it robs a bowler of pace and spin, increases the tendency to bowl down the leg-side. It is also a posture from which it is easier to throw rather than to bowl.

The coach should create situations which will make the bowler turn into his action. This can be done by placing a stump on the bowling crease just wide of the wickets themselves and another stump on the batting crease in line with the nearest wicket to the bowler. He must then run and bowl through the corridor created, running more into his action and bowling more across his front foot. The coach should also watch for the bowler who runs up too quickly and does not look behind his front arm and at the spot on the pitch on which he hopes to bounce the ball.

The bowler opens up his action too early in the delivery stride
Some bowlers position themselves correctly at the bowling crease yet open their action too early in their delivery stride. This is generally indicated by an inclination to throw the front arm towards the slips and to rotate the hips early, pointing the front toe towards slips, and by a low bowling arm and slinging action. Opening your action too early and slinging in this way will produce inaccuracy. If you release the ball too early it will pass down the leg-side and if you release it too late it will pass wide on the off-side.

Your action should stay with the front arm as long as possible. Remember that where the front arm goes, the bowling arm follows. If you open your action early you will veer off quickly away from the pitch and push the ball down the leg-side. You cannot run in one direction and project the ball in another with any degree of accuracy. You should literally run after the ball, at the same time avoiding running on the wicket.

Again the coach may use stumps to indicate the path that the bowler should follow, with more stumps being used to outline the path of the bowler's follow through.

The bowler does not follow through
If you don't follow through, your approach is probably too slow and does not provide enough impetus to force you down the wicket. Lack of follow through is a dangerous fault. The follow through is the shock absorber of the action. If you take one or two steps after releasing the ball, your body is absorbing all of the violent shock of the explosive final stride and gymnastic action. This places tremendous strain on the muscles and you will tire quickly.

Run after the ball. Throwing your front arm and leg down the wicket will help you follow through just as proper acceleration in your approach will.

Faults in the grip
Most faults in the grip stem not from ignorance of how to hold the ball but from lack of understanding about where the seam of the ball should be pointing at the moment of release. To swing the ball the seam should point in the direction of the desired movement when you release the ball. To spin the ball the seam must be revolving in the direction of the desired turn on release. The position of your wrist and your body action play an important part in the skills of swing and spin.

A common fault in spinners is to hold the ball too close to the palm and not in the fingers. There must be tension between the top knuckles of your fingers to spin the ball. In swinging the ball it is also advisable to hold the ball out of the palm. This is difficult for children whose hands are too small for them to grip the ball in the fingers. Wherever possible use a suitable junior ball with under-age children.

Faults in the grip can only be cured by observation on the part of the coach. He should position himself in front and to the side of the bowler or behind so that he can observe the position of the seam at the moment of release. He will then be able to make suggestions about alterations to the grip. If a bowler adopts an unorthodox grip, however, and achieves the desired results, there is no point in suggesting that he changes his grip to a more conventional one.

31 Wicketkeeping

The wicketkeeper is the most important fieldsman in cricket. Theoretically he may have to stop every ball. He takes more catches, stumps more batsmen, and runs out more players than any other fieldsman. There is no substitute for a good 'keeper: he has to be consistently proficient and can inspire his side.

Remember: Be balanced.
Watch the bowler, the batsman and the ball.

How to keep wicket

Equipment

Always wear and use comfortable clothes and equipment—small light pads and gloves are preferable to big and heavy ones. The gloves protect the hands but must allow you to 'feel' the ball as you take it. A pair of inner chamois gloves should always be worn in addition to the wicketkeeping gloves themselves. Push fingers of both your hands hard into the tops of the inners and gloves. It is an idea to shorten the length of the hard finger stall protection at the end of fingers. The stall protection is standard in most gloves but it can reduce the flexibility of the fingers. Never allow the glove surface to become worn and smooth and your gloves should have a good hollow or 'cup' in the palm. Comfortable boots are essential. To avoid sore feet on hard grounds wear inner soles or two pairs of socks. Clothes should be loose fitting for comfort and quick movement. A cap helps concentration and reduces glare from the wicket.

Stance

It is difficult to set a standard stance for wicketkeepers. Some prefer to squat on their toes, others balance on the balls of their feet. Whichever stance you adopt, it should be comfortable with your weight distributed evenly between your legs and feet. The comfortable balanced squatting stance will ensure essential speedy footwork.

Stand back far enough to fast bowlers to receive the average ball as it stops rising. Judge how far outside the off stump you should stand. Naturally this will vary with different bowlers and conditions. A left-hand bowler over the wicket on a 'green' pitch will demand a different 'keeping position to a right-handed bowler on a good wicket. The critical point is that the bowler's hand must be clearly visible throughout the run-up and delivery.

Simplified hints

Push your fingers hard into the top of your inners and gloves to feel the ball. Be comfortable in your equipment and not weighed down.

Speedy footwork is important to good wicketkeeping and this starts from a comfortable squatting stance, with the body balanced and the feet apart. Squat in a position just outside off stump from where a clear view can be obtained of the bowler's hand and always have the stumps within reach when standing up to the wicket.

To a pace bowler the 'keeper should be in a position far enough back to gather the average ball as it stops rising.

For slow bowlers you must judge how far outside the off stump you need to stand. It will generally be just outside off stump but will vary according to the type of bowler. It is essential that you are near enough to the stumps to reach them with one movement and effect a stumping when the opportunity arises. For medium-paced bowlers you must decide whether you stand up to the stumps or back. This will depend on the state of the game and the wicket. If in doubt it is better to stand back since in that position you will take a high percentage of the straightforward edged catches.

Movement of the feet

Quick movement is essential to good wicketkeeping. You will need at all times to drive your legs to achieve this. Try to move into a position behind the ball or where you can take the ball on the side of the body closer to the stumps.

Here comes a fine edge down the leg-side; now *drive* yourself at the ball and try to take it on the side of the body nearer the stumps.

When standing back to any bowler, be prepared to spring up to the stumps, every ball if necessary, to deter the batsman from taking quick singles and to be prepared for run-out attempts. Unless there is a chance of a run-out, you should always move to the thrown balls and try to take returns from the fieldsmen on the full, thus preserving the shine of the ball for bowlers and showing the batsmen that you are alert. If you cannot take the ball on the full toss, move back, gaining time to see its height and direction and minimising the risk of an awkward bounce and possible injury.

England needs a single to win the game with one ball remaining. The batsmen have made up their minds to run, even if the striker misses the ball. Now, from a standing back position, move up to the wicket as quickly as you can to run the batsman out or take the return from the field. Drive your legs.

The hands

To avoid damage to the fingers in taking the ball it is essential that you always point your fingers up or down when taking the ball, sometimes slightly to the side. Never point them towards the ball.

Point your fingers at 6 or 12 o'clock and never towards the bowler and ball.

Give with your hands, arms and body as you take the ball to prevent it bouncing out and to avoid sore hands. Never snatch at the ball.

When you are taking the ball imagine that you are catching a raw egg and you don't want to break it. Let your hands give like a mattress.

Head and eyes

Never take your eyes off the ball while it is in play. Ignore the swing of the bat and assume that every ball will come to you. Hold your head steady.

Watch the ball all the time. The batsman and his bat do not exist. Take every ball.

Stumping

Always be in a position to stump the batsman who has left his crease. Keep the stumps within reach in a single movement. Never retreat to take the ball. Watch the batsman's feet and the ball all the time. Rise with the ball according to its bounce and let the hands give as you gather it. Concentrate on taking the ball before moving your hands towards the stumps. When you see the batsman leave his crease, never be hurried into snatching at the ball.

First things first. Make haste slowly. You can't stump anyone unless you take the ball first. Watch the ball and striker. Let the ball come and the hands give. After that comes the time for speed in striking at the stumps which should be within reach.

The following are the most frequent wicketkeeping faults:

Incorrect gloves and equipment
Faulty balance
Poor footwork
Wrong positioning at the stumps
Uncomfortable stance
Lack of drive in the movement to the ball
Inability to reach the stumps standing up
Wrong positioning of the hands when taking the ball
Snatching at the ball and not allowing the hands to give
Taking the eyes off the ball
Trying to stump the batsman before taking the ball
Retreating when taking the ball.

Stance standing up

Taking the ball

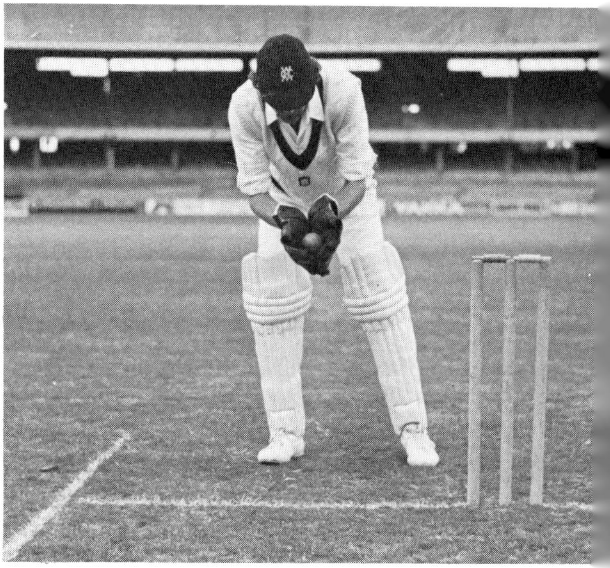

Stumping on the off-side

Stumping on the leg-side

Check list
Emphasise points in this order.

Watch the ball all the time. The batsman and his bat do not exist. Take every ball.
Push your fingers hard into the top of your inners and gloves to feel the ball. Be comfortable in your equipment and not weighed down.
When you take the ball, point your fingers at 6 o'clock or 12 o'clock and never towards the bowler and the ball. Imagine that you are catching a raw egg and you don't want to break it. Let your hands give like a mattress.
Speedy footwork is important to good wicket-keeping. This starts from a comfortable, squatting stance, with the body balanced and the feet apart. Squat in a position just outside the off stump from where a clear view can be obtained of the bowler's hand. Always have the stumps within reach when standing up to the wicket. To a pace bowler be in a position far enough back to gather the average ball as it stops rising.
Here comes a fine edge down the leg-side; *drive* yourself at the ball and try to take it on the side of the body nearer the stumps.
England needs a single to win the game with one ball remaining. The batsmen have made up their minds to run, even if the striker misses the ball. Now from a standing back position, move up to the wicket as quickly as you can to run the batsman out or take the return from the field. Drive your legs.
First things first. Make haste slowly. You can't stump anyone unless you take the ball first. Watch the ball and the striker. Let the ball come and the hands give. After that comes the time for speed in striking at the stumps which should be within reach.

Remember: Be balanced.
Watch the bowler, the batsman and the ball.

1 Stance standing back
2 Taking the ball on the leg-side having moved across
3 Taking the ball on the leg-side
4 Taking the ball on the off-side
5 Taking the ball above the waist

Field placements

(for a right-handed batsman)

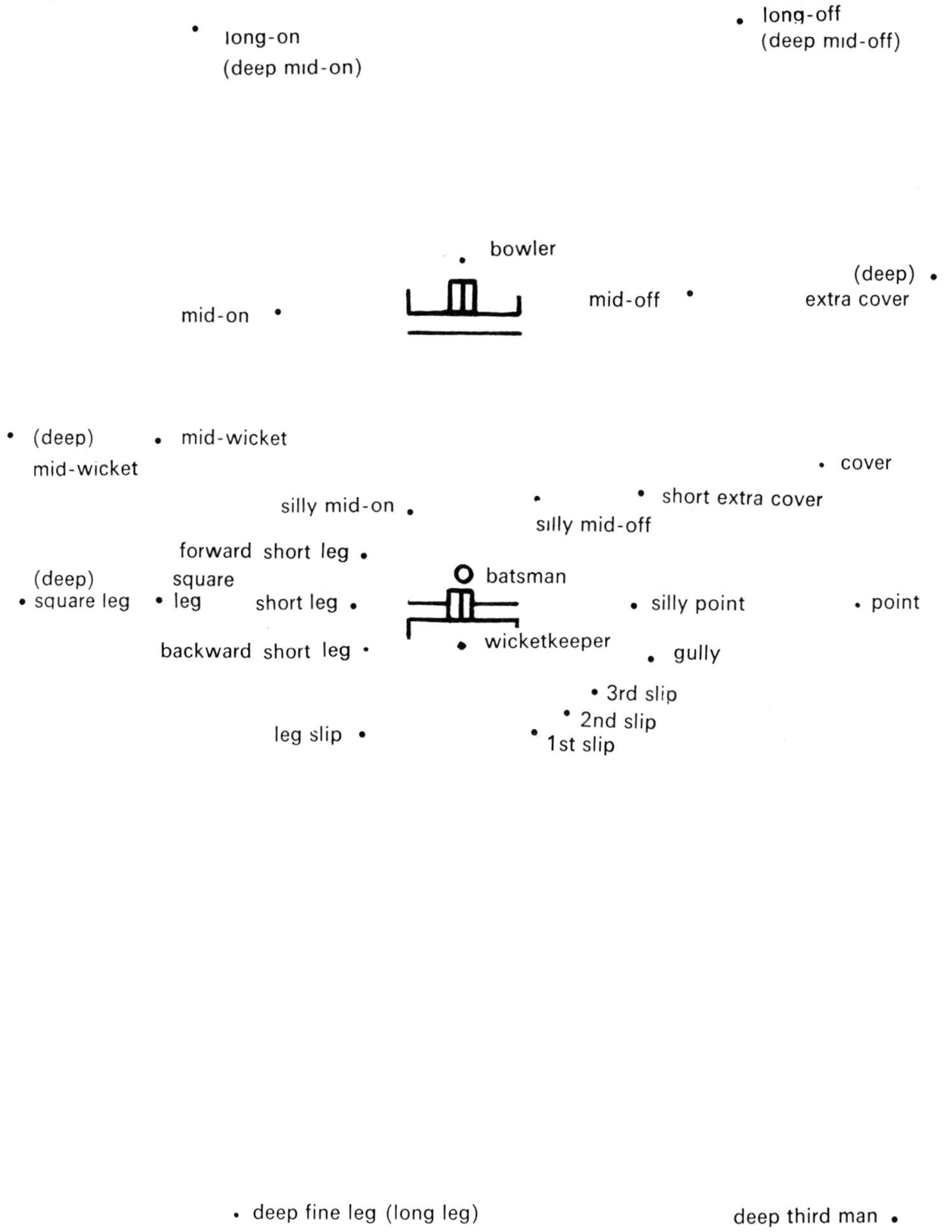

32 The attacking outfielder

A player fields in an attacking way in the outfield in order to assist the bowler and wicketkeeper to dismiss the batsman by catching or running them out. The attacking outfielder not only helps dismiss batsmen, but he saves runs and makes the batsmen unsure in the judgement of runs and pressurises them into mistakes.

The close-to-the-wicket fieldsmen attack by catching the batsman. The attacking outfielder is to be found in all positions away from the wicket: the third man area, deep point, cover, extra cover, mid-off on the off-side, mid-on, mid-wicket, square leg, fine leg on the on-side. The outfielder should defend only when the ball is struck past him or at him hard enough to make stopping the ball his first consideration.

Remember: Be balanced.
Watch the ball and the batsman.

How to field in an attacking way

The stance

As the ball is bowled you should be upright, on your toes, leaning forward slightly and moving in at a walk towards the pitch or batsman, ready to accelerate in any direction towards the ball.

Head and eyes

Hold your head steady. Your eyes should be fixed first on the ball and bowler and then on the batsman. His actions will lead you to anticipate the direction of the stroke. After the ball is struck the eyes should be firmly on the ball until it is out of play, or it comes right into your hands and you return it to the 'keeper or the bowler.

Movement to the ball and stop

As the ball is struck move quickly to left, right or forward until your body is in line with the ball. Step forward towards the line of the ball, your front toe pointing towards the target wicket. As you stoop to pick it up bending your knees, place your rear foot behind the ball and at right angles to its path. Your weight should be on the rear foot with your front side and foot still pointing towards the stumps at which you will throw. Pick the ball up in front of your rear foot, the fingers of your hands pointing downwards and both hands cupped together. Watch the ball right into your hands.

The throw

With one movement take your throwing arm back with wrist cocked until it is level with your rear shoulder. At the same time point your front arm and shoulder, which were previously aligned at the target stumps. Keep your eyes on the target as you throw a fast, flat return along the line of your front arm, transferring your weight on to the front foot as the rear arm and shoulder follow through. Aim your return to arrive just over the top of the stumps on the full.

Simplified hints

Attack the ball in the field whenever you can. Be on your toes like a boxer and ready to move off towards the ball like an upright sprinter.

Keep your eyes glued on the bowler, the ball, the batsman and the 'keeper until the ball is dead.

Swoop after the ball like a bird. As you gather it, have your back foot behind it and your front side, foot and arm pointing at the target wicket. Fingers point to 6 or 12 o'clock.

In one movement, throw hard along the line of the body and front arm, with your eyes on the target area, just above the stumps into the 'keeper's gloves on the full or at the fieldsman who is covering the stumps at the bowler's end.

Draw your gun then pull back the string of your bow, before letting go of the arrow.

Backing up

Outfielders should always back up the wicketkeeper or bowler when returns come to the stumps from the opposite side of the pitch, moving quickly into line behind the throw in case the wicketkeeper or bowler misses it. When a ball is struck and the batsmen think of a run, fieldsmen such as mid-off and mid-on close to the bowler's stumps move to the wicket to take any return that may come to that end. Close-to-the-wicket fieldsmen perform the same service for the wicketkeeper when he does not have time to come up to the stumps for a fast return. A fieldsman must never presume that the player closer to the wicket will stop the ball. He must back him up in case the batsman's stroke penetrates the first line of defence.

Don't throw runs away; back up your mates and get behind them.

Catching in the outfield

In general, outfield catches arrive as a skimming head high catch or as a high lofted catch. In both cases position is important. Between balls retire behind your post in the field and move up to that position as the ball is bowled. When a catch comes your way, don't move forward too early. Watch the ball closely and judge the flight of the catch and the spot where it should bounce before moving into position. Movement too early may cause you to misjudge the flight of the catch and then you will be forced to run backwards which is very difficult. Movement too late may cause you to arrive too late on the spot where the ball descends. Remain out only until you have judged the catch and them move quickly into line and under it.

More haste, less speed. Look and judge before you catch and run. Eyes on the ball right into your hands. Catch just below or above your eyes and sight the ball between the fingers pointing upwards or downwards. Hands together. Let your hands give as though you were catching a raw egg.

The most effective catching is achieved just above or just below eye level. Cup your hands together with your fingers pointing upwards or downwards at those levels. Above eye level sight the ball between the back of the fingers of the hands cupped together level with the forehead. Watch the ball right into the hands and give with your hands as the ball enters them to stop it bouncing out, and avoid injury. Never snatch at the ball.

Check list
Emphasise points in this order.

Keep your eyes glued on the bowler, the ball, the batsman and the 'keeper until the ball is dead. More haste, less speed. Look and judge before you catch and run. Eyes on the ball right into your hands. Catch just below or above your eyes and sight the ball between the fingers. Hands together. Let your hands give as though you were catching a raw egg.
Attack the ball in the field whenever you can. Swoop after the ball like a bird. As you gather it, have your back foot behind it and your front side, foot and arm pointing at the target wicket. Fingers point to 6 or 12 o'clock.

In one movement, throw hard along the line of the body and front arm, with your eyes on the target area, just above the stumps at the 'keeper's or bowler's end. Draw your gun then pull back the string of your bow before letting go of the arrow.
Don't throw runs away; back up your mates and get behind them.
Be on your toes like a boxer and ready to move off towards the ball like an upright sprinter.

Remember: Be balanced.
Watch the ball.

33 The defending outfielder

The object of fielding in the outfield in a defensive way is to prevent the batsmen scoring runs. All positions on the field are defensive when the ball penetrates that position or is struck hard towards it. Stopping the ball and saving runs is then the fieldsman's first consideration.

Remember: Be balanced.
Watch the ball.

How to field in a defensive way	Simplified hints
	Everyone in the field must be prepared to die in order to save runs.
Stance As the ball is bowled you should be upright, on your toes, leaning forward slightly and moving in at a walk towards the pitch or batsman, ready to accelerate towards the ball in any direction.	Be on your toes like a boxer, and ready to move off like a sprinter from a standing start.
Head and eyes Keep your head steady and your eyes fixed first on the ball and the bowler, then on the batsman whose actions will lead you to anticipate the direction of his stroke. After the ball is struck watch the ball until it is dead or it comes into a fieldsman's hands and he returns it to the 'keeper.	Keep your eyes glued on the bowler, the ball, the batsman and the 'keeper until the ball is dead.
Movement to the ball, the stop and retrieve As the ball is struck move quickly to the left, right, forward or back until your body is in line with the ball and the bounce or roll of the ball suitable for a good stop. In stopping the ball use your body as a barricade or second line of defence so that, if you miss the ball with your hands, your body will prevent it going for runs. Do this either by kneeling in a side-on position with the front side of the body behind the line of the ball and gathering the ball beside your front leg, or by standing with your feet and legs together and behind the ball as you stoop to gather it. Fingers point to 6 or 12 o'clock and the hands give as they gather the ball.	Swoop after the ball like a bird. Move into line and put up the 'barricades' of your legs and body. Fingers point to 6 or 12 o'clock. Imagine you are stopping a raw egg.
If the ball penetrates the field, chase it. As you stoop to retrieve the ball your back will be towards the target wicket and your weight on your heels as you stop inside the boundary. Your back should be pointing directly at the target wicket so that when you pick up the ball, you can spin on your rear foot and throw accurately in the direction of the 'keeper or bowler's wicket. In some instances close to the boundary if you are supported by another player, flick the ball backhand to the fieldsman backing you up so that he can return to the target wicket.	Turn your back on the target—and as you stop, scoop up the ball, swivel and throw in the opposite direction, right into the 'keeper's hands on the full or first bounce.

The throw

Throw the ball without delay. Don't run two or three steps in order to gain power. With one movement carry your throwing arm back with wrist cocked until it is level with your rear shoulder. At the same time point your front arm and shoulder, which have already been aligned with the target stumps at the wicketkeeper or bowler. Your eyes should be on the target as you throw a high lofted return in order to gain distance. Throw with your elbow leading, transferring your weight on to the front foot as your rear arm and shoulder follow through. Aim your return to arrive just over the top of the stumps on the full or after one bounce. The speed of a long return can be increased if the ball is relayed via a fieldsman who backs up halfway to the boundary. Your throw can then be flat, but it must be accurate.

Point your front arm and side like a signpost at the target wicket. Look at the 'keeper and throw high for distance along the path of the signpost arm and into his gloves on the full or first bounce.
Draw your gun then pull back the string of your bow before letting go of the arrow.

Backing up

Backing up is one of the most important aspects of defensive fielding. Outfielders should always back up the wicketkeeper or bowler when returns come from the opposite side of the pitch, moving quickly into line behind the throw in case the wicketkeeper or bowler misses it. When the ball is struck and the batsmen think of a run, fieldsmen such as mid-off and mid-on close to the bowler's stumps move in to them to take any return that may come to that end. A fieldsman must never presume that the player closer to the wicket will stop the ball. He must back him up in case the batsman's stroke penetrates the first line of defence.

Don't throw runs away—back up your mates and get behind them.

Check list
Emphasise points in this order.

Keep your eyes glued on the bowler, the ball, the batsman and 'keeper until the ball is dead.
Swoop after the ball like a bird. Move into line and put up the 'barricades' of your legs and body.
Fingers point to 6 or 12 o'clock. Imagine you are stopping a raw egg.
Turn your back on the target—and as you stop, scoop up the ball, swivel and throw in the opposite direction, right into the 'keeper's or bowler's hands on the full or first bounce.
Be on your toes like a boxer, and ready to move off like a sprinter from a standing start.

Everyone on the field must be prepared to die in order to save runs.
Point your front arm and side like a signpost at the target wicket. Look at the 'keeper and throw high for distance along the path of the signpost arm and into his gloves on the full or first bounce.
Draw your gun, then pull back the string of your bow before letting go of the arrow.
Don't throw runs away—back up your mates and get behind them.

Remember: Be balanced.
Watch the bowler, batsman and ball.

1 Move to the ball
2 Stop

3 Cock the elbow
4 Throw
5 Follow through

34 The close-to-the-wicket fielder

The close-to-the-wicket fielder's job is to assist the bowler to dismiss the batsmen by catching or running them out. Most dismissals in cricket result from catches in the field when a bowler forces a batsman into producing a false shot which travels in the air. Many of these catches are taken in close-to-the-wicket positions. The close-to-the-wicket fieldsman also has to stop the ball to prevent the scoring of runs.

The close-to-the-wicket fieldsmen are positioned in front of the wicket and behind. Behind the wicket on the off-side are the slips whose number can vary. Generally there are three slips standing in an arc from the wicketkeeper to the off-side. Their distance back from the stumps is governed by the pace of the bowler and wicket so that an edged stroke from the batsman which carries as a catch will reach the slips at comfortable height between the knees and waist. The greater the contact a ball makes with the bat, the wider it will deflect from the bat, and the shorter the distance it will carry. Thus second and third slips and gully should be correspondingly closer to the bat and stumps in 'staggered' lines. The gully fieldsman is on a 45-degree angle behind the wicket, whilst point is at right angles to the stumps and close on the off-side. First slip stands to the off-side of the wicketkeeper and as wide as the 'keeper—who is aware of the territory he can cover—wants. The slips and gully should be able to touch hands when their arms are outstretched leaving no gap through which a catch can escape.

Leg slips occupy the same position on the leg-side as the orthodox slips on the off. Short leg corresponds to gully on the off-side, whilst short square leg is the on-side equivalent of point. In front of the wicket on the off-side just off the pitch and at a distance which varies between half the length of the pitch and a few yards is silly mid-off. Wider on the off-side of silly mid-off is short extra cover. Their equivalents on the leg-side are silly mid-on and forward short leg. All the fieldsmen in front of the wicket are stationed for the shot played in their direction and in the air.

How to field close to the wicket

Stance

Since most of the close-to-the-wicket fieldsmen are placed as catchers, their stance is stationary. Squat on the balls of your feet or toes, with your feet comfortably apart and your weight evenly distributed. You must be able to move very quickly from this position. It is easier to raise than lower the centre of gravity suddenly from a squat position. Move into your stance as the bowler turns to bowl.

Head and eyes

Your head should be still with your eyes fixed first on the bowler. As he bowls first slip should watch the ball, since its path and behaviour is clearly and constantly visible. The other slips, gully and point should watch the ball and the edge of the bat. The leg-side fieldsman does not have as clear a view of the ball as the slips and gully and may need to anticipate a catch by the batsman's movement. Your eyes must follow the ball whenever possible but in the positions squarer of the wicket, you may have to anticipate the batsman's movement.

Simplified hints

Quick movement is important to close-to-the-wicket fielding. This starts from a comfortable squatting stance, with the body balanced and the feet apart. When you prepare to take the ball, point all your fingers at 12 or 6 o'clock and never towards the bowler or ball.

Watch the ball in play all the time. Try to anticipate from the batsman, the bat and the path of the ball which way the ball will travel.

Check list
Emphasise points in this order.

Watch the ball in play all the time. Try to anticipate from the batsman, the bat and the path of the ball which way the ball will travel.
When you are taking the ball, cup your hands like a bird's nest and imagine that you are catching a raw egg and you don't want to break it. Let your hands give like a mattress.
Put up the barricades of your body behind the line of the ball.
Quick movement is important to close-to-the-wicket fielding. This starts from a comfortable squatting stance, with the weight equally balanced between the feet slightly apart.
When you prepare to take the ball, point all your fingers at 6 or 12 o'clock and never towards the bowler or ball.
Don't throw runs away—back up your mates and get behind them.
A quick flick.

Remember: Be balanced.
Watch the ball and the batsman.

Stance

Move to the ball

Catch

The catch and stop

In stopping or catching always cup both hands together and point your fingers down or up, sometimes to the side but never at the ball. Give with your hands as the ball enters them to stop the ball bouncing out of them and to avoid injury. Never snatch at the ball. The most effective catching is done just above or just below eye level. Cup your hands together with your fingers pointing upwards or downwards, at those levels. Watch the ball right into the hands.

When you are taking the ball, cup your hands like a bird's nest and imagine that you are catching a raw egg and you don't want to break it. Let your hands give like a mattress.

When you stop the ball use your body as a second line of defence, so that if you miss the ball, your body will prevent it going for runs. Kneel in a side-on position with the front side of your body behind the line of the ball or by standing with the feet and legs together behind the ball as you stoop to gather it.

Put up the barricade of your body behind the line of the ball.

The throw

In close-to-the-wicket fielding positions the throw required most often is an underarm flick at the stumps as the batsman moves outside his crease.

A quick flick.

Backing up

Close-to-the-wicket fieldsmen quite often need to back up the wicketkeeper who may not have time to come from a standing back position up to gather a quick return. On these occasions short leg, point, silly mid-off or on fill the 'keeper's role. Close-to-the-wicket fieldsmen also act as a second line of defence to the 'keeper for returns from the outfield or for flick throws from fellow close-to-the-wicket fieldsmen.

Don't throw runs away—back up your mates and get behind them.

Position of the slip field

35 Correction of fielding faults

The remedying of fielding faults depends largely on the diagnosis of those faults. The following are the most frequent errors.

Inattention or failure to keep the eyes on the ball or the captain whilst the ball is in play and the game in progress.

Failure to be on the toes and on the move in the outfield when the ball is bowled.

Failure to move behind the line of the ball.

Failure to have all the fingers pointing to 6 or 12 o'clock in gathering the ball.

Failure to allow the hands to give with the ball.

Failure to line up the body sideways to the target before the ball is gathered.

Taking two or three steps before throwing the ball and thus delaying the return.

Failure to use the front arm in order to aim at the target.

Failure to transfer the weight on to the front foot in returning the ball.

Failure to return the ball on the full to the 'keeper or bowler's wicket.

Failure to back up on both returns and on possible misfields.

Failure to support a fellow fieldsman in a chase to the boundary.

Failure to attack the ball whenever possible in the outfield.

Failure to adopt the correct position when fielding close to the wicket.

Failure to keep the eyes on the ball, bat or batsman when fielding close to the wicket.

Moving in too hastily in the outfield and misjudging a catch or gather.

Moving from your position in the field without instructions from the captain or bowler.

Since you will be fielding for 75 per cent of the time you spend playing cricket, you must practise the skills you will need constantly. Fielding practice can be boring and can lack the glamour of the other skill practices so the coach should try to make fielding practice as varied and as interesting in match terms as possible.

The 'keeper should not practise only in the nets where the ball does not beat the bat enough to present the 'keeper with the varied situations which occur in a match. He cannot stand back in the nets nor can he take returns from fieldsmen so 'keeping should be practised constantly as a specific skill along the lines suggested in the group activities and situations practice sections of the book.

A fieldsman is a pawn on the captain's chessboard and is moved around accordingly. When you are fielding watch your captain between balls and overs to find out what he wants you to do.

Fielding contains many useful skills which are only needed infrequently: the flick throw from close to the wicket, the flick back to a supporting fieldsman and the relay throw from the outfield. Remember to practise these skills.

Fielding requires a lot of thought. Concentrate while the ball is in play. Think about throwing at the stumps when there is no-one to take the ball and no-one backing-up. Ask yourself 'is there a possible run-out here?' Think about the type of throw that you should make from the outfield: if there is no possibility of a run-out, it would be wiser to throw slowly and accurately rather than quickly and erratically thus increasing the possibility of overthrows. Remember to ask yourself: 'is this chance worth the risk of overthrows?'

36 Captaincy

The good captain of a cricket team should provide it with a leader qualified and capable of executing a single, well-planned policy aimed at winning the match in an ethical manner. He should be a tactician to guide his side, and to ensure the maximum participation and enjoyment in cricket for every player in it. He should be able to communicate with all the players and with officials and outside agencies. In junior clubs he will need to be an organiser who can co-ordinate selection and availability of players, transport, net duties, etc. and to organise a practice routine which will set players on a right path towards cricket proficiency.

There is no easy answer on how to be a good captain. In junior sides the coach may guide his captain in conduct and tactics, or the captain can be a more experienced player.

The captain takes responsibility for the direction of the side on the field. He is in authority but he should not necessarily be authoritarian. He should lead because his side consents to it and supports him because of his knowledge of tactics, his ability to make decisions on the field, his playing ability, his personality and his ability to command respect and obtain obedience.

The captain can communicate with and unify his side. In this respect his role is like the coach's. He should encourage the players by praising success, criticising minimally and being objective and unemotional in his comments. He should outline and discuss the aims and tactics of the side, about the policy for the day or for the match, pinpointing the weaknesses and strengths of the opposition and in every way improve his side's knowledge about the game. He should also know the members of his team and talk to them to gain the best out of them.

The best way for a captain to command his side's respect is by being a good example by his alertness, his sportsmanship, his self-discipline and his competency both in the skills themselves and in his ability to use the talents of his team to best advantage. He should be a competitive, thoughtful and impartial leader of his team.

As a tactician the captain's first decision is whether to bat or bowl upon winning the toss. He should bat if:

The wicket is hard and firm, with little or no green grass in evidence.

The weather or wicket look as if they might worsen with the onset of rain, or the dampening or crumbling of the pitch.

The wicket and weather are moderately good and look as if they might improve quickly.

He should bowl if:

The wicket is green, i.e. covered with green grass, a condition which normally helps the fast or medium bowler to 'move the ball off the seam' after it pitches. (The captain must have faster seam bowlers in his side if he is to take advantage of these conditions.)

The wicket is soft because of rain and will help the fast and slow bowlers to make the ball kick, turn, seam or cut off the wicket.

The wicket is green or soft and it looks as if batting will be easier at a later stage. Under these circumstances the captain takes advantage of temporarily good bowling conditions.

The day is overcast and humid and produces conditions suitable for a fast or medium bowler to swing the ball. The lack of excessive heat means that his bowlers will be more effective for longer periods of time.

The batting strength of the opposition appears suspect against the bowling side's attack. The opposition might have a poor record against fast bowling over the season, and the bowling strength of the captain's side might rest on two or three good fast bowlers.

In most instances the junior captain should decide to bat to put 'runs on the board' and thus create a psychological hurdle for the opposition.

The captain's responsibility does not end with the decision to bat or bowl according to the conditions. He must also watch his players' performances in the match situation. Thus a bowler who pitches consistently short on a wicket helpful to the seam bowler who bowls a full length must be instructed to modify his length. The batsman who fails to take advantage of the good wicket and a misdirected attack must be advised about how to attack the bowling. The leg spinner pitching too short on a slow wicket must be guided into a fuller length. The counselling role of captain never ends.

The captain must base his decisions on the strengths and weaknesses of the opposition. If an opposition batsman shows he is weak against inswing, leg spin, outswing or rash in certain favourite strokes, the captain should pick the faults and direct his attack accordingly with an appropriate field. If an opposing bowler has an effective and dangerous delivery, he must warn his batsmen about it. Should an opposition fieldsman excel in a certain position, the man must be pinpointed.

It may become obvious that the opposition is attacking in a certain way, and the tactic has to be countered. Thus a deep off-side field with the bowlers attacking the off stump short of a length will call for instructions for the batsmen to concentrate on singles. A restrictive opposition bowling and fielding policy, with a declaration approaching, may call for adventurous instructions to his batsmen. A hitting policy on the part of the opposition batsmen, or an inclination to go for quick singles demands a knowledge of sensible field changes to increase the batting risks and prevent the flow of runs.

The captain must know his own batsmen's, bowlers' and fieldsmen's strengths. He must realise that the batsman who combats the new ball well should be batted high in the order and that the stroke makers should be shielded from the new ball in the middle order. He must know the fast bowler who uses the new ball best and moves it most. He should be able to decide which of his bowlers will be most effective against certain batsmen and which of his batsmen will counter a certain attack most effectively. He must know which of his fieldsmen are best in specialist positions. He must also be aware of the psychological makeup of his own side and who will best stand up to crises and pressures. He must realise when his bowlers are tired and need to be relieved. He must know when a certain type of bowler is ineffective under certain conditions and against certain types of batsmen and change them accordingly. He must appreciate when to take the new ball, when to attack for quick runs, when to pressurise a batsman newly arrived at the crease, and when to attempt to slow down the opposition's scoring rate. His judgement must tell him when to enforce the follow-on and when he should ask his batsmen to consolidate.

The captain's task is not easy. Throughout his job he should give immediate specific instructions to individuals. He must have a general plan of campaign when going on to the field but must be adaptable, since original plans always need modification. He must also keep the game moving and see that no time is wasted through a slow over rate. A great part of the captain's responsibility in the field lies in consultation with the bowler and at times with other players and in the placement of the bowler's field.

A few basic precepts need to be observed in the setting of a field.

In the close-to-the-wicket position such as the slips, there should be no gaps in the field. The slips should be able to touch each other's fingers at arm's length. They should be staggered, with the squarer fieldsmen closer to the bat than the fine positions. The ball travels less distance in the air when the hit is squarer. The distance back from the bat is governed by the state of the wicket and the distance travelled by the ball in the air when it is edged. The behind-the-wicket fieldsmen should be placed to take the ball at comfortable height according to its carry, between the waist and the knees.

No short fieldsman should be in the same line as the deeper fieldsman. This means that two men are covering the same angle of a possible hit, and the fieldsman at the rear does not have a clear sight of the ball because his view is obstructed by the closer man.

Boundary fieldsmen should remain on the boundary. It is easier to run forward towards the wicket than backwards. Moreover there is more time to prevent a possible boundary hit by running around the perimeter of the field.

The captain should insist that his fieldsmen watch him whenever the ball is not in play. He may need to make slight, tactical changes in the field.

The captain should place as many men as possible in catching positions. His fieldsmen are there to catch and attack, to save a single, and to save a boundary. There are no in-between positions. The field settings in the diagrams on pages 94 and 95 show the orthodox field placements for the different types of bowlers. Attacking variations in placements are indicated.

A captain should field mostly at mid-off or mid-on where he can observe the game from close to the centre of the activity yet not be in a critical position which demands complete concentration on the fielding skill. He needs time to think about captaincy. This is not an absolute rule, however, and varies according to individuals such as Ian and Greg Chappell, Bobby Simpson or Len Maddocks who were specialist slip fieldsmen or wicketkeepers. Watching senior games will help him learn about field placements.

A captain should always observe a commonsense approach to his field placement and set his field according to the standard of cricket in which he plays. It is no use setting a 'Dennis Lillee' field of five slips and no third man or fine leg if there is no 'Dennis Lillee' in his side. As a general rule a junior captain should always place a deep third man and fine leg. Similarly he should never place his fieldsmen in positions of danger.

If there is any hesitancy on the part of two or more fieldsmen going for a catch, the captain should nominate the fieldsman to take the catch by shouting his name.

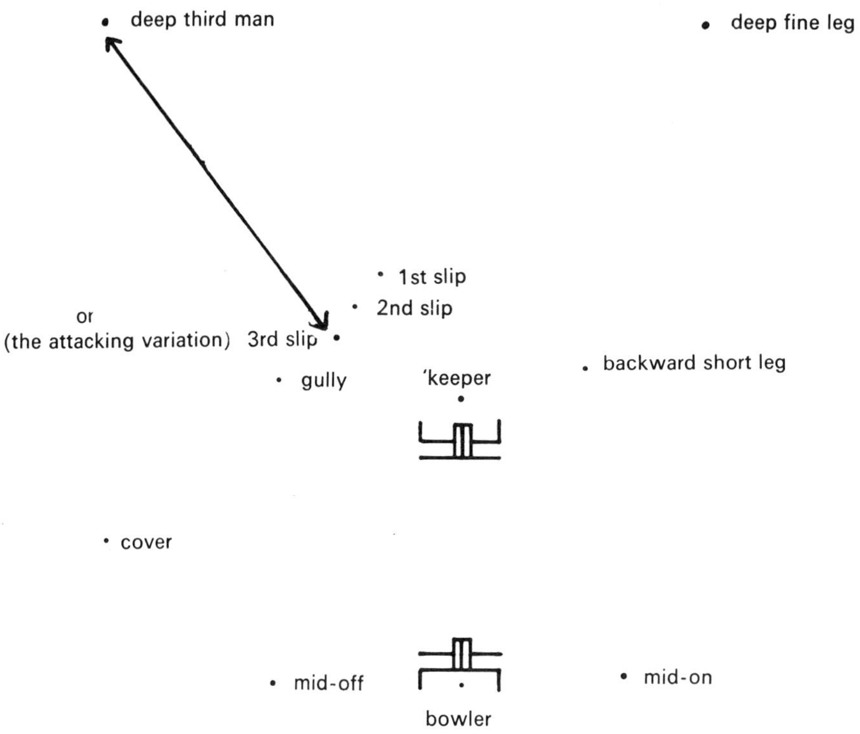

Orthodox field placings for fast-medium, outswing or leg cutting bowler

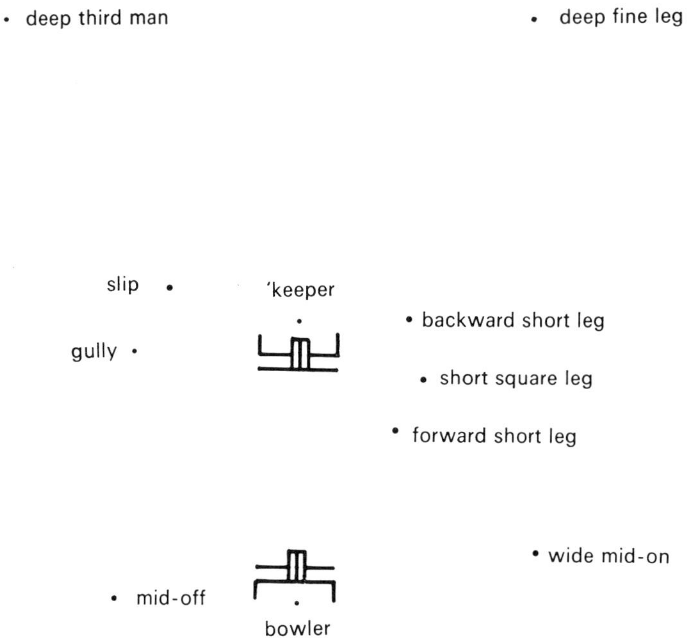

Orthodox field placings for fast-medium, inswing or off cutting bowler

(for a right-handed batsman)

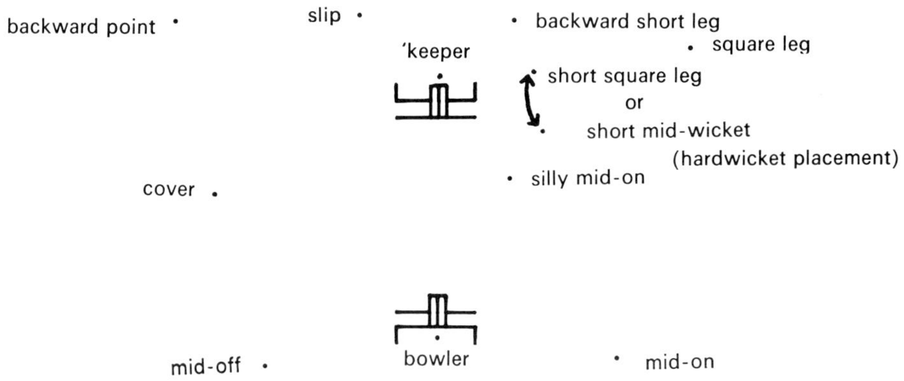

Orthodox field placings for slow off spin bowler

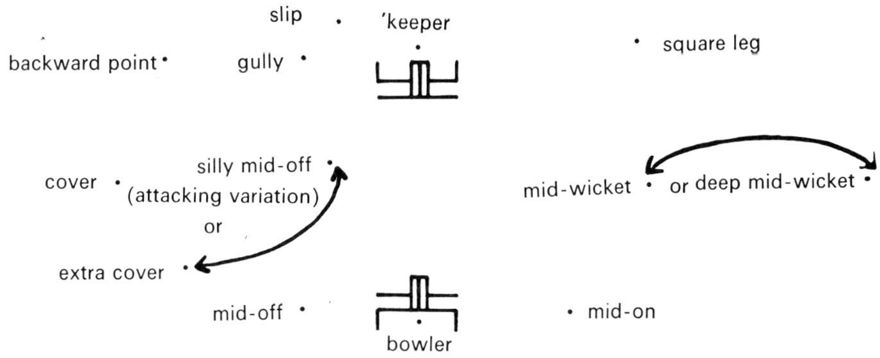

Orthodox field placings for slow leg spin bowler

(for a right-handed batsman)

37 Physical training programmes for cricket

In the past physical training programmes for cricket have aimed at producing a general level of fitness without any regard for the specialised needs of batsmen, bowlers, wicketkeepers and fieldsmen whose physical requirements must differ widely. For instance, the stamina and gymnastic action required of a wicketkeeper is different from that needed in batting; the batsman needs to be more nimble and the bowler stronger. It is logical therefore that fitness training programmes designed specifically for these different qualities in the different activities of cricket should be clearly defined.

As a preface to specific fitness in cricket, however, a general level of fitness is mandatory. This general fitness can be achieved by conventional methods. These include pretraining jogging, short sprints, flexibility and strength exercises such as press-ups, squats, leg raises, burpees, back arches, toe touching, sit-ups, trunk rotations, step-ups, etc. Even at general fitness level training should be supervised by qualified coaches who do not overstrain the physical capabilities of their students. This overstrain can be avoided by applying the principles of circuit training, that is, by first establishing the maximum number of repetitions of any exercise which each student can perform or the highest achievement level they can attain within a time limit and then setting a training dose which is usually half this maximum. The general fitness programme should be as carefully planned as any more sophisticated programme so that no one aspect is neglected and so that the exercises are graded for improved performance.

Physical training programmes for cricket observe the principles guiding any training schedule. The body adapts according to a number of influences, the most important of which for a cricketer is exercise. Exercise should improve muscular strength, muscular endurance, flexibility and the efficiency of his heart and breathing functions. Properly planned it should adapt the cricketer's body according to the particular demands made upon it.

To plan an exercise programme it is necessary to identify the functions and skills which need developing. Thus, for example, a bowler's programme will include specific exercises for those muscles subject to strain in his action, that is, his trunk, legs, shoulders and arms. To identify these specific needs the player can determine which muscles need strengthening from a feeling of strain, weakness or tiredness after the skill is performed or the coach can make an expert judgement on the movements needed in a particular cricket skill. He may experiment to test which parts of the body require development, for instance, determining the strength of a bowler's trunk muscles by measuring the number of wall pulley exercises which the bowler can perform in a minute against a set weight. He may forecast the demands on a player's body by measuring the effort required in a specific skill, for instance, measuring the distance per day a cricketer has to run in a game. For example, Ian Redpath batted on an average 97 minutes each day in the course of a season, during which time he ran 1170 metres each day. The coach may also analyse which muscles are used in a certain skill by film analysis or by calculating the strength and effort needed by electrodes attached to the muscles.

Having established which areas need development, the next step is to select exercises which impose demands on that area. Thus a wicketkeeper needs specific exercises to strengthen the knee extensors (quadriceps) and the hamstring because of his continual squatting during the match. In an average first class day in the field the wicketkeeper performs over 600 squats. His exercises may include knee straightening, that is, sitting on a chair with weights attached to the insteps of the feet and straightening the legs in a set number of repetitions, or squats with barbells on the shoulders. A fast bowler will need to do specific work on the shoulder extensors, for example, exercises with wall pulleys which also develop the lateral muscles of the trunk.

The final step would be to apply the selected exercises with gradually increasing intensity. To produce improvements in the physical performance of a skill the student should exercise at a level beyond that at which he is tired. This is the principle of overload. To produce continued improvement, exercise must be progressive in its demands. A gradual intensification of the imposed demand can be achieved by:

Increasing the intensity of the activity by increasing the weight or resistance against the muscles used or increasing the speed of the exercise.

Increasing the duration of the activity by increasing the time spent on the exercise or increasing the numbers of repetitions of the exercise.

Increasing the intensity and the duration of the activity at the same time.

The best method is to increase the duration of the exercise first and then the intensity.

To avoid boredom a coach should explain the exercise programme with its desired effects on the game. He should vary the activities and location of the training, use 'self testing' activities so that the students can appreciate their improvement and include a moderate amount of competitive activities.

Strength programmes entail progressive resistance exercises which demand a high degree of resistance or weight against the muscles used and a low number of repetitions, for example, heavy weight training for a few repetitions. Muscular endurance programmes entail a low resistance or weight against the muscles used but an increased number of repetitions, for example, using light weights with increased repetitions. Cardio-respiratory exercises are designed to combine speed, time and repetitions to apply overload and progression, for example, repeated wind sprints.

Hints on fitness work

The activities should be as specific to the game of cricket as possible and they should be carried out under conditions similar to those encountered in the game. Batsmen should wear pads and carry a bat in doing interval-type work.

Fitness work should be interspersed with skill practice. Fitness work will probably be most effective at the beginning of the season.

A car inner tube can be used instead of wall pulleys or chest expanders. Broom handles with weights on ropes can be used for wrist rolling. Instead of barbells, pipes with concrete on the ends may be used. Use tree limbs instead of parallel bars or beams for pull-ups or chins. Use the outer ground or pavilion steps for stair running or step-ups.

Specific fitness programme: A programme designed to increase strength
The progressive resistance exercise
Test the individual to determine the number of repetitions that he can perform with a maximum weight. Begin at half the maximum number of repetitions with the maximum weight, then work on alternate days until the number of repetitions regularly exceeds the proven maximum. Increase the maximum weight and reduce the repetitions to the original number, that is, half the possible maximum. Repeat until the repetitions consistently exceed the possible maximum, then increase the weight again.

The isometric exercise
In isometric exercises the muscles are flexed against an immovable resistance for periods of 5 to 12 seconds, such as pulling on a fixed rope or pushing against a wall. Perform the action at different angles.

A programme designed to increase muscular endurance
Muscular endurance exercises require the use of lighter fixed weights than in progressive resistance exercises but the number of repetitions is increased. If time is restricted, then progression can be achieved by increasing the weights or resistance or by performing the maximum number of repetitions in a set time.

Example: fitness circuit for batsmen

	Test time or repetitions	Training dose 1	Training dose 2
20.1 m (22 yd) interval sprints	4 reps, 5 sec. intervals	4 reps, 15 sec. intervals	4 reps, 10 sec. intervals
Shoulder extension (chins or weights)	Max. against fixed weight	½ of max.	⅔ of max.
20.1 m (22 yd) intervals	as above	as above	as above
Wrist rolling (weights)	Max. in 2 mins against fixed weight	½ of max.	⅔ of max.
20.1 m (22 yd) intervals	as above	as above	as above
Shoulder flexion (push-ups or weights)	Max. in 2 mins against fixed weight	½ of max.	⅔ of max.
20.1 m (22 yd) intervals	as above	as above	as above
Forearm curls	Max. in 2 mins against fixed weights	½ of max.	⅔ of max.
Step-ups	Max. in 2 mins	½ of max.	⅔ of max.
Sit-ups	Max. in 2 mins	½ of max.	⅔ of max.

NOTE: All weights used should be suited to the individual cricketer.

Each player should keep a record card to show:

The initial time taken to complete the circuit three times on the first occasion.
The target time set for the subsequent set of three circuits (normally ⅔ of the initial best time).
The times achieved at subsequent training sessions.
An outline of the circuit itself.

An interval training programme (cardio-respiratory)
The students should run a set distance in a set time, followed by a period of complete or partial rest, then repeat. To intensify the activity reduce the rest periods, increase the duration or extent of the activity, increase the speed of the activity or increase the extent and speed of the activity and reduce the rest period.

The principles of circuit training
Design a series of simple activities for a specific purpose, for example, for a fast bowler who needs to strengthen back, leg, shoulder, arms and lateral muscles and increase cardio-respiratory efficiency. Practise each activity in an established order, for example, trunk rotation, interval wind sprints for the length of the run-up with 30-second rests, arm extensions, further wind sprints, lateral trunk stretches, further wind sprints, sit-ups for trunk flexibility, bench jumping, leg raising for hip flexibility. Then establish the maximum number of repetitions which they can perform of each exercise within a time limit. Establish a training dose, usually half the maximum of each exercise.

Practise your own specific circuit until you are familiar with the exercises and the number of repetitions required. Establish an initial time for three laps of the circuit by running the three circuits as fast as possible and set a target time, which is generally

Example : fitness circuit for bowlers

	Test time or repetitions	Training dose 1	Training dose 2
Trunk rotation (arms outward stretched, wall pulley in one hand, arms move in horizontal lateral movements)	Max. in 2 mins against fixed weight	$\frac{1}{2}$ of max.	$\frac{2}{3}$ of max.
Run-up wind sprints at length of run	8 reps, 5 sec. intervals	8 reps, 15 sec. intervals	8 reps, 10 sec. intervals
Arm extension (bowling action of arm only downwards against resistance of wall pulleys)	Max. in 2 mins against fixed weight	$\frac{1}{2}$ of max.	$\frac{2}{3}$ of max.
Run-up wind sprints	as above	as above	as above
Lateral trunk flexion (body action in bowling with the arm pulling against pulleys)	Max. in 2 mins against fixed weight	$\frac{1}{2}$ of max.	$\frac{2}{3}$ of max.
Run-up wind sprints	as above	as above	as above
Trunk flexion (sit-ups, etc.)	Max. in 2 mins	$\frac{1}{2}$ of max.	$\frac{2}{3}$ of max.
Bench jumping	Max. in 2 mins	$\frac{1}{2}$ of max.	$\frac{2}{3}$ of max.
Hip flexion (leg raising from a prone position on back)	Max. in 2 mins	$\frac{1}{2}$ of max.	$\frac{2}{3}$ of max.

Example: fitness circuit for wicketkeepers

	Test time or repetitions	Training dose 1	Training dose 2
Sideways run ('keeper drives himself over a distance of 15 metres)	8 reps, 5 sec. intervals	8 reps, 15 sec. intervals	8 reps, 10 sec. intervals
Squats	Max. in 2 mins against fixed weight	½ of max.	⅔ of max.
Forward run (wicketkeeper drives himself forward over 15 metres)	as above	as above	as above
Rotary wall touches (feet astride, arms raised; bend to touch right toe with left hand then leap to touch wall behind your back high to the left with your right hand. Repeat touching left toe with right hand, then wall high behind you to the right with left hand)	Max. in 2 mins	½ of max.	⅔ of max.
Sideways run	as above	as above	as above
Forearm curls	Max. in 2 mins against fixed weight	½ of max.	⅔ of max.
Step-ups	Max. in 2 mins	½ of max.	⅔ of max.
Sit-ups	Max. in 2 mins	½ of max.	⅔ of max.
Forward run	as above	as above	as above

2/3 of the maximum speed. The players then train the circuit until they achieve their target time which is that originally achieved at maximum speed.

The programme can be intensified by reducing the target time, by increasing the repetitions or by re-establishing a harder circuit.

The following is a précis of the training programme evolved by Dr Frank Pyke for the Australian fast bowler, Dennis Lillee.

The intensive 5-second effort involved in his approach and delivery demands a great degree of explosive power. Because these short bursts have to be repeated many times during a game—sometimes only 30 seconds apart—any fast bowler needs stamina as well as strength and flexibility of the lower back and upper body muscles.

Running training

For the first three weeks of the six week programme Lillee ran continuously at a comfortable pace for 20 minutes in each session. The initial runs were at about 80 per cent of the maximum speed for the distance but, as his fitness improved, he was running 3000 metres in each session and trying to improve his time each day.

For the last three weeks, interval running, sprinting at a little below maximum speed for 5 seconds followed by a 15-second walk, was repeated twelve times at first and progressively extended.

Strength and power training

The first training sessions were spent familiarising the bowler with the technique and weights of weight training. Light weights were used, and the emphasis placed on correct technique.

After three sessions Lillee was loaded with a weight that he could lift 30 times consecutively. After six sessions this load was increased so that only 15 repetitions could be completed consecutively.

As the playing season approached, the strengthening programme was modified to explosive movements more typical of fast bowling. The number and sets remained the same but the weights were altered to 50 per cent of the maximum weight that could be lifted for the 15 repetitions.

Common exercises such as bicep curls and bench presses were used to strengthen the upper body; half squats and leg presses for the leg muscles. A pulley system was used to simulate the bowling action and overload the muscles involved. Both sides of

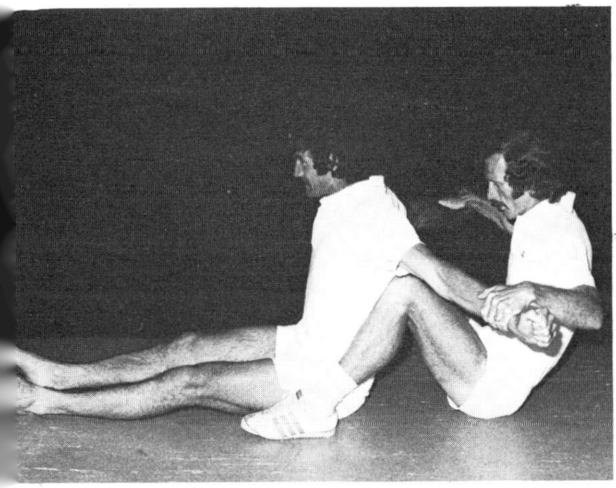

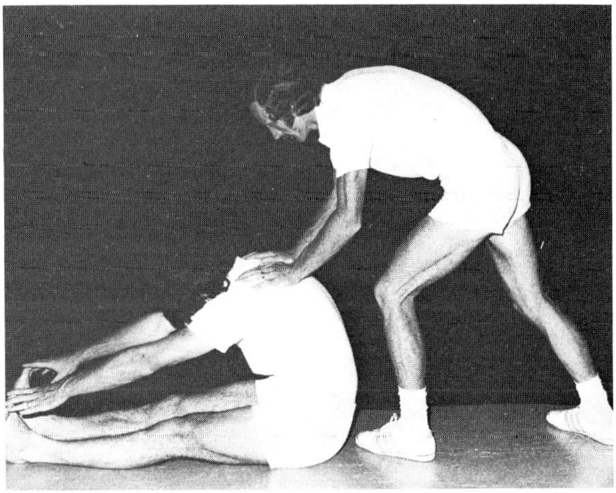

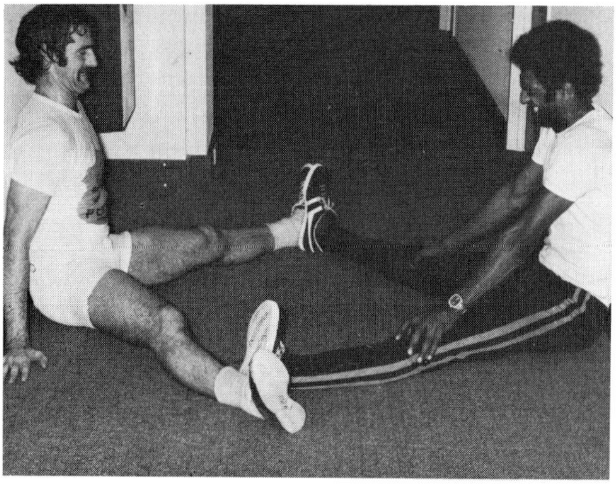

the body were exercised with 4 sets of 10 repetitions, again performed more explosively later in the programme. This was supplemented by bowling a lightweight (2 kg) medicine ball. Reverse wrist rolling was included for wrist development. Sit-ups with bent knees and curled trunk were performed in 4 sets of 10 repetitions with a 45-second rest between each set. This load was increased progressively by using an inclined board.

Flexibility training
Flexibility exercises for the muscles involved in fast bowling were done with a partner. The subject stretches his muscles as far as possible by himself, then while in this position he contracts the muscles isometrically for 6 seconds against the movable resistance provided by his partner. He then stretches to a new position as a result of increased flexibility and repeats the exercise four times. After a short rest, the partners complete a second and third set. In these exercises concentrate on the muscles of both sides of the lower back and hamstrings and the groin and shoulders.

Several precautions should be taken with these exercises:

The isometric contraction should never be explosive but involve a gradual increase in effort in the first 2 seconds, then sustained for an additional 4 seconds.

Perform the exercises with less than maximum effort until you are used to them and confident that no injury will result.

After the isometric contraction, the partner should not force the subject into a new position of improved flexibility. This movement must be unaided and done smoothly.

38 Group activities

Group activities must have certain ingredients. They must:

Provide communication, interaction, and feedback between the participants to promote a learning and an improvement situation.

They must produce interest, fun, rewards and be meaningful. They must promote the interest and stimulation which flows from the normal game of cricket.

They must produce the pressures that the player meets in the game. In isolation a player may be able to execute a skill such as fielding well, but can he perform well as a cover fieldsman when the batsman hits a ball towards him and goes through for a quick single?

They must produce enough repetitions of a skill to ensure an improvement in that skill. At the higher levels, improvement in a cricket skill is only achieved by many repetitions of the action.

It must aim at physical improvement; a situation which is produced by extending and overloading the pupil. Coaches should be careful not to overtax the student, since fatigue will cause a fall off in skill performance.

They must produce a sense of achievement in the pupil. Improvement continues when the student sees he is improving. The coach should try to build some degree of measurement of performance into group activities. If the batsman practises an off-drive, it is good for him to see that he can hit the shot four times out of six through a 10-metre area of the covers. The group activity should incorporate a set task for the student.

Group skill practices must be mobile and occupy the student all the time. There is little learning value if only one member of a group is occupied whilst four others listen and watch. If there is to be an interchange of activities and groups, the coach must ensure that the change is made without wasting time and that the flow is continuous and smooth.

The group activity must lead to an extension of the skill. If the batsman can drive a ball between an area 10 metres wide in the covers, the coach should see whether he can penetrate a narrower region, or place one ball in three squarer of the wicket.

A suggested teaching method

The following method is suitable for groups of no more than 20 at one time. Larger classes should be divided and one half given an activity as an alternative to the coaching segment of the lesson, e.g. half of the class plays fielding football whilst the other half is being coached.

Step 1

The pupil discovers for him or herself why and when a certain stroke or technique is necessary. It should be a discovery which has meaning in terms of the pupil's experience, e.g. boy X imagines that he is playing in the famous tied Test in Brisbane in 1960 and is facing Wes Hall with one over to go and four bouncers to come. Eleven runs are needed. Four boys in boy X's group field at deep fine leg and one throws bouncers from a short distance for accuracy outside leg stump. In this way he discovers his technique is either adequate to the situation or not good enough, and he asks himself why it is inadequate. When should he hook? Each boy in the group attempts the skill.

Step 2

Having discovered why and when a certain technique is necessary the pupil now learns how to perform it. Feedback information from the boy to the coach shows why boy X is failing. He may not have moved his back foot far enough back and across inside the line of the bouncer. By offering as a model himself, or using a good boy performer, the correct movements are established.

Step 3

A good boy performer or the coach demonstrates the shot, and describes the movements in simple terms related to the pupil's previous experience until the movement is identified sufficiently for imitation. The speed of the repetitions may be slowed up for identification but should always finish with a normal speed repetition. The coach should not theorise about the skill and the pupil should not be overloaded with information.

Step 4
The pupils now try the skill again in group formation. The coach moves around giving encouragement and never criticism. He should assess performance and possible future groupings. The ball should be delivered over short distances for accuracy and to save time.

Step 5
Transfer the class activity into an interest, group or game situation. Not too much time should be spent at an early age (7-12) in dull repetitive drills. Young children demand game activity and movement with their peers. Spend a maximum of 10 minutes on the skill instruction, with a return to the lesson at a later date. The rest of the lesson should be taken up with a game or group activity. Of course it is impossible to achieve a high degree of skill without frequent repetitions and these must be done with older pupils. For youngsters, however, the coach should be satisfied with a lesser mastery of skills and a greater degree of enjoyment and participation especially when the group is not particularly skilled.

Suggested dramatic interpretative situation for step 1
Forward defensive shot
Boy Y is batting in a Test in which Australia, with their last man in, needs 150 runs to win and has 10 balls to survive to draw the game. Boy Y has to survive against 10 good length balls on the stumps.
Jim Laker is bowling on a 'turner' at Old Trafford and Australia's wickets are falling like ninepins at the other end. Rain is in the air and the match can be saved if boy Z can survive 20 good length off spinners just outside the off stump.
(Similar situations can be imagined for the back defensive stroke.)

Off drive
Victoria is playing Queensland and with only an over to go, and Francke bowling. Victoria, with boy X batting, needs 20 runs to win. Francke is bowling to 7 men on the off-side and keeping the ball well up outside the off stump. What can be done to win?
(Similar situations can be built up for all the attacking strokes. Thus Lillee may be bowling four bouncers an over with 20 needed to win, and three men waiting for the mishook at deep fine leg. What will boy C do if he cannot hook downwards?)

Bowling: Outswing
Batsman X has a known fallibility against outswing; he is being partnered by the last man in, and bowler Z has 8 balls to bowl before the end of the match to batsman X. The ball is reasonably new and the opposition only need 10 runs to win; what will bowler Z do?
(Again similar situations can be built up around inswing, leg and off spin, etc.)

Fielding
Australia is playing the West Indies and the scores are tied with one ball remaining. Max Walker faces Lance Gibbs and hits a steepling catch to long-on, where fieldsman D is waiting underneath it. If he drops the catch, Australia wins; if he takes the catch the match is a tie. How should fieldsman D take the ball?
(Similar situations can be imagined for ground fielding, and for running between the wickets, e.g. four singles needed in the last over of the game with a bowler bowling short outside the off stump with seven men on the off. How should the batsmen run?)

To make the group activity situation productive for both student and coach, the coach should prepare the content and organisation of the coaching session carefully. Players should be grouped according to their ability, size, age and compatability and the coach should decide when these groupings are required within the context of the lesson. Will he, for example, demonstrate first and then work in groups or will he create a self-discovery situation involving group work before he demonstrates? These groups should be moved into position quickly and set working for there is no single factor more destructive to group activities than the waste of time and the opportunity to fool around because of boredom. There should be a smooth flow between activities throughout the coaching session and players should not have to spend too long listening to instructions.
Activities should be simple at first, working up to the more complex ones later.

Taking the above guidelines the coach could come up with the following suggested general outline for an hour's activity for 24 pupils:

He aims at teaching the off drive, attacking fielding, 'keeping and bowling at the off stump. He divides his class into three groups of eight pupils each graded by age and ability and organises the practice area to include a centre wicket practice with equipment, a net practice with equipment and a demonstration area with equipment.

He decides that ten minute spells will be allocated to practise net, demonstration and centre wicket activities. The off-side of the practice area is not protected by a net but left open for fielding. The demonstration area is placed in a safe position close to the other activities for quick interchange. The groups of boys change activities quickly upon a cue after ten minutes. In the demonstration area the coach either creates a self-discovery situation about the off drive, or demonstrates the skill to be learned in broad outline, followed by repetition drills with a student throwing the ball and another batting.

In the nets two batsmen each bat for five minutes and are bowled to by two bowlers. There are three fieldsmen in the covers and a 'keeper at the bowler's end taking the returns from the field. Bowlers and fieldsmen rotate after bowling a set number of balls.

The group in the centre wicket situation perform pre-determined tasks. The bowlers aim at the off stump, the batsmen attempt the off drive, the fieldsmen in the covers try to stop the shots and return to the 'keeper at the batsman's end. Five men field in the covers, one bowler operates at a time sending down 6 balls and the batsmen face 6 balls before giving way to the next pupil. Fieldsmen, bowlers and batsmen rotate.

After half an hour of such group activity, the coach could then move his 24 pupils into a centre wicket match situation with each batsman facing a set number of balls, and each bowler sending down a similar number. There would be 12 players on each side. Pads and batting gloves could be used together with other protective equipment according to the time available.

Further coaching hints in the group situation

Cues

The greatest difficulty about executing a cricket skill is knowing when to do it. The performer receives certain cues, that is, the ball is on a good length therefore demands a forward defensive stroke since it is on the stumps. This is a visual cue. A coach can say to the pupil 'forward defence' as the ball is coming down the wicket and help make the decision for him. Similarly a coach can imitate the 'whistle-clunk' sound of the ball through the air and on the bat to help build up a pattern of timing in the mind of the striker. Visual cues can be given by means of placards or signs placed at strategic points on the training ground. The disadvantage of all these cues is that they may distract the batsman.

Target

When coaching, always give the student something to strive for both in the long and short term. If a bowler is trying the inswinger, give him something to aim for. Tell him to start the inswinger on a certain line outside the off stump so that when the ball moves it will finish in line with the wicket. Tie a piece of cloth on the back net for the bowler to aim at and give him a goal to achieve.

Learning to spin is best achieved by teaching beginners to spin the ball underhand. The exercise can be carried out against a wall with the student aiming to hit a target on the ground and then a target on the wall. The wall target is to the left or right of the ball's bounce according to the desired turn. If the wall target gives off a sound (that is, if it is wood or metal), it will add to the student's sense of achievement.

Stumps and front foot in bowling

To ensure the correct positioning of the front foot in the delivery stride, a stump can be used along the line of the popping or batting crease. The coach can insist that the bowler passes to one side of the stump to gain the correct side-on position. For the follow through a corridor can be laid out by means of pairs of stumps.

The driving net

Group coaching of driving off the front and back feet is made safer if there is a tennis net between the server of the ball and the striker. The server throws the ball from one side of the net and the batsman drives it into the net on the other. This also saves time spent retrieving the ball.

Group Activities—Batting

1 *Survival on the Front Foot*

Bowler A throws 10 balls for Australia from a distance of 3 metres against England's batsman B. The ball is thrown rather than bowled to increase accuracy and to give more time for repetitions. They are on a good length. There is a 'keeper C and fieldsmen D, E, and F at silly mid-off, silly mid-on and short leg. The batsman has to surive for 10 balls, For each ball he keeps on the ground he receives one run; he receives one run for every ball not thrown accurately on a good length. He gives up a run if he misses a good length ball or drives it rather than defending. He is said to have lost a wicket but remains at the crease for every catch he gives to the fieldsmen. After 10 balls the batsmen, thrower and fieldsmen rotate. The batsman with the least number of dismissals and greatest number of runs wins. An extension of the experience is gained by allowing the thrower to bowl from 15-20.1 metres (15-22 yd).

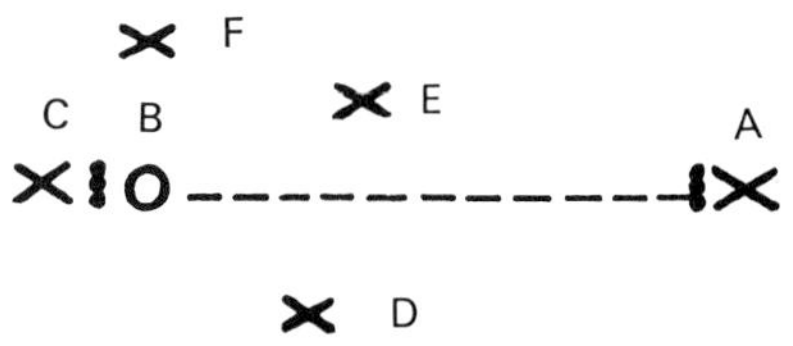

2 *Attack on the Front Foot*

Bowler A throws 10 balls for England from a distance of 3 metres against Australian batsman B. They are of half-volley length. He has 'keeper C and cover and mid-off fieldsmen D, E, F (these positions can be altered according to the direction of the drive). The batsman has to score 10 runs in 10 balls. A ball driven through the field counts 4, whilst the batsman can run singles to a wicket 10 yards away for any stroke worth the run. He can be run out or caught and is said to have lost a wicket but remains at the crease. He is penalised a run for every ball missed and for every shot misdirected. The bowler is penalised 1 run for every misdirected throw. The batsmen rotate after 10 balls each, and the winner is the one with the best average number of runs per wicket. Note that the minimum number of runs must be 10. The experience can be widened by bowling from 15 metres, and then 20.1 metres (15-22 yd).

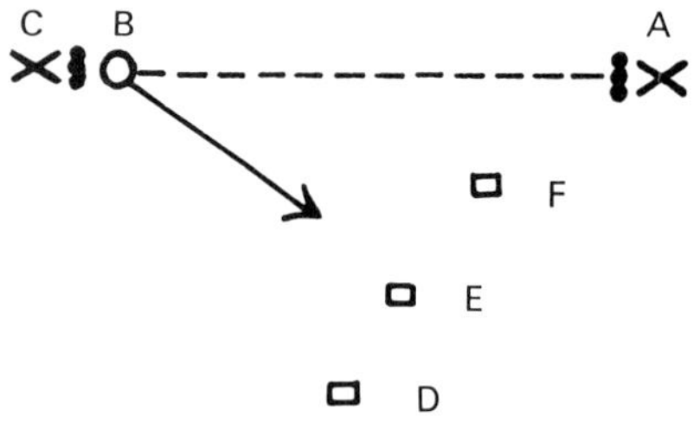

3 *Survival on the Back Foot*

Bowler A throws 10 balls for England short of a length to batsman B for Australia. They pitch in line with the stumps from the throwing point 3 metres away. The field is 'keeper C and fieldsmen D, E and F at short leg, silly mid-off and slip. The batsman has to survive for 10 balls. For each ball he keeps on the ground he receives one run and he receives one run for each ball not thrown accurately by the bowler. He gives up a run if he misses a short ball or drives rather than defends. He is said to have lost a wicket each time he is caught but remains at the crease. After 10 balls the batsmen, fieldsmen and thrower rotate; the batsman with the least number of dismissals and highest number of runs wins.

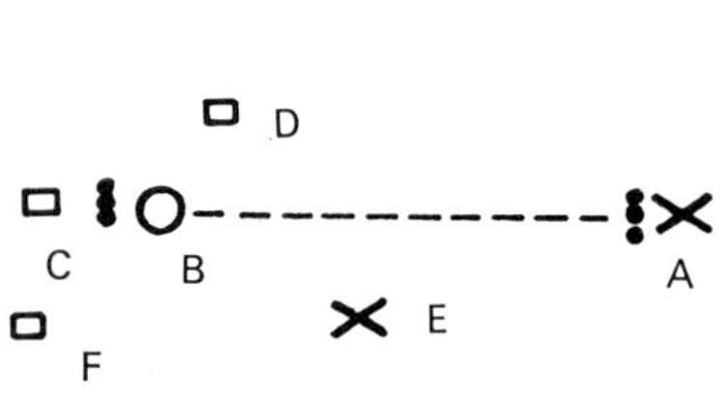

4 *Attack on the Back Foot*
Bowler A throws 10 balls for Australia from a distance of 3 metres against English batsman B. They are long hops and there is a field of a 'keeper C and cover and mid-off fieldsmen D, E, and F (these positions can be varied according to the direction of the drive). The batsman has to score 10 runs in 10 balls. A ball driven through the field counts 4 runs whilst the batsman can run singles to a wicket 10 metres away for every stroke worth a run. He can be run out or caught and is said to have lost a wicket but remains at the crease. For every ball missed he is penalised a run, as he is if the shot is misdirected. The bowler is penalised a run for every misdirected throw. The batsmen and fieldsmen rotate after every 10 balls and the winner is the one with the best average number of runs per wicket, provided he has scored a minimum of 10. The experience can be widened by bowling from 15-20.1 metres (15-22 yds).

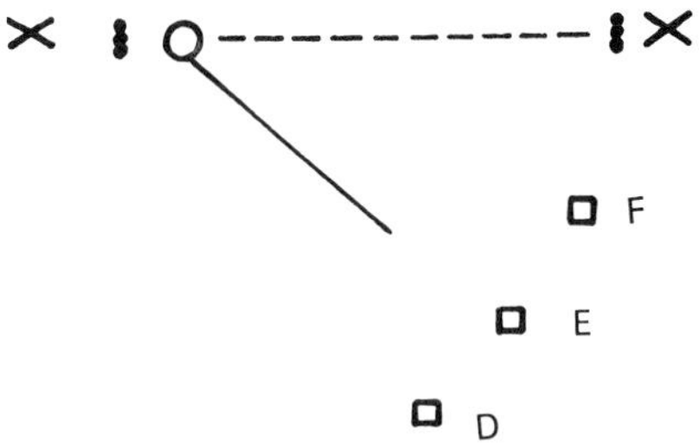

5 *Successful Cutting*
Batsman A for Australia needs 10 runs from 10 balls with bowler B for England throwing balls from 3 metres away, short of a length and well wide of the off stump. C is the 'keeper and in the square cover area are fieldsmen D, E, and F. Batsman A receives 4 runs for every square cut that penetrates the field, and can run to a wicket 10 metres away for every shot which is fielded but deserves a run. If he misses the ball or misdirects his shot, he is penalised 1 run. He can be caught out or run out and is said to have lost a wicket but remains at the crease. The bowler is penalised 1 run for every misdirected throw. The batsmen rotate with the fieldsmen and 'keeper after every 10 balls and the winner is the scorer of the highest number of runs at the best average—provided they exceed 10.

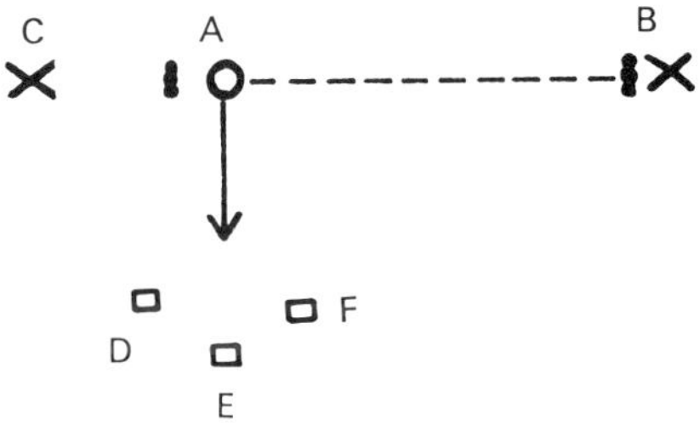

6 *Hooking and Pulling*
Batsman A for Australia needs 10 runs in 10 balls with bowler B for England throwing balls from 3 metres away in the form of bouncers down the leg-side. C is the 'keeper and in the area of deep square leg and fine leg are fieldsmen D, E, and F. Batsman A receives 4 runs for every hook which penetrates the field and can run to a wicket 10 metres away for every shot which is fielded, yet deserves a run. If he misses a ball or misdirects his stroke he is penalised 1 run. He can be run out or caught and is said to have lost a wicket but remains at the crease. For every ball he misses he is penalised a run as he is if a shot is misdirected. The bowler is penalised 1 run for every misdirected throw. The batsmen rotate after 10 balls each and the winner is the one with the best average number of runs per wicket provided that the minimum of 10 runs has been exceeded. To expand the activity bowl from 15-20.1 metres (15-22 yd).

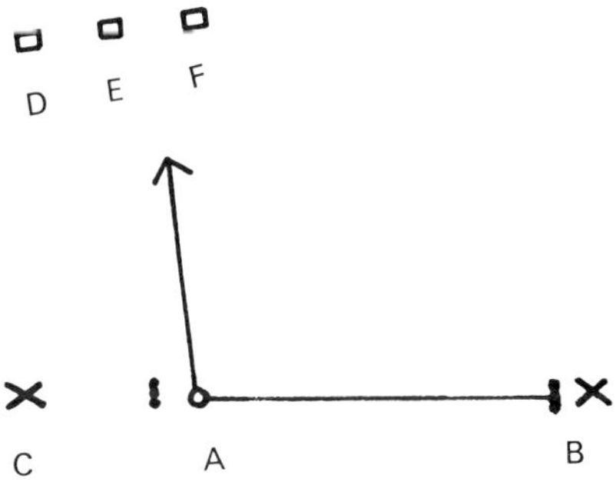

Note: Similar sorts of drills can be created for the full range of the shots in cricket.

7 *Target Batting* (*tennis or rubber ball to be used for bounce*)
Five strokes are attempted in sequence. The batsman takes his stance and the ball is served by a player dropping the ball on to a target vertically, one stride in front of the batsman. He hits the ball on the second bounce. Back foot shots are served from a distance of approximately 10 metres from the batsman. The batsman attempts to hit his stroke between two skittles or stumps set 6-10 metres apart at a distance of 30-50 metres from the bat, according to the degree of skill required. Fieldsmen are placed in the anticipated area of the shot ready to return the ball to the server. Each stroke is attempted 6 times and for each successful attempt, the batsman receives a point, making a total of 36 points for the full range of 6 strokes. The ball is struck so that it bounces once before passing through the markers at a reasonable speed. The lofted drive must carry beyond the markers before bouncing. The range of strokes includes: the pull, the on-drive, the straight drive, the off-drive, the cover drive (all drives off either the back or front foot), and the square cut.
Note: The ball can be teed-up rather than served, if the young batsman lacks batting co-ordination.
If young players are not able to play a full-scale game of cricket, a match of 'teed cricket' could be organised on this format complete with fieldsmen. The only skill omitted is the bowling skill and it would still be possible to teach batting, fielding, wicketkeeping in an enjoyable game context.

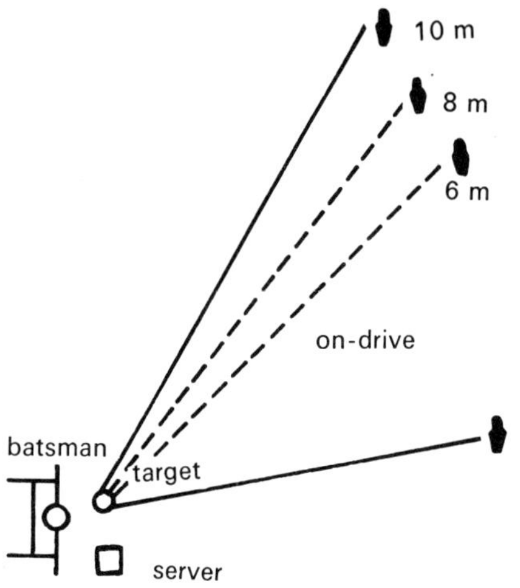

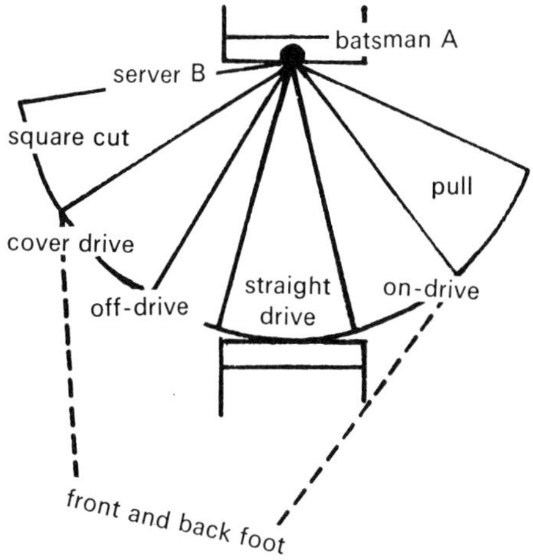

Group Activities—Bowling

8 *Relay Running Up*
Two groups of bowlers face one another at points A and B. The first bowler at A practises his run-up without bowling and at the end of his approach and follow through hands the ball to the first bowler at B who repeats the exercise to A, and so on. Because of the varying lengths of the bowlers' run-ups, groups should stand at the side of the bowlers' paths

9 *Competitive Bowling*
Each bowler sets himself a task, for example, he must bowl 8 balls in succession of a certain type (i.e. off-spin, leg-spin, outswing, inswing, short of a length outside off stump, on a full length on leg stump, bouncers (here a target of a mop head can be used above the off stump). The ball must hit a length area on the pitch and the intended target (wicket or to one side and above the stumps). Points are awarded for success. If the bowler hits the area on the pitch = 3

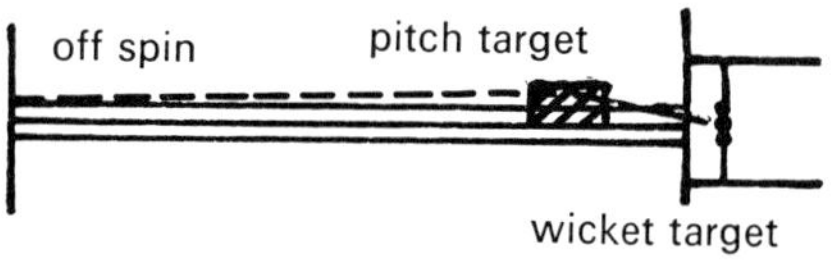

points; if he hits the intended target = 2 points; if he misses all targets hit for 4. He sees how many points (or wickets) he can gain in 8 balls. Bowlers can pressurise themselves by trotting back to their marks. They can extend the task by setting themselves a succession of tasks (fast bowlers—outswing, inswing, short outside off stump, etc.). Nets are used without batsmen and the number of bowlers limited.

For juniors such tasks can be made easier by allowing them to aim at 5 or 4 stumps, and extending the area to be hit on the pitch. An extension of this skill would be to ask the bowler to pick a batsman's weakness and to see how many times in an over he can hit the spot that would best exploit that weakness with a suitable ball.

10 *Disc Bowling*

A group of four or five seam bowlers in a circle. They bowl a flat wooden disc the diameter of a cricket ball to each other around the circle. If the disc spins flatly like a wheel, the seam has been held correctly. Any distortion in the flight means that the grip is wrong.

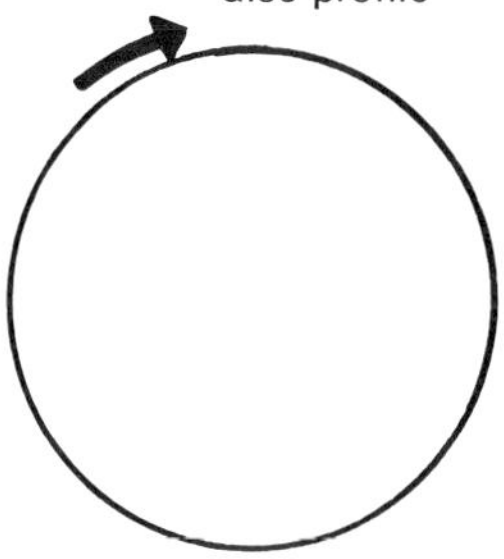

A substitute for a wooden disc could be a wheel of a plastic toy approximately the same circumference as a cricket ball. The correct fast bowler's grip makes the disc rotate pointing down the wicket and in the direction of the desired swing. The slow bowler's grip makes the disc spin across the wicket in the direction of the desired turn.

11 *Length and Direction*

Two bowlers bowl to one another over a full length pitch, aiming at the stumps. On a length in front of the stumps, a circle is drawn. The bowlers score a point for hitting the circle and another for hitting the stumps. A further incentive is sometimes added by placing a coin in the circle to be hit. After 20 deliveries each, the winner is the bowler with the most points.

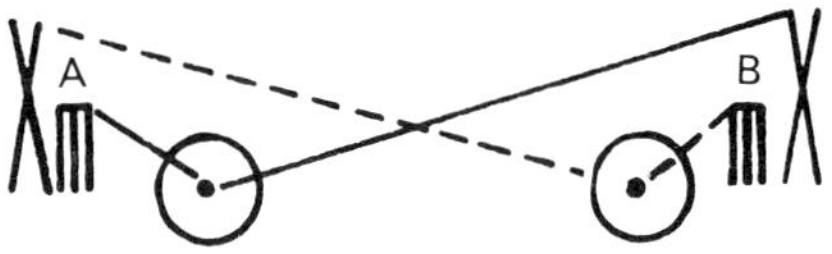

12 *Spin Tennis*

Two or more players in teams play over an area of any size according to their numbers, but laid out like a tennis court. The ball is bowled underarm into the court of the opposition and, as it is delivered, spin is imparted to deceive the opponent. In a team game the ball should be delivered to each opponent in turn. The receiver allows the ball to bounce once before gathering it. If it bounces twice, or is dropped the point goes against him. The score is kept as in tennis. There is no necessity for a net. If the ball goes out of court, the point goes against the deliverer. The skill can be extended to overarm bowling.

Group Activities—Fielding

13 *Measured Returns*
The ball is fed along a line (20, 30, 40 metres from the target area grid). Running from the opposite end of the line the fieldsman picks the ball up on the run and returns to the 'keeper standing in the centre of the grid on square 4. Points are awarded according to where the ball lands in the grid. After returning the ball the fieldsman returns to the starting point and the next fieldsman in line takes his turn. Further pressure could be added by having two batsmen running to complete a single (or two runs according to the throw).

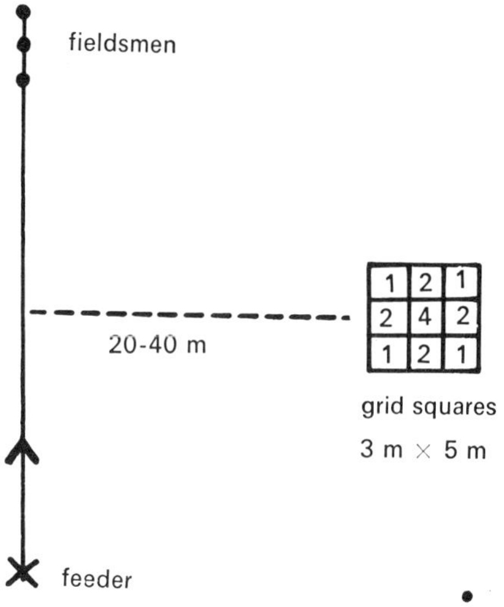

14 *Race Against Time*
A continuous effort to field six balls by one fieldsman. The balls are fed in turn from a distance of 20 (or 40) metres. The fieldsman moves in from a marker, fields and throws at the target. The target could be a 'keeper standing between two stumps 1 metre apart or a target on the wall. Then the fieldsman returns to his marker and moves in again for the next ball. The time is taken from start to finishing back at the marker having fielded and thrown all 6 balls. Three seconds bonus is given for each throw which hits the target at reasonable speed. Less than 20 seconds (for 20 metres mark) gains 10 points, 20-25=8 points, 25-30=6 points, 30-35=4 points, and 35-40= 2 points.

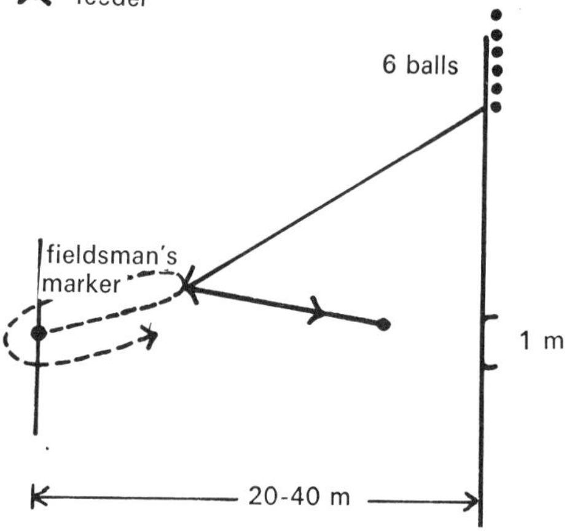

15 *Timed Shuttle Run*
The fielder is timed whilst running to pick up and throw at a target, 5 balls placed at appropriate distances along a line returning to his starting position each time before running to pick up the next ball. Time is taken from the start to the final return. Three seconds bonus is awarded for each throw that passes through the target with reasonable speed. The same points are awarded for the times indicated in activity 14. This activity could also be organised as a relay race between two teams of fieldsmen each picking up successive balls.

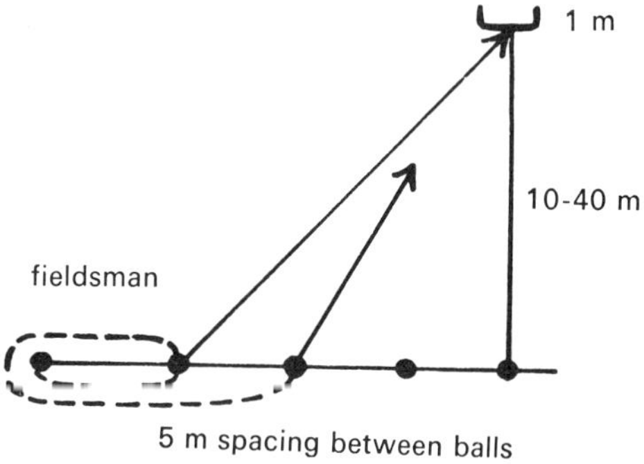

16 *Mobile Backing Up*
Fieldsmen A, B and C are placed in a circle around a stump with A and B on one side and C backing up the throw of A. A throws at the stump and immediately moves around ready to back up B's throw. Having gathered A's throw, fieldsman C moves around to take B's place in reserve, having returned the ball to B, who then throws at the stump. Points are awarded for the times on which the fieldsmen hit the stump. The distance of the fieldsmen from the stump can be varied.

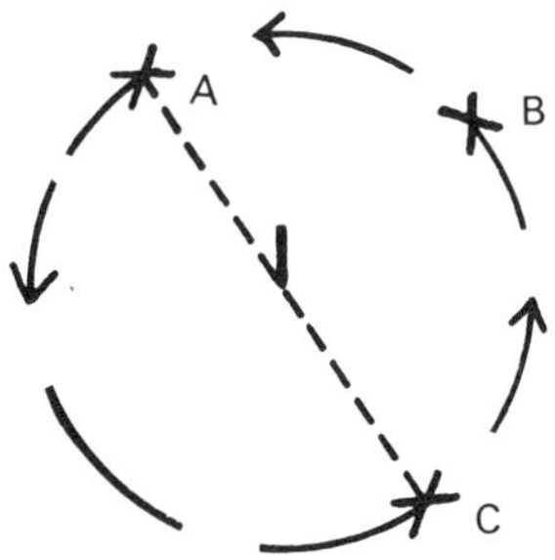

17 *Fielding Football*

This can be played outdoors, on a tennis court, basketball court or gym, between teams of no more than 8 to avoid congestion. Two skittles, 2 metres apart, act as goals at each end of the playing area. They are guarded by a goalkeeper, and goals are thrown between those skittles. The teams are divided into four forwards, three defenders and a goalkeeper. The ball is thrown between team members NO HIGHER THAN SHOULDER LEVEL. If a pass is dropped the other side takes a free throw. If the man in possession is touched by an opponent, he must part with the ball. He can take no more than one step before throwing. A ball passing outside the playing area is thrown in by an opponent of the man who last touched it. Play halves of 10 mins.

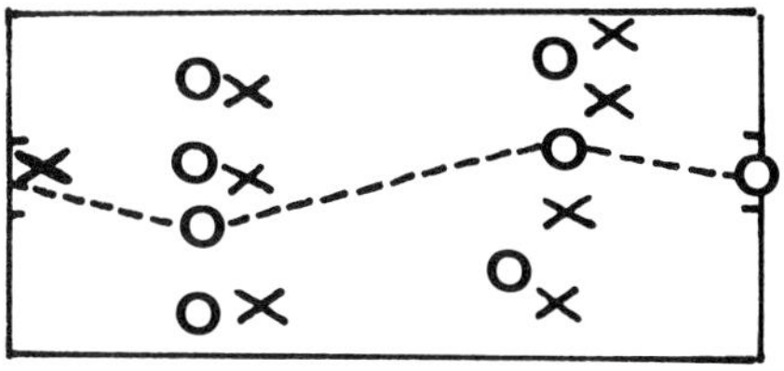

18 '*Yours*'

A group of 8 or 10 fieldsmen stand in a circle around the coach or leader with their eyes closed, having previously numbered off. The coach or leader may vary the distance of the fieldsmen from him. The leader then throws the ball high in the air within catching distance of the fieldsman shouting: 'Yours Number 3'. Number 3 then opens his eyes and tries to catch the ball. The player to make three successful catches replaces the leader.

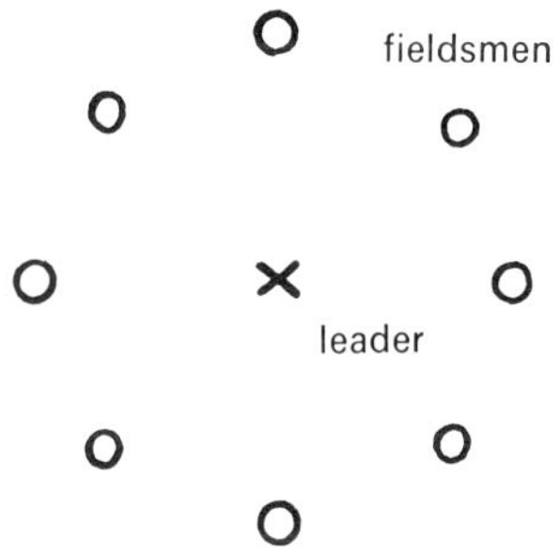

19 *Surprise Ball*

A group of 5 fieldsmen crouch as though they were in the slips 10 metres from a wall. The coach or leader stands behind them and throws a hard rubber ball against the wall in such a way that it carries as a catch to one of the fieldsmen. The fieldsman completing three successful catches replaces the leader.

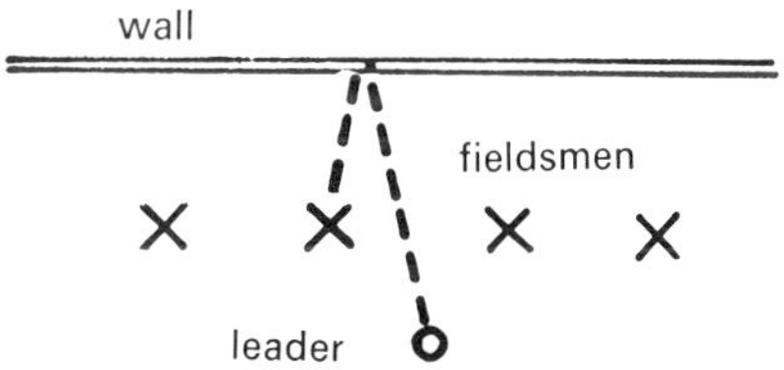

20 *Slip Promotion*

A group of fieldsmen crouch in an arc around the leader. The leader throws random catches to each in an attempt to surprise the fieldsmen. If the fieldsman is successful in the catch he moves up one place in the arc towards first slip. The others move down. If the first slip holds three catches he replaces the leader.

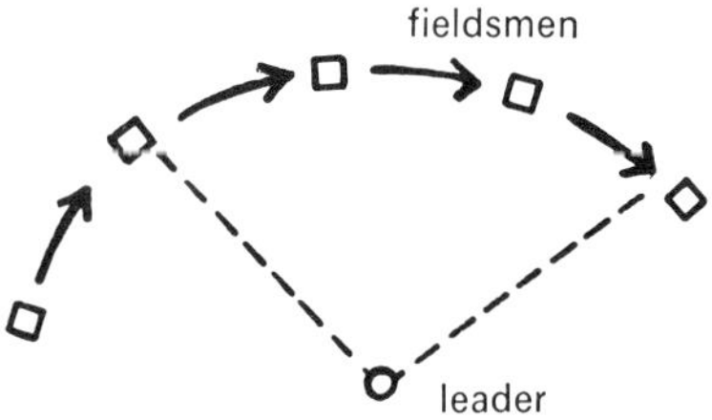

21 *The Middle Man*

A fieldsman stands in the middle of a circle of half a dozen fieldsmen who must not approach closer to the centre man than 5 metres. The player in the centre attempts to intercept and catch throws between the fieldsmen, who must throw across the circle no higher than shoulder level. When the middle man intercepts a catch the thrower takes his place in the centre of the circle.

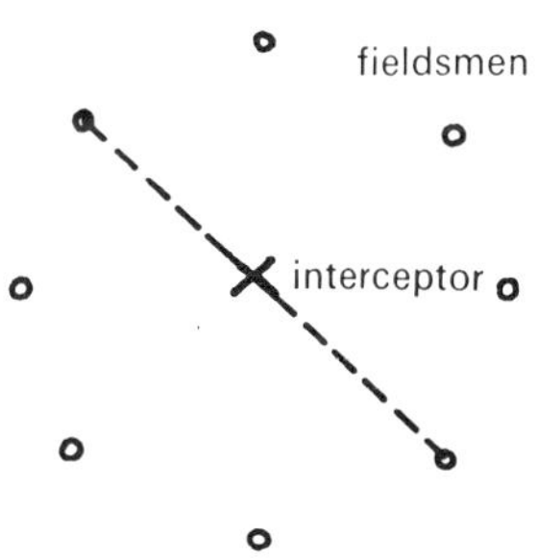

22 *Scurry Ball*
Two batsmen attempt to sneak a quick single. They stand at each end of a 20.1 metre (22 yd) wicket. In the covers there is a full cordon of five fieldsmen and a 'keeper behind the striker's stumps. A server of the ball stands at short leg and rolls or throws the ball past one of the batsmen at the supposed striker's end at varying speeds and to the left or right hands of the fieldsmen. The batsmen have to judge the value of the run and run or not accordingly, making the appropriate call. The fieldsmen try to run the batsmen out at the keeper's end. This exercise could be helped if the batsman on the side of the server wears a blinker. Such a blinker could be a piece of cardboard inserted under the batsman's cap to prevent his seeing the direction of the serve. Instead of the ball being served it could be teed up for the batsman to play into the covers.

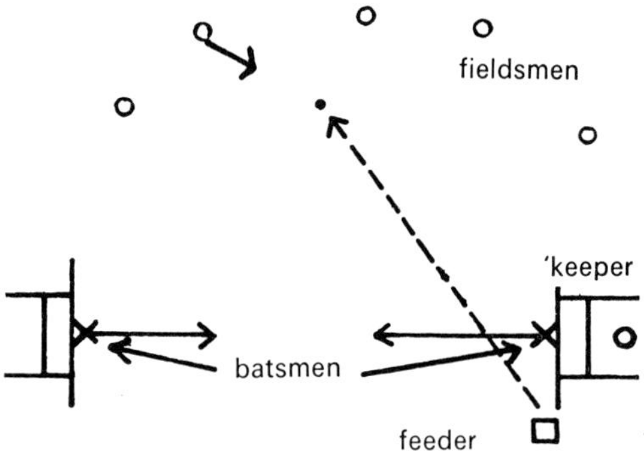

Group Activities—Wicketkeeping
Since a wicketkeeper is unique in the cricket team it is almost impossible to devise group activities which incorporate only the 'keeping skill. Thus he has to combine with other skills. It is equally true however, that a 'keeper is often grossly underworked at practice, through no fault of his own. If he keeps in a net situation, too few deliveries pass the batsman, and he is unable to stand back to the fast bowlers. Exercises must therefore be devised to keep the 'keeper working in a match situation.
Note: The following activities should be executed in full equipment, i.e. pads, protector, gloves, etc.

23 *The Slip Cradle*
The wicketkeeper and one slip take charge of one side of the slip cradle with fieldsmen A, B, and C on the other side. The 'keeper takes all the catches on his side of the cradle and the slip fieldsman throws catches to fieldsmen A, B and C who return in kind. The same sort of exercise can be carried out with the aid of a roller instead of a cradle.

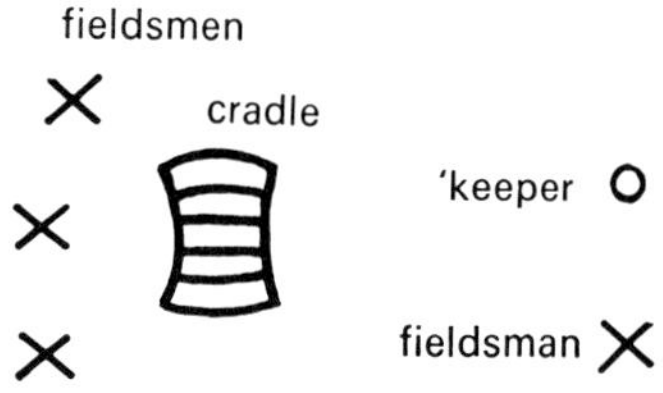

24 *Juggling*
In 'keeping, the 'hands maketh a man'. Therefore the 'keeper should practise such tricks as keeping three balls in the air at one time. Any other sleight of hand exercises are good.

25 *Drive Ball*
The 'keeper stands with his back to a net and a batsman drives the ball on the half-volley at the 'keeper and to his left and right. The 'keeper attempts to take every ball. The ball should be driven fairly hard since the match situation will bring the ball to him at that speed. An extension of this skill would be to feed the ball to the 'keeper at a slower speed or as a catch in front of the wicket so

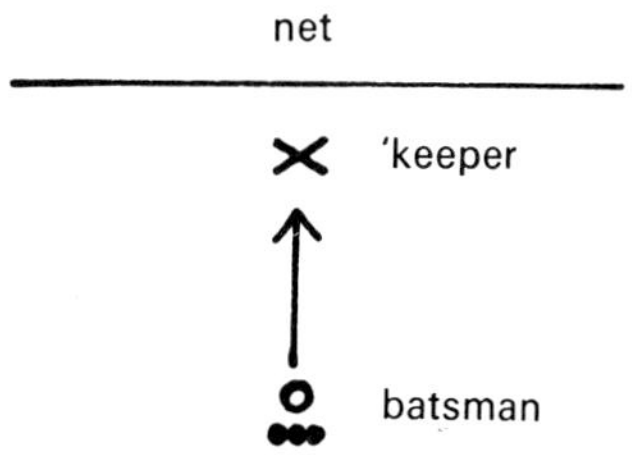

that he has to come around a stump to take the catch or collect the ball and flick it backwards towards the stump.

26 *Keeping Rough Shod*
On a stretch of uncut outfield with the 'keeper standing with his back to a net, a bowler either throws or bowls the ball at a stump with the 'keeper standing up. The 'keeper has to take the ball. The exercise is aimed at sharpening the reflexes. Much of the 'keeper's work in times of crisis consists of taking the ball which does the unexpected off the edge of the bat at the last minute. The rough outfield provides the 'unexpected' element in this exercise.

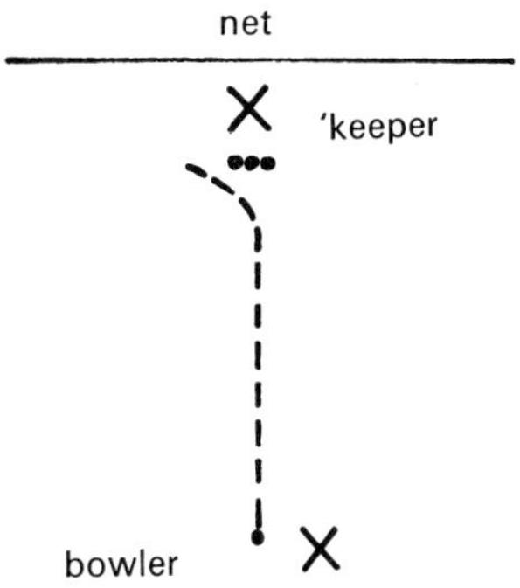

27 *Standing Up*
In a net situation, with a batsman taking strike and three spin bowlers operating, and varying their deliveries down the off and leg side, the 'keeper takes every ball with the batsman not hitting the ball but 'shadowing', i.e. pretending to play at the ball. The 'keeper must take each delivery and remove the bails. He gains a point for every successful take and stumping, and measures his efficiency by his score out of the maximum. The bowlers can measure their success in bowling balls of a certain kind.

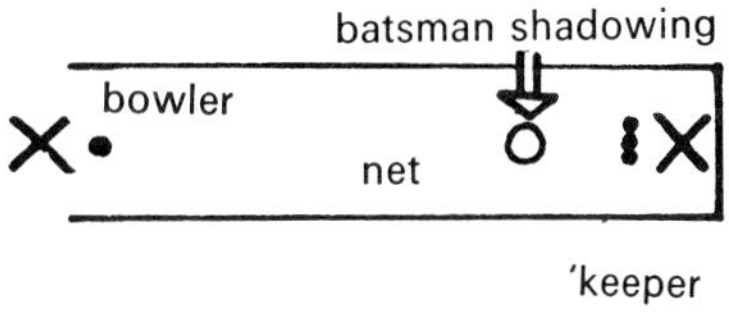

28 *Driving to the Wicket*
The leader or coach stands at the wicket and hits a ball along the ground or as a catch to fieldsmen A, B and C stationed at various points in front of the stumps and at different distances. The 'keeper is standing back from the stumps and each time a ball is struck drives himself forward to the stumps to take the return. For each return taken he gains a point. Perform the exercise 8 times, timing the 'keeper, not counting any wild returns, and then repeat, awarding the 'keeper a bonus of 5 points if he can improve on his earlier time. The fieldsmen at the same time may be measuring their efficiency by gaining 1 point for a clean stop or catch, 1 point for a good return, minus 2 points for a muffed catch or stop and minus 2 points for a bad return. The same penalties can be imposed on the 'keeper if he fails to gather the ball which is a good return (within 5 metres of the stumps).

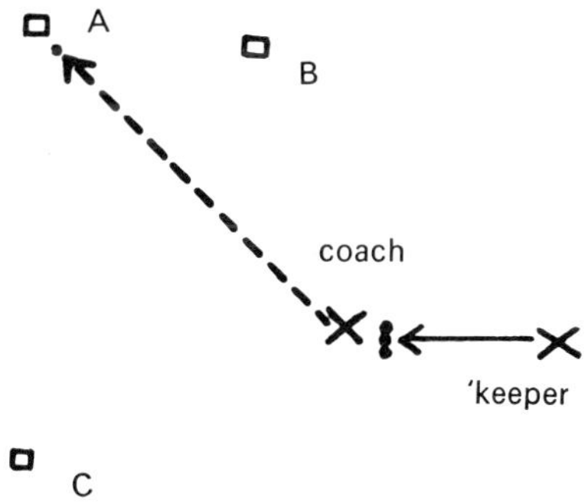

29 *Standing Back*
The coach stands 10 metres in front of the wicket with the 'keeper standing back. The coach then throws 8 deliveries, varying them in length and direction down the off and leg-side at fast speed. The 'keeper must take these balls cleanly and at the correct height as they begin their downward path. For each clean take he gains 1 point and for each miss is penalised 2 points. Assess the performance by the number of points gained at the end of the over.

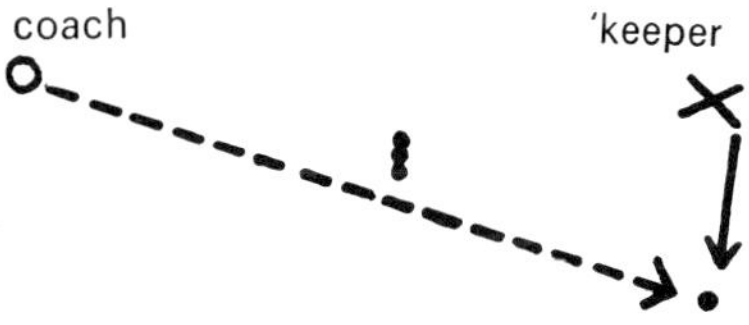

Group Activities—Elementary Skills

30 *Ball Chase* (*Skills—Catching, Throwing*)
A group of fieldsmen stand in a circle. They pass two or more balls around the circle trying to overtake the ball in front. The spacing of the circle can be varied according to the type of catch and throw being practised.

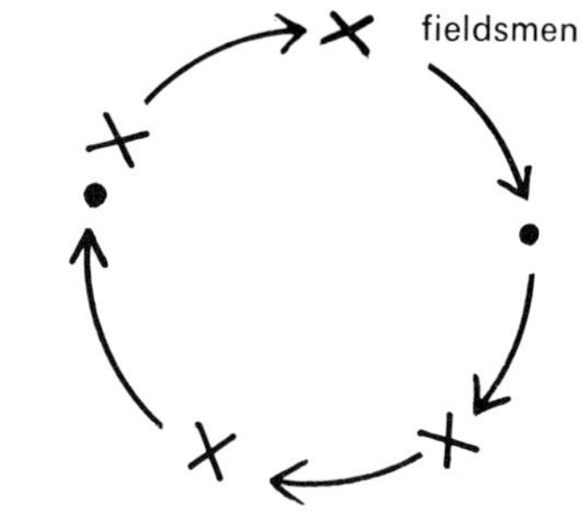

31 *Bogey Ball* (*Skills—Catching, Throwing*)
A ball is placed on line AB, and the group lines up behind line CD (10 or 20 metres distance according to requirement of practice). No. 1 team member runs to retrieve the ball and throws to No. 2 who must remain behind line CD. The throw is made from line AB, after which No. 1 goes to the back of the queue. Repeat through the team.

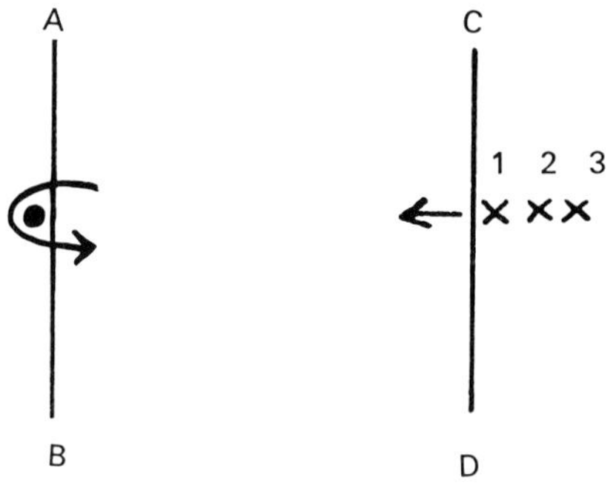

32 *Catching Relay* (*Skills—Catching, Throwing*)
Each player receives the ball from, and returns it to, the leader, except the last person in the line who runs as fast as possible to take the leader's place. The whole team moves along one place with the leader moving to place No. 1. The procedure continues until the leader is again in front of the team with the ball. The distance between the leader and the team varies according to the required distance of the throw and catch.

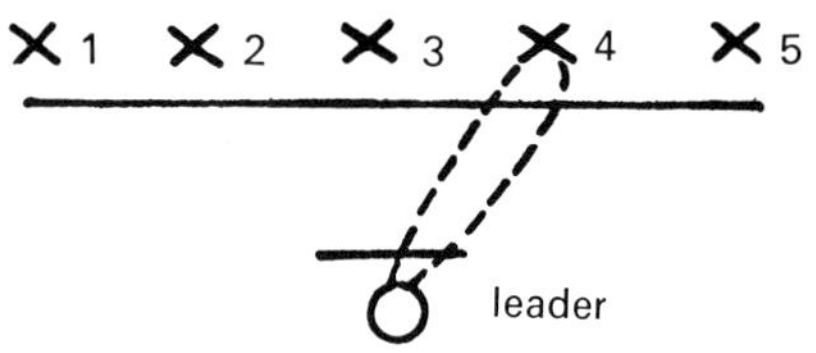

33 *Exchange Ball Relay* (*Skills—Catching, Throwing*)
No. 1 has the ball. He runs to line C, passes the ball to No. 2 and then runs to line up behind No. 6. No. 2 runs to line D, passes the ball to No. 3 and then runs to line up behind No. 5. This procedure continues until team members are back in their original positions.

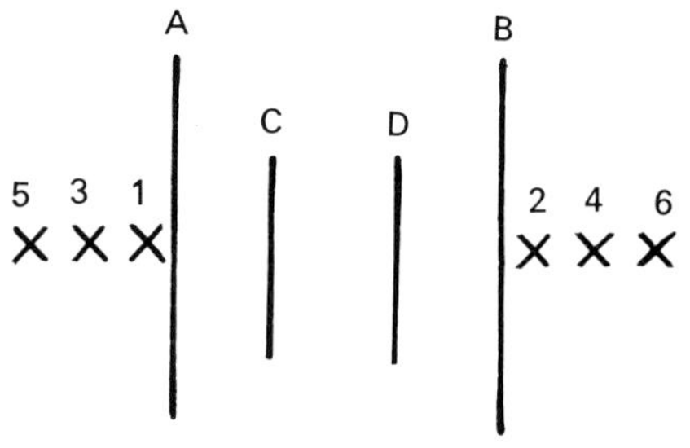

34 *Force Back* (*Skills—Catching, Throwing*)
In pairs or teams equidistant from a centre line. A throws the ball towards B, throwing for distance. B returns the ball from the spot where the ball is caught. Each player tries to force the opponent back until he is able to catch the return throw on the opponent's side of the centre line.

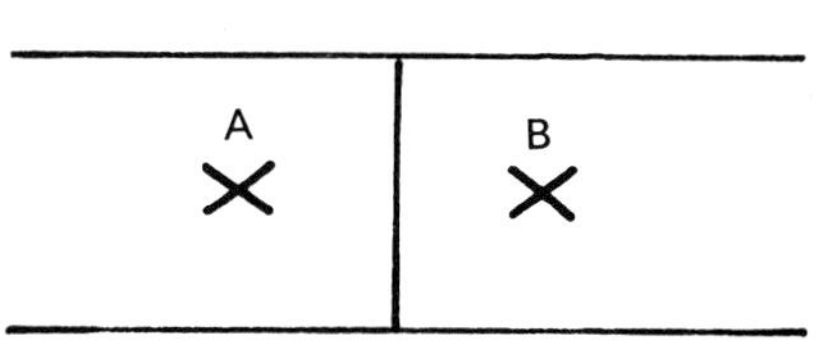

35 *Interception in Threes* (*Skills—Stopping, Hitting, Catching, Throwing*)
A and B try to make as many passes as possible without C intercepting the ball. The ball may be rolled, thrown or struck.

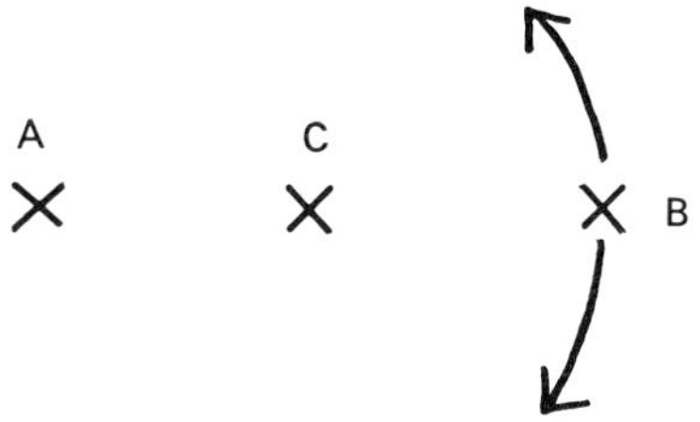

36 *Pepper* (*Skills—Throwing, Hitting, Catching, Stopping*)
Whoever fields the ball bowls or throws the ball immediately at the batsman. After a certain number of hits the batsman changes place with a fieldsman.

37a *Progression Ball* (*Skills—Catching, Throwing*)
A and B are equidistant from a centre line. A throws the ball to B. If the ball is caught, B takes one step backwards, but if the ball is dropped he takes one step forward. The winner is the one who is the greatest distance from the centre line when the signal is given.

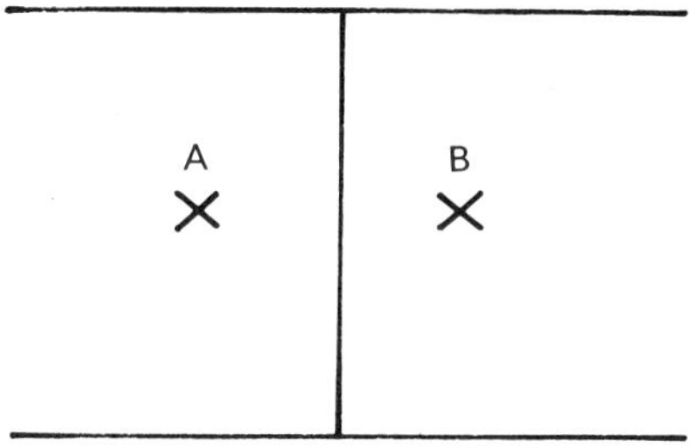

37b *Progression Ball*
The leader throws the ball to any player who catches the ball and returns it to the leader. A player taking three catches becomes the new leader. A misfield cancels the previous catches.

38 *Rebound Ball* (*Skills—Throwing, Hitting, Catching, Stopping*)
No. 1 throws a rubber ball (or hits it) at the wall and moves quickly to the end of the team allowing No. 2 to move up and catch the ball. The game continues with the players following in sequence.

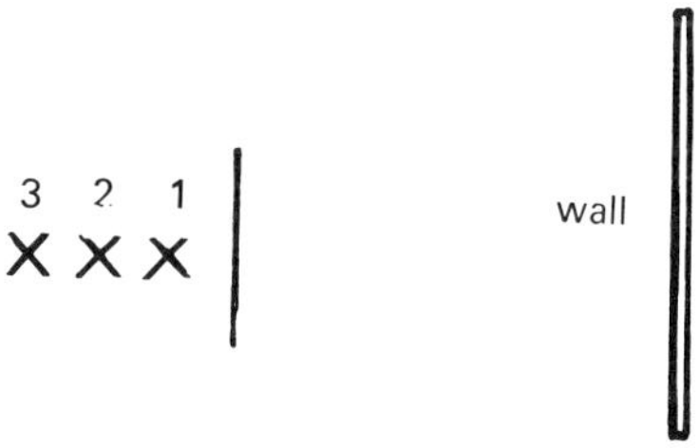

39 *Roll a Goal* (*Skills—Stopping, Throwing*)
The players are in pairs. Each player in turn tries to roll the ball through his opponent's goal. The opponent defends. The distance between goals can be varied.

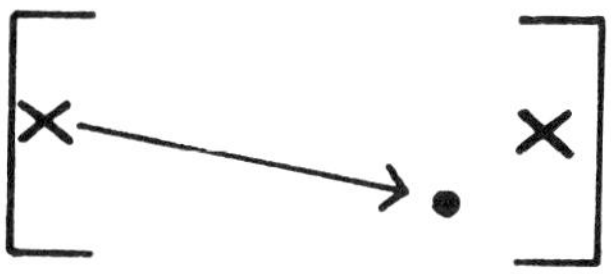

40 *Shuttle Ball Relay* (*Skills—Throwing, Catching*)
No. 1 throws the ball to No. 2 then runs over to line B. No. 2 throws the ball to No. 3, then runs to line A. No. 3 throws the ball to No. 1 and so on.

41 *Return Relay* (*Skills—Catching, Stopping, Throwing*)
No. 1 runs up to A and as he passes line BC he places the ball on it. He runs around point A and back towards his team. As he returns he picks up the ball and throws it underarm to No. 2. No. 2 runs out and places the ball on the line BC and then runs around point A and so on until the leader returns to the head of his team. The distance between the lines can be increased.

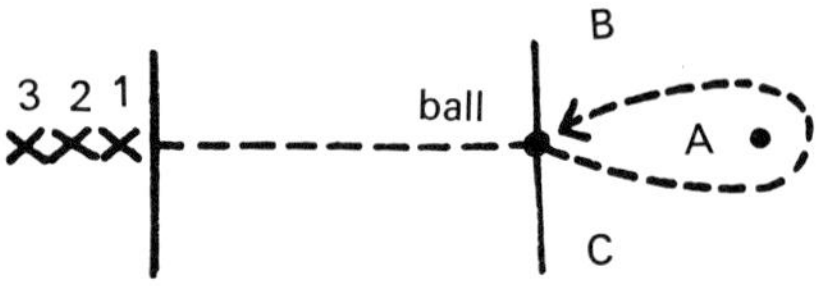

Elementary Skills—Games

42 *Bouncing Ball* (*Hitting*)
Each player is allocated a number. All players stand behind a restraining line AB 5 metres from a wall. No. 1 player hits the ball against the wall from any position behind the restraining line. As the ball bounces back from the wall No. 2 player attempts to hit the ball back against the wall with his hand. Play continues with Nos 3, 4, 5, 6 taking their turn to hit the ball. A player is allowed to pat bounce a ball before hitting it, but the ball must be hit from behind the restraining line and must bounce behind the line. The player who misses the ball incurs a penalty point. The player with the lowest score over a specified time wins.

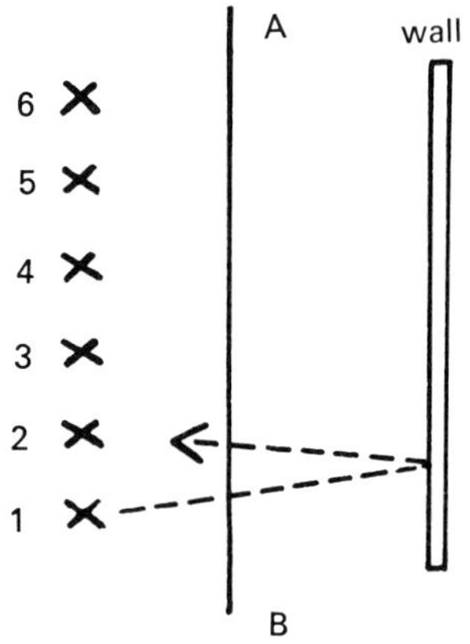

43 *Bombardment* (*Rolling, Throwing*)
Two equal teams, one defending, one attacking, and one in each half of a tennis court. The players move about freely in their own court bar a 2 metre square target area in each court. In each target area place some skittles or wooden blocks. One player holds the ball and on the signal 'go' puts it into play by rolling it at the target on the opposite side. Players try to hit and knock their opponents' target with the ball, at the same time protecting their own. The winner is the team that first knocks down the target of the other team.

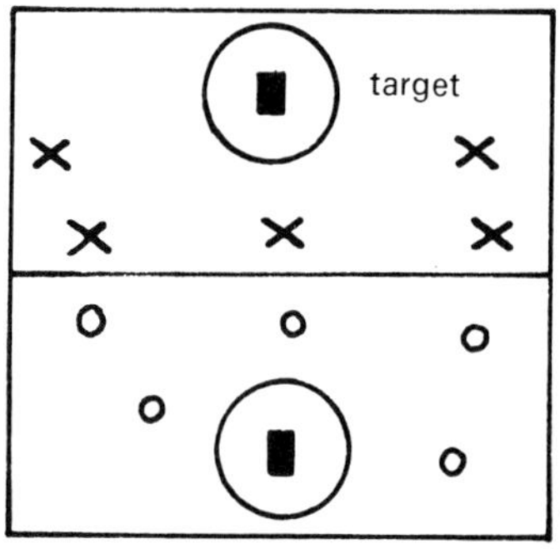

44 *Boundary Ball* (*Throwing, Catching*)
Two teams. Players stand anywhere within their own team's half of the playing area. The game is begun by giving the ball to a player near the centre line. This player attempts to throw the ball over the opponents' end line providing he bounces it once within his opponents' court. The opposing team try to stop the ball from passing over the end line. If the ball is stopped from passing over the end line, a member of the team having possession may pass the ball to another team member in a better position to throw the ball over the opponents' end line.

One point is scored if the ball crosses the opponents' end line, providing it has touched the ground at least once in the opponents' territory. The player catching the ball may take only one step before throwing the ball. If a ball crosses a side line, it is awarded to an opponent of the player who last touched the ball before it went out of bounds.

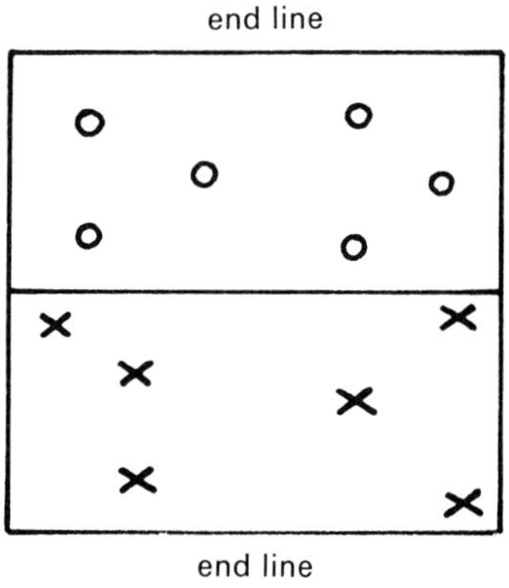

45 *Continuous Cricket* (*Hitting, Throwing, Stopping, Catching*)
Two teams. The ball is bowled to the No. 1 batsman. If he hits the ball, he drops the bat, runs around the post as indicated in the diagram to score a run, picks up his bat and prepares to face the bowler again. The ball is fielded and thrown to the bowler who immediately bowls again, whether the batsman has returned or not.

When the No. 1 batsman is out, he immediately drops the bat and No. 2 batsman runs to pick it up and take his place. The bowler may continue to bowl during the changeover and, if he hits the wicket, No. 2 is out. Then No. 3 batsman runs in, and so on until the whole team is out. The teams then change over. The side scoring the greater number of runs wins.

A run is scored each time the batsman runs around the post and back to his wicket without going out. The batsman is out if the bowler hits the wicket, if he hits his own wicket, and if he is caught from a hit.

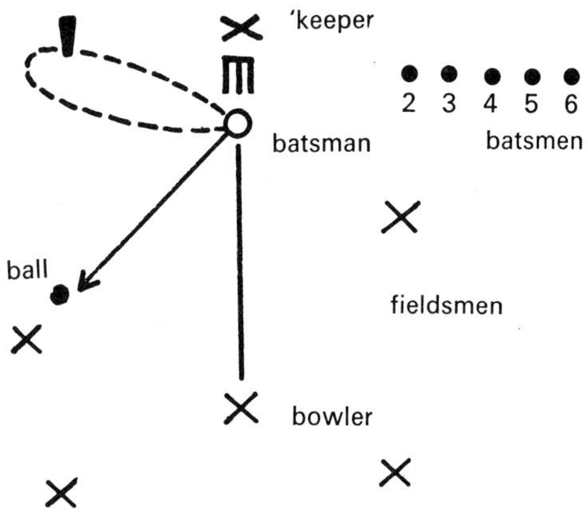

46 *Danish Rounders* (*Hitting, Throwing, Catching*)
Two teams, up to 12 members each, one batting and one bowling. The pitcher throws a high lob upwards between himself and the first batsman. The batsman hits at the ball and whether he hits or not, runs to first base; he may continue running to the other bases. However, if the pitcher grounds the ball in the pitching circle and calls 'stop' whilst the runner is between bases, then the runner is out. If the runner is on a base when the call is made, he is safe. Batsman No. 2 takes his turn as soon as the pitcher has the ball and the game continues until five batsmen are out. Any number of batsmen may be on the same base at the same time; batsmen may also pass one another when running between bases. The team scoring the greater number of points is the winner.

The batsman scores a point each time he gets to home base. If the ball is caught the batsman is out. All batsmen between bases when the bowler calls 'stop' are out. The ball must not be hit behind the lines joining the fourth, first, and home and third bases. The penalty is that the batsman is out.

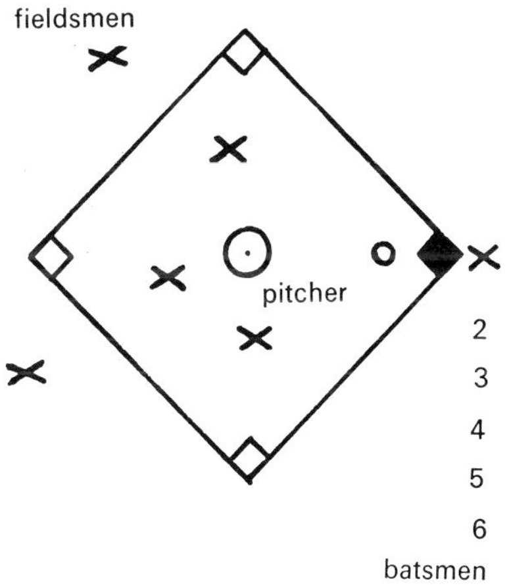

47 *Hit and Run* (*Hitting, Throwing, Catching, Stopping*)
Two teams of 8-10 players each, a bat, soft rubber ball and stumps. To begin the game a fielder near the batsman bowls the ball underarm to the batsman. If the batsman hits the ball he runs to the opposite stumps and continues running between the stumps until he is out. A successful journey from one stump to the other scores one run. When the ball is fielded, it is returned to a fielder close to the running batsman. This fieldsman tries to hit the batsman with the ball below shoulder level. The batsman can defend himself by hitting the ball with his bat, but

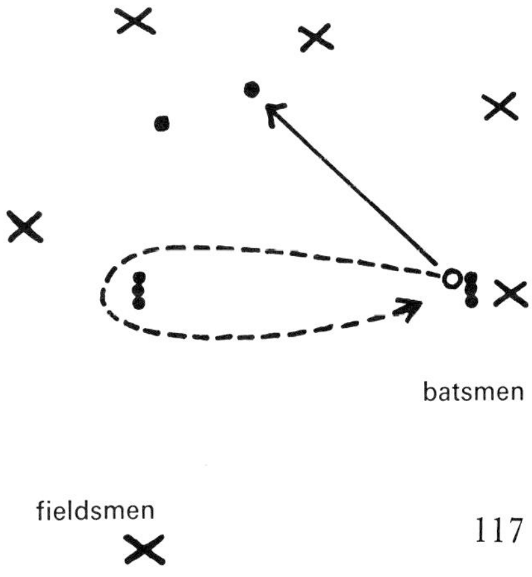

is out if the ball hits his body or legs. No. 2 then becomes the batsman. The team scoring the greater number of runs is the winner. When aiming at the batsman the fieldsman may only take one step forward.

48 *Long Ball* (*Hitting, Throwing, Catching, Stopping*)
Two teams of 8-10 players each, a small ball, bat and bases. Can be played on a basketball court. One of the teams bats and the other fields. The playing area has a home plate, a long base and a pitcher's box. The fielding team has a pitcher, a catcher, a long baseman and fielders. When the batsman hits the ball he runs to long base and, if possible, returns home. If successful he scores a point for his side. There are no fouls in this game: any hit is good. A base runner may stay on long base if it is not safe to return home. Any number of runners may be on long base at the same time. A runner on long base may run only when a ball has been hit by a batsman, unless it is a catch. In this case the runners must return to long base. One point is scored per return run. A runner may not steal home. The batsman is out if he strikes out, or hits a catch, is touched off base by a fieldsman with the ball, steals a run to home base, reaches long base after the ball is received by the long base man or throws his bat after the hit is made.

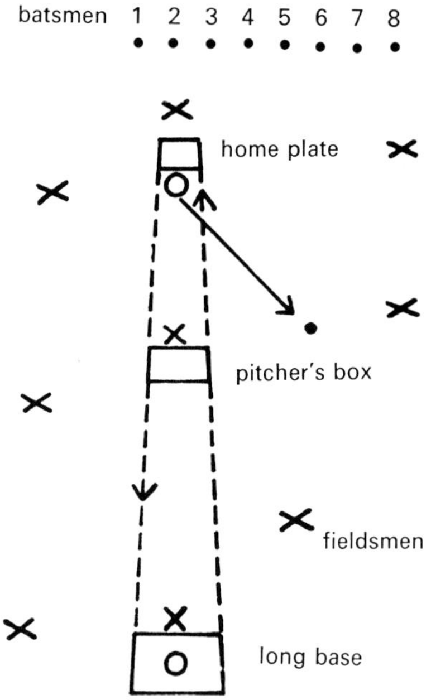

49 *Ruler Cricket* (*Hitting, Throwing, Stopping*)
Two teams of 8-12 players each, with two circles and a ball in each circle. No. 1 player in each team goes in the centre of the other team's circle. The players around the circle aim the ball at the centre player who hits it with a ruler. He can move freely within the circle. The players outside must not enter the circle. The outside team scores one point if the centre player is hit below the knee, while he scores one point if he succeeds in hitting the ball through the ring of players. The game continues for about 10 minutes until the coach gives the signal to change places. No. 2 then takes his position in the opponents' circle. When all the players have batted the batsmen's scores are added to find the team's score. The team gaining the higher number of points is the winner. Players outside the circle should pass the ball amongst themselves before aiming at the centre player.

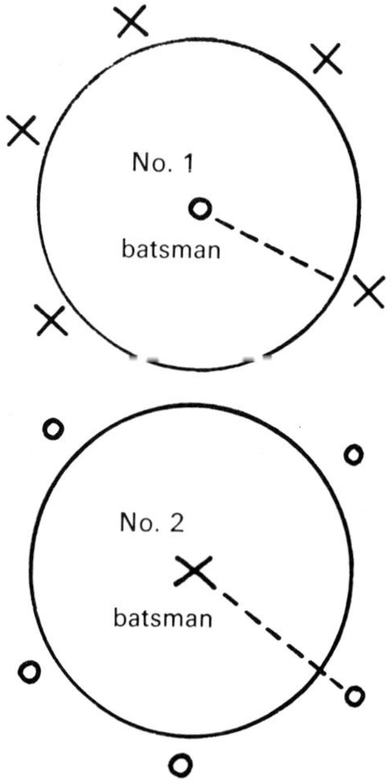

50 *Running Circle Catch* (*Throwing, Catching*)
A group of 6-8 players run in a circle around a centre player who throws the ball in turn to each. After catching each player throws it back to the centre player who passes it to the next and so on round the circle. Beginners must learn to catch the ball without stopping. Increasing the size of the circle makes the game more difficult. The direction of the run can be altered, and players can run sideways whilst facing the thrower.

51 *Net Cricket or Tennis Court Cricket* (*Hitting, Stopping, Catching, Bowling*)
In a net situation this game can be played between two teams of eleven players with a narrow bat and a rubber ball. The batsman bats to a bowler delivering from 20.1 metres (22 yd). There is a 'keeper and across the pitch of the net practice area are drawn lines at distances of 5, 10 and 15 metres from the batsman. Two fieldsmen are stationed on the end of each of these lines next to the net. A further fieldsman is stationed behind the bowler. The bowler bowls and the batsman attempts to hit the ball past the fieldsmen without lofting the ball out of the net. If he succeeds in hitting past the first two fieldsmen he scores one run; past the second line of defence he receives 2 runs, past the third, 3 runs, and past the bowler and deep fieldsman four runs. There is no running between wickets. The batsman can be out in every way in the Laws of Cricket except lbw and run out. If he lofts the ball out of the net he is out. The batsman faces a limited number of overs. The bowler is changed after every over, with the fieldsmen rotating. The batting side wait outside the net to take their place at the batting crease. For this game there is no need of protective equipment. The side scoring the highest number of runs wins. A similar game is possible using the markings of a tennis court and fieldsmen placed behind the 'tramlines', the net line and the base line, with runs awarded for penetrating those limits.

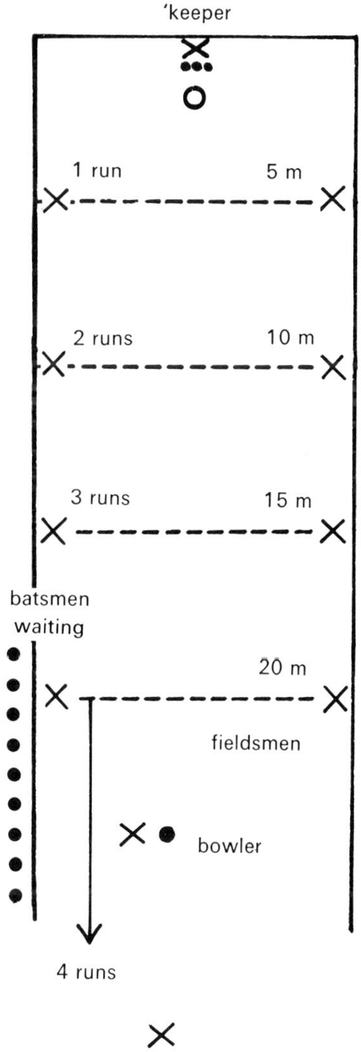

39 Recommended games for juniors

Too often in the past, junior cricket has been played as though it were a Test Match. There was no difference in the format of an England-Australia game and an under 14 or primary school match. Consequently some individuals monopolised the game and others would find themselves fielding at deep fine leg and not bowling and not having a chance to bat since they were too far down the batting line.

The aim in recommending junior forms of cricket is to increase the participation of the individual junior player, and with this increased participation bring added fun and a greater desire to continue to play the game. It is strongly recommended that associations and schools adopt the one or two day format and it is hoped that teachers of physical education will find the single and double wicket, and the six- and eight-a-side games suitable for curriculum activities. The games of cricket included in the following section are recommended not only on a participation and temporal basis but also because they bear a close resemblance to the more serious parent game.

Games suitable for one or two physical education periods within school time

Six-a-side cricket

Each match shall be played between two teams consisting of six players. Each team shall have one innings.

The match ends when a win is gained even though the five overs have not been bowled.

Each team member shall bat once and thereafter bowl one over. The wicketkeeper shall not bowl.

The match shall be played under the Laws of Cricket wherever applicable.

The five players of the fielding side shall each bowl one over of six balls including wides and no balls.

Wides and no balls shall each count four runs against the fielding side and shall be added to the opponents' score.

The normal boundary shall count six runs instead of four.

The normal six boundary shall count ten runs.

All six players shall bat until out or until their personal score is 25, whichever is the sooner. The maximum score for one person is 34. (24 plus a 10 hit off the last ball the batsman is eligible to face.)

The batsman will lose his personal score if he fails to add to the score on three consecutive deliveries. If the batsman is out on the third ball (e.g. run out) he will still lose his score.

The last batsman will continue to bat on his own. The next to the last batsman will stay in to run with him but will not take strike.

The team with the highest aggregate runs in the five overs, or by the time all six of their batsmen are out, whichever is the sooner, will be the winner.

Individual scores will be noted against each player's name (runs scored), be marked in bowling squares and also indicated on the accumulative runs in the score book.

Any runs forfeited will be deleted in the runs scored column. No corresponding cancellation is made on the accumulative runs or bowling columns in the score book until the end of the innings. Any further runs are recorded and when the player is out totalled.

The minus runs (those forfeited) are also totalled and entered in the appropriate square under minus scores. On completion of the team's innings, the minus scores should be totalled and deducted from the total of the accumulative runs.

A player retires immediately on scoring 25 or over (i.e. 24 plus a boundary).

Runs and extras are recorded in the normal way, but with special values as follows:

a boundary six extra = 10 runs

a boundary four extra = 6 runs

a wide = 4 runs

a no ball = 4 runs.

Eight-a-side cricket

The time required for an eight-a-side game is approximately 60-75 minutes. This is the time for each side to bat for 12 overs. It is advisable that the master-in-charge or coach should keep the score and umpire at the bowler's end, with a member of the batting side filling the role of square leg umpire.

The game shall be played under the Laws of Cricket whenever applicable.

Each team shall comprise 8 players. All shall bat but only 4 players in each team shall bowl.

The team scoring the highest average number of runs per wicket lost shall be the winner.

The fielding side shall provide a wicketkeeper and seven fieldsmen, four of whom shall each bowl three overs—a double change of bowlers shall occur at the end of the sixth over.

The batting side shall provide one or two umpires, two or three fieldsmen, two batsmen and two batsmen padded up.

The two fieldsmen from the batting side shall not be permitted to bowl or keep wicket whilst their side is batting.

Batsmen shall have an unlimited number of dismissals but each shall be recorded on the score sheet as a wicket lost.

Each pair of batsmen shall change after the third, sixth and ninth overs.

If a pair of batsmen each complete their innings without being dismissed a bonus of half the total runs scored during their partnership shall be added to the score of the batting side.

It is possible to lengthen the extent of the match or shorten it. If it is required to shorten the game to 8 overs, the pairs of batsmen will change after each two overs. Each bowler will be limited to two overs and changes in bowling will occur after the fourth over. More flexibility is permissible in bowling and it is not necessary to insist that bowlers deliver two consecutive overs from one end. If it is desired to lengthen the game to 16 overs, the pairs of batsmen change after the fourth, eighth, and twelfth overs and the bowling change occurs after the eighth over.

It is important to remember that when each pair of batsmen change places, and those retiring take off their pads, they should immediately come on to the field to enable the next pair of batsmen to pad up. It is also possible to add scoring value to a shorter game by making a 6 boundary = 10, and a 4 boundary = 6 runs.

Single Wicket and Double Wicket Cricket

Single Wicket Cricket

Single wicket competitions can be played within groups of 12 or more players.

One player competes against another.

The remainder of the group act as wicketkeeper and fieldsmen. They are not allowed to bat or bowl.

Each batsman is entitled to face one over of 8 balls.

He cannot be out, but should he be dismissed he will be debited with one wicket.

Each bowler must deliver one over of 8 balls.

No balls, wides, shall count as legitimate balls in the over, but for each no ball and wide the batsman will be credited with 6 runs.

The normal 6 boundary shall count 10 runs and the normal 4 boundary, 6 runs.

The player averaging the highest number of runs per wicket lost shall be the winner.

The Laws of Cricket shall be applicable whenever possible.

After one pair of players has completed its game, they will be succeeded by the next pair of single wicket contestants.

There are certain variants possible in this game. It is permissible to increase or decrease the number of balls received by each batsman according to the time available, and the number of players participating. It is also possible to vary the boundary rule, and the no dismissal rule. These are recommended, however, as rewarding and increasing participation. It is permissible to vary the law concerning lbw. In games for juniors it could be ignored completely or even applied to balls pitching outside the leg-stump.

Double Wicket Cricket

Double wicket cricket shall be played within groups of 12 or more players.

Two players within the group shall compete against another two.

The remainder of the group shall act as wicketkeeper and fieldsmen. They are not allowed to bat or bowl.

Each pair of batsmen is entitled to face two overs or 16 balls.

Each bowler shall deliver one over of 8 balls. Both players on the bowling side must bowl.

The batsman cannot be dismissed, but should he lose his wicket, he will be debited with that wicket.
No balls and wides shall count as legitimate balls in the over, but for each no ball and wide, the batsman will be credited with 6 runs.
The normal boundary for 6 shall count as 10 runs; the normal 4 boundary, 6 runs.
The side averaging the highest number of runs per wicket lost shall be the winners.
The Laws of Cricket shall be observed whenever applicable.
After two pairs of players have completed their game, their places will be taken by the next two pairs of contestants.

The observations on the variations of single wicket cricket also apply to double wicket.

Games suitable for school situations embracing one morning's or afternoon's play of 3 hours

One Day (Morning) Game

The game shall be played under the Laws of Cricket wherever applicable.
The game shall be of one morning's (afternoon's) duration and the hours of play shall be from 9 a.m. to 12 noon (2 p.m. to 5 p.m.) except as herein provided. If the side batting first has not completed its innings, the innings shall be compulsorily closed on the completion of 144 balls (24 x 6 ball overs, or 18 x 8 ball overs). The side batting second shall then face the same number of balls. If the innings of the side batting first has been completed before 144 balls the side batting second shall be entitled to bat for a maximum of 144 balls. Thereafter the side batting first shall begin its second innings.
No bowler shall be permitted to bowl more than 4 x 6 ball overs (or 3 x 8 ball overs).
A batsman shall be compulsorily and temporarily retired when he has scored 25. He may resume batting in turn after all the other batsmen have been dismissed or retired. The maximum score before retirement is 30 (24 plus a 6 boundary).
A batsman can be retired at the discretion of the coach, provided he has been batting for a minimum of 3 overs. A batsman retired in this manner is 'out'.
There shall be no follow-on law.
There shall be adequate adult supervision of the game controlling both umpiring and scoring. Adults should be allowed to assist the boys by coaching or organising provided this does not lead to wastage of time. On the field coaching should not cause delay in play.

Optional Laws

The bowler's run up shall be limited to 10 yards.
The over shall be 6 (or 8) deliveries, irrespective of whether any wides or no balls were bowled in the 6 (8) deliveries.
A no ball shall be called for any normal violation of the law and for a ball which lands off the wicket area or a ball which first lands in the bowler's half of the wicket.
A wide ball shall be called when the ball passes the batsman as he stands in his normal position, out of his reach and on the full toss.
There shall be no lbw decisions given OR the lbw law shall be applied to the ball that pitches outside the leg-stump as well as the ball which pitches on the stumps or outside the off-stump.
Unless injured the wicketkeeper shall not be replaced during a session of play (this rule is to prevent wastage of time).
No junior player shall be forced to field closer to the bat than ½ the pitch length—except in the slips area.

Two Day (Morning) Game

The game shall be played under the Laws of Cricket wherever applicable.
The game shall be of two mornings (afternoons) duration and the hours of play shall be three hours on each morning. On the first day if the side batting first has not completed its innings, the innings shall be suspended (or compulsorily closed) on the completion of 144 balls (24 x 6 ball overs or 18 x 8 ball overs). The side batting second shall face the same number of balls. If the innings of the side batting first has been completed before 144 balls the side batting second shall be entitled to bat for no more than a maximum of 144 balls. Thereafter it can be decided according to the local

rules whether to begin the second innings of the side batting first or to delay that innings until the second day and initiate a practice situation.

If a team in either session on the first day has not been dismissed, then the first innings of the team or teams must continue on the second day until either a further 24 x 6 ball (18 x 8 ball) overs have been delivered or the side has been dismissed. If the side batting first on the second day is dismissed before the expiration of the 24 x 6 (18 x 8) ball overs, the side batting second shall be entitled to face the same number of balls. The remainder of the time may be occupied by the second innings based on divided time.

An alternative to the above second day situation is to declare each side's first innings compulsorily closed after they have faced 144 balls each on the first day. On the second day, the batting must be opened by the batsmen who have not batted on the first day. The second day will be occupied by the second innings based on the same compulsory closure as the first innings (i.e. 144 balls).

No bowler shall be permitted to bowl more than 4x6 (3x8) ball overs in each innings.

A batsman shall be compulsorily and temporarily retired when he has scored 25. He may resume batting in turn after all the other batsmen have been dismissed or retired. The maximum score before retirement is 30 (24 plus a 6 boundary).

A batsman can be retired at the discretion of the captain or coach, provided he has been batting for a minimum of 3 overs. A batsman retired in this manner is 'out'.

There shall be no follow on rule.

In a junior game there shall be adequate adult supervision of the game controlling both umpiring and scoring. Adults may assist boys by coaching or organising, provided that this does not waste time.

The optional laws may also apply to the two day game.

Crickball

Crickball is a modified game of cricket aimed at increasing participation and accelerating the scoring rate.

The Laws of Cricket shall apply to Crickball.

The hours of play and numbers of players shall be agreed to by the opposing sides.

The wicket area shall be marked with white lines as in the accompanying diagram.

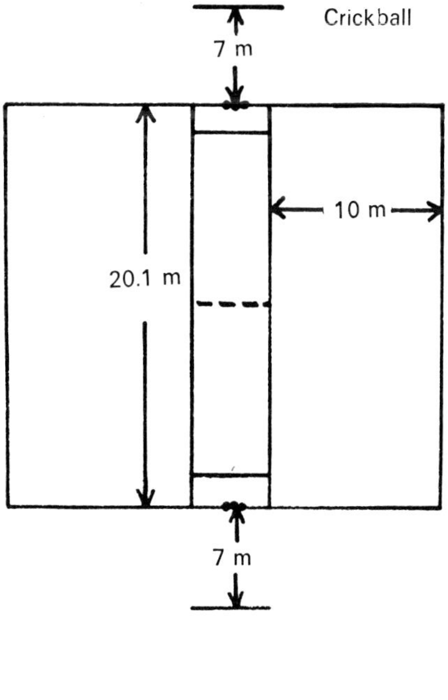

The bowler shall not commence his run-up further than 7 metres from the bowling wicket.

No fielder shall enter the area 10 metres on each side of the pitch before the ball leaves the bowler's hand.

If the ball bounces in the bowler's half of the wicket, 'no ball' shall be called.

The batsmen must score 16 runs in 4 overs. Failure to do so will cause the dismissal of one batsman, beginning with the first batsman in the team and working through the team.

At the end of its allocated number of overs, the side batting first must close its innings. The opposing side will then face the same number of balls.

A commonly agreed number of players in each fielding side shall bowl an agreed number of overs.

40 Recommended equipment

Satisfactory and adequate equipment suitable to the age group of the juniors should be used. The following should be included:

set of stumps and bails
4 pairs of batting gloves and pads
1 pair of 'keeper's gloves and pads
thigh pads
boxes
4 cricket bats
1 cricket ball
1 score book

The following sizes of equipment are recommended:

Bats
Over 16 years old (up to 170 cm (5′ 7″) in height)—Harrow size (above 170 cm (5′ 7″) full size)
14-16 years (up to 165 cm (5′ 5″) in height)—size 6 (Harrow above 165 cm (5′ 5″))
11-14 years (up to 158 cm (5′ 2″) in height—size 5 (size 6 above 158 cm (5′ 2″))
8-11 years (up to 145 cm (4′ 9″) in height)—size 4 (size 5 above 145 cm (4′ 9″))
Weight and the 'pick up' of the bat are important. Remember that the heavier bat does not make the player hit the ball harder. If he hit the ball with a lamp post he would only increase his hitting efficiency by 7 per cent.

Balls
For junior players up to the age of 14—a 135-142 g (4¾-5 oz) ball, in composition or plastic.

Stumps
Full size as the club players 71.12 x 22.86 cm (28″ x 9″).

Wicketkeeping gloves
These must be of the correct size and flexible enough to allow the 'keeper to feel the ball. His fingers must be able to reach the end of the glove fingers, which should not be too rigid. The finger stall must not be too long and the palm must not be worn smooth.

Pads
These are not made in any specific sizes outside those of boys', youths' and seniors'. Your equipment should cater for the differing sizes of the team members. It should not be so cumbersome as to prevent free movement between the wickets and in execution of strokes. Batting gloves should also ensure comfort and freedom of movement.

The pitch
It is strongly recommended that the pitch length for players under 12 years be shortened to 17.7 m (19⅓ yards) (a length of the concrete strip on most junior pitches) and that the game be played on concrete without the laying of matting. No boundary shall exceed 50 (60) metres from the centre of the pitch. (Either option may be adopted.) They should be clearly marked by lines or flags and the creases clearly marked.

The following cricket equipment is available from most sports stores.

Cricket balls
Leather—Available in 156 g (5½ oz) (156-163 g (5½-5¾ oz) 22.4-22.8 cm ($8\frac{13}{16}$-9″ circumference))
142 g (5 oz) (142-149 g (5-5¼ oz))
135 g (4¾ oz) (135-142 g (4¾-5 oz) 21.6-22 cm ($8\frac{11}{16}$″ circumference))
Plastic coated—Available in 156 g (5½ oz) and will be available in 135 g (4¾ oz)
Composition—Available in 156 g (5½ oz) and 142 g (5 oz).

Leg guards
Batting leg guards—Generally available in five sizes, to suit players as indicated:
Small boys' 53-56 cm (21-22″) overall suits boys to about 122 cm (4′) tall.
Boys' size 58-61 cm (23-24″) overall to 142 cm (4′ 8″).
Youths' 63.5 cm (25″) overall to 157 cm (5′ 2″).
Men's 68.6 cm (27″) overall to 183 cm (6′).
Large Men's 71 cm (28″) overall over 183 cm (6′).
Wicketkeeping—Available in men's and youths' sizes. From experience, it has not been necessary to have a boys' wicketkeeping pad as they generally find batting pads acceptable.
Thigh guards—Available in a senior size only, which would be too bulky for boys under about 152 cm (5′) tall.

Kit bags
Generally available in two sizes, 91.4 x 27 x 30 cm (36 x 10½ x 12″) which is satisfactory for junior teams and 91.4 x 30 x 38 cm (36 x 12 x 15″) generally used by senior teams.

Protectors
Padded protectors are available in standard men's and junior sizes with and without tapes. Athletic supports designed to carry the protector without tapes are available in the following sizes:
Small 76-81 cm (30-32″) waist; Medium 86-91 cm (34-36″); Large 96.5-102 cm (38-40″).
Protectors in unpadded plastic are available also in men's and junior sizes which also fit into the support pouch. Wicketkeeping protectors with abdominal guards are available in men's sizes only.

Cricket bats
Bats are readily available in full size, Harrow size, size 6, size 5. (Size 4 bats are available in limited quantities only.) Cheaper fabric wrapped Indian bats are also available, including size 4.
The following are suggested standard bat specifications:

SIZE	HANDLE LENGTH	BLADE LENGTH	BLADE WIDTH	OVERALL LENGTH
3	26.0 cm	46.0 cm	9.5 cm	72.0 cm (28.3″)
4	27.0 cm	48.0 cm	9.8 cm	75.0 cm (29.5″)
5	28.0 cm	50.0 cm	10.1 cm	78.0 cm (30.7″)
6	29.0 cm	52.0 cm	10.4 cm	81.0 cm (31.9″)
Harrow	30.0 cm	54.0 cm	10.6 cm	84.0 cm (33.1″)
Men's short handle	30.0 cm	56.0 cm	10.8 cm	86.0 cm (33.9″)
Men's long handle	32.0 cm	56.0 cm	10.8 cm	88.0 cm (34.6″)

Cricket gloves
Batting: Spiked rubber batting gloves are available in boys', youths' and men's sizes and also the sausage type batting gloves are available in men's, youths' and boys' sizes.
Wicketkeeping: available in boys', youths' and men's sizes.
Inner gloves: junior and senior sizes.
The boys' size would generally fit boys up to 11 or 12 years, youths' size would fit 12 to 16 years, thereafter they would use men's.

Stumps and bails
Stores stock full-size stumps and bails for club use and smaller sizes in their toy range.

Footwear
The following range is available:
All makes and sizes of conventional boots.
White sandshoes—canvas upper tennis shoe, available in all sizes.
White cricket shoes—rubber sole, leather upper, available from size 5 upwards.
Predominantly white warm-up shoe with canvas uppers are now sold in large volume.

41 The Laws of Cricket and their interpretation

Some of the Laws of Cricket are clear and easily understood, others may need interpretation for the coach and player. The Laws are set out here in full, but where some explanation may be helpful, a brief comment is included in the right-hand column. The comments are subject to amendment under the provisions of local cricket associations.

The Players, Umpires and Scorers

1 A match is played between two sides of eleven players each, unless otherwise agreed. Each side shall play under a Captain who before the toss for innings shall nominate his players who may not thereafter be changed without the consent of the opposing Captain.

Notes

1 If a captain is not available at any time, a deputy must act for him to deal promptly with points arising from this and other Laws.

2 No match in which more than eleven players a side take part can be regarded as First-class, and in any case no side should field with more than eleven players.

Substitutes

2 Substitutes shall be allowed to field or run between the wickets for any player who may during the match be incapacitated from illness or injury, but not for any other reason without the consent of the opposing Captain; no Substitute shall be allowed to bat or to bowl. Consent as to the person to act as substitute in the field shall be obtained from the opposing Captain, who may indicate positions in which the Substitute shall not field.

Notes

1 A player may bat, bowl or field even though a substitute has acted for him previously.

2 An injured batsman may be 'Out' should his runner infringe Laws 36, 40 or 41. As *striker* he remains himself subject to the Laws; should he be out of his ground for any purpose he may be 'Out' under Laws 41 and 42 at the wicket-keeper's end, irrespective of the position of the other batsman or the substitute when the wicket is put down. When *not the striker* the injured batsman is out of the game and stands where he does not interfere with the play.

2 It is the *right* of a captain to use any substitute fieldsman or any batsman's runner, when the man whom the substitute is replacing is incapacitated during the match. The opposing captain need not be consulted.
The *consent* of the opposing captain for a substitute fieldsman or runner is needed if the replaced player is absent or cannot run between the wickets for any other reason than incapacitation during the current match. Thus a player leaving to attend a wedding can only be substituted with the consent of the opposing captain. The opposing captain has the right to say where the substitute *may not field* and who the substitute may be. Thus he can prevent a substitute 'keeping wicket. Custom normally dictates that the twelfth man shall be nominated by each team before the game, and this man acts as substitute fieldsman.

The Appointment of Umpires

3 Before the toss for innings two Umpires shall be appointed one for each end to control the game as required by the Laws with absolute

impartiality. No Umpire shall be changed during a match without the consent of both Captains.

Note
1 The umpires should report themselves to the executive of the ground 30 minutes before the start of each day's play.

The Scorers
4 All runs scored shall be recorded by Scorers appointed for the purpose; the Scorers shall accept and acknowledge all instructions and signals given to them by the Umpires.

4 The scorers act on the instructions of the umpires.

Note
1 The umpires should wait until a signal has been answered by a scorer before allowing the game to proceed. Mutual consultation between the scorers and the umpires to clear up doubtful points is at all times permissible.

The Ball
5 The Ball shall weigh not less than 5½ ounces (155.9 g), nor more than 5¾ ounces (163 g). It shall measure not less than 8 13/16 inches (22.4 cm), nor more than 9 inches (22.9 cm) in circumference. Subject to agreement to the contrary either Captain may demand a new ball at the start of each innings. In the event of a ball being lost or becoming unfit for play, the Umpires shall allow another ball to be taken into use. They shall inform the Batsmen whenever a ball is to be changed.

Notes
1 All cricket balls used in First-class matches should be approved before the start of a match by the umpires and captains.
2 In First-class matches, the captain of the fielding side may demand a new ball after the prescribed number of overs has been bowled with the old one. The Governing Body for cricket in the country concerned, shall decide the number of overs applicable in that country, which shall be not less than 75 overs, nor more than 85 overs (55 to 65 eight ball overs).
In other grades of cricket, these regulations will not apply unless agreed before the toss for innings.
3 Any ball substituted for one lost or becoming unfit for play should have had similar wear or use as that of the one discarded.

The Bat
6 The Bat shall not exceed 4¼ inches (10.8 cm) in the widest part; it shall not be more than 38 inches (96.5 cm) in length.

The Pitch

7 The Pitch is deemed to be the area of ground between the bowling creases, 5 feet (1.52 m) in width on either side of the line joining the centre of the wickets. Before the toss for innings, the executive of the ground shall be responsible for the selection and preparation of the Pitch; thereafter the Umpires shall control its use and maintenance. The Pitch shall not be changed during a match unless it becomes unfit for play, and then only with the consent of both Captains.

7 The width of the pitch may vary according to local requirements. The width of an artificial pitch is the width of the surface.

The Wickets

8 The Wickets shall be pitched opposite and parallel to each other at a distance of 22 yards (20.12 m) from stump to stump. Each Wicket shall be 9 inches (22.9 cm) in width and consist of three stumps with two bails upon the top. The stumps shall be of equal and of sufficient size to prevent the ball from passing through, with their top 28 inches (71.1 cm) above the ground. The bails shall be each $4\frac{3}{8}$ inches (11.1 cm) in length, and when in position on the top of the stumps, shall not project more than $\frac{1}{2}$ inch (1.3 cm) above them.

Notes

1 Except for the bail grooves the tops of the stumps shall be dome-shaped.

2 In a high wind the captains may agree, with the approval of the umpires, to dispense with the use of bails (*See* Law 31, Note 3).

The Bowling and Popping Creases

9 The bowling crease shall be marked in line with the stumps 8 ft 8 ins (2.64 m) in length; with the stumps in the centre. The popping crease shall be marked 4 ft (1.22 m) in front of and parallel with the bowling crease and shall extend a minimum of 6 ft (1.83 m) either side of the line of the stumps. The return crease shall be marked at each end of the bowling crease, at right angles to it, and shall extend forward to join the popping crease, and a minimum of 4 ft (1.22 m) behind the wicket. Both the return and popping creases shall be deemed unlimited in length.

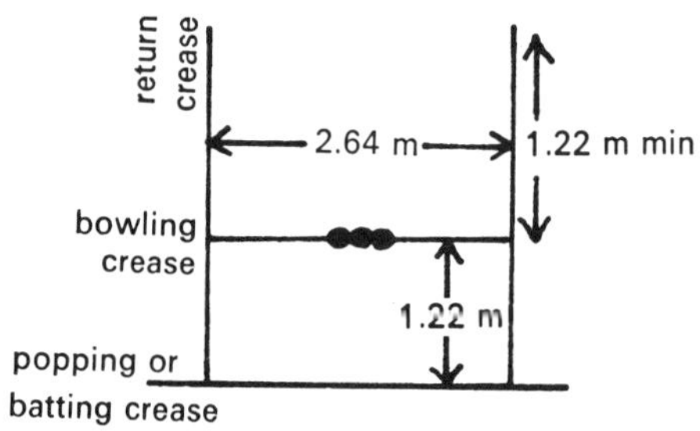

Notes

1 The distance of the Popping crease from the wicket is measured from a line running through the centre of the stumps to the inside edge of the crease.

2 Whenever possible, the popping crease and the return crease shall be redrawn during each interval.

Rolling, Mowing and Watering
10 Unless permitted by 'Special Regulations', the Pitch shall not be rolled during the match except before the start of each innings and of each day's play, when, if the Captain of the batting side so elect, it may be swept and rolled for not more than 7 minutes. In a match of less than three days' duration, the pitch shall not be mown during the match unless 'Special Regulations' so provide. In a match of three or more days' duration, the pitch shall be mown under the supervision of the Umpires before play begins on alternate days after the start of a match, but should the pitch not be so mown on any day on account of play not taking place, it shall be mown on the first day on which the match is resumed and thereafter on alternate days. (For the purpose of this Law a rest day counts as a day.) Under no circumstances shall the Pitch be watered during a match.

Notes
1 The umpires are responsible that any rolling permitted by this Law and carried out at the request of the captain of the batting side, is in accordance with the regulations laid down and that it is completed so as to allow play to start at the stipulated time.
The normal rolling before the start of each day's play shall take place not earlier than half an hour before the start of play, but the captain of the batting side may delay such rolling until 10 minutes before the start of play should he so desire.
2 The time allowed for rolling shall be taken out of the normal playing time if a captain declare an innings closed either, (*a*) before play starts on any day so late that the other captain is prevented from exercising his option in regard to rolling under this Law, or (*b*) during the luncheon interval later than 15 minutes after the start of such interval.
3 Except in the United Kingdom, if at any time a rain affected pitch is damaged by play thereon, it shall be swept and rolled for a period of not more than ten consecutive minutes at any time between the close of play on the day on which it was damaged and the next resumption of play, provided that:

(i) The umpires shall instruct the groundsman to sweep and roll the pitch only after they have agreed that damage caused to it as a result of play after rain has fallen warrants such rolling additional to that provided for in Law 10.
(ii) Such rolling shall in all cases be done under the personal supervision of both umpires and shall take place at such time and with such roller as the groundsman shall consider best calculated to repair the damage to the pitch.

(iii) Not more than one such additional rolling shall be permitted as a result of rain on any particular day.

(iv) The rolling provided for in Law 10, to take place before the start of play shall not be permitted on any day on which the rolling herein provided for takes place within two hours of the time appointed for commencement of play on that day.

Covering the Pitch

11 The Pitch shall not be completely covered during a match unless 'Special Regulations' so provide; covers used to protect the bowlers' run up shall not extend to a greater distance than 3½ ft (1.07 m) in front of the Popping creases.

Note

1 It is usual under this Law to protect the bowlers' run up, before and during a match, both at night and, when necessary, during the day. The covers should be removed early each morning, if fine.

Maintenance of the Pitch

12 The Batsman may beat the Pitch with his bat, and Players may secure their footholds by the use of sawdust, provided Law 46 be not thereby contravened. In wet weather the Umpires shall see that the holes made by the Bowlers and Batsmen are cleaned out and dried whenever necessary to facilitate play.

Innings

13 Each side has two innings, taken alternately, except in the case provided for in Law 14. The choice of innings shall be decided by tossing on the field of play.

Notes

1 The captains should toss for innings not later than 15 minutes before the time agreed upon for play to start. The winner of the toss may not alter his decision to bat or field once it has been notified to the opposing captain.

2 This Law also governs a One-day match in which play continues after the completion of the first innings of both sides (*See also* Law 22).

Following Innings

14 The side which bats first and leads by 200 runs in a match of five days or more, by 150 runs in a three-day or four-day match, by 100 runs in a two-day match, or by 75 runs in a one-day match, shall have the option of requiring the other side to follow their innings.

Declarations

15 The Captain of the batting side may declare an innings closed at any time during a match irrespective of its duration.

Note

1 A captain may forfeit his second innings. In this event, the interval between innings shall be 10 minutes and his decision must be notified to the opposing captain and umpires in sufficient time to allow seven minutes rolling of the pitch.

16 When the start of play is delayed by weather Law 14 shall apply in accordance with the number of days' play remaining from the actual start of the match.

Start and Close of Play and Intervals

17 The umpires shall allow such intervals as have been agreed upon for meals, 10 minutes between each innings and not more than 2 minutes for each fresh batsman to come in. At the start of each innings and of each day's play and at the end of any interval the Umpire at the Bowler's end shall call 'Play', when the side refusing to play shall lose the match. After 'Play' has been called no trial ball shall be allowed to any player, and when one of the Batsmen is out the use of the bat shall not be allowed to any player until the next Batsman shall come in.

Notes

1 The umpires shall not award a match under this Law unless (i) 'Play' has been called in such a manner that both sides can clearly understand that play is to start, (ii) an appeal has been made, and (iii) they are satisfied that a side will not, or cannot, continue play.
2 It is an essential duty of the captains to ensure that the 'in-going' batsman passes the 'out-coming' one before the latter leaves the field of play. This is all the more important in view of the responsibility resting on the umpires for deciding whether or not the delay of the individual amounts to a refusal of the batting side to continue play.
3 The interval for luncheon should not exceed 45 minutes unless otherwise agreed (but *see* Law 10, Note 2). In the event of the last wicket falling within 2 minutes of the time arranged for luncheon or tea, the game shall be resumed at the usual hour, no allowance being made for the 10 minutes between the innings.
4 Bowling practice *on the pitch* is forbidden at any time during the game.
5 No bowler shall have a trial 'Run-up' after 'Play' has been called in any session, except at the fall of a wicket, when an umpire may allow such a trial 'Run-up', if he is satisfied that it will not cause any waste of time.

17 Unless local Laws provide to the contrary, there is no provision for the batsman to be declared out or the match awarded, unless the umpires are satisfied that a side will not or cannot continue to play. The 2 minute law is designed to prevent wastage of time.

18 The Umpires shall call 'Time', and at the same time remove the bails from both wickets, on the cessation of play before any arranged interval, at the end of each day's play, and at the conclusion of the match. An 'Over' shall always be started if 'Time' has not been reached, and shall be completed unless a batsman is 'Out' or 'Retires' within 2 minutes of the completion of any period of play, but the 'Over' in progress at the close of play on the final day of a match shall be completed at the request of either Captain even if a wicket fall after 'Time' has been reached.

Notes

1 If, during the completion of the last over of any period of play, the players have occasion to leave the field, the Umpires shall call 'Time'. In the case of the last over of the match, there shall be no resumption of play and the match shall be at an end.

2 The last over before an interval or the close of play shall be started, provided the umpire standing at square leg, after walking at his normal pace, has arrived at his position behind the stumps at the bowler's end before time has been reached. The above provision will apply if the batsman is 'Out' off, or 'Retires' after the last ball of an over when less than two minutes remain for play at the conclusion of the match.

3 In the final stages of a match, the umpires shall indicate when one hour of playing time remains (according to the agreed hours of play). From that moment, and providing a result is not reached earlier, the game will continue for a minimum of 20 6-ball overs (15 8-ball overs).

In the event of play being interrupted (including intervals or stoppages for rain, bad light, etc.), the number of overs to be bowled shall be reduced in proportion to the time lost, in the ratio of one over for every three minutes (four minutes for 8-ball overs) or part thereof lost.

If a new innings starts within the last hour of a match, the minimum number of overs to be bowled shall be calculated on the basis of one for each three minutes, or part of three minutes (four minutes for 8-ball overs) remaining for play, when the innings is started.

Whenever the minimum number of overs has been bowled before the agreed time for the close of play, the match shall continue (in the absence of a result) until the agreed time for close of play.

(Both captains may agree before the match to forgo the conditions of this Note subject to such agreement being permitted by 'Special Regulations'.)

18 An over shall always be started if the umpire at the bowler's end has reached his position and time for close of play has not been attained. The over shall always be completed unless the batsman is out or retires within 2 minutes of the time fixed for completion of play.

Note 3 governing the minimum number of deliveries to be sent down in the period commencing one hour before the scheduled close of play can be varied according to the local rules applying. Care should be taken to find out what the local conditions are.

Local rules can also control the completion of the final over when a wicket falls before the end of that over.

Scoring

19 The score shall be reckoned by runs. A run is scored:

1st—So often as the Batsmen after a hit, or at any time while the ball is in play, shall have crossed and made good their ground from end to end; but if either Batsman run a short run, the Umpire shall call and signal 'One short' and that run shall not be scored. The Striker being caught, no run shall be scored; a Batsman being run out, that run which was being attempted shall not be scored.

2nd—For penalties under Laws 21, 27, 29, 44 and boundary allowances under Law 20.

Notes

1 If while the ball is in play, the batsmen have crossed in running, neither returns to the wicket he has left except in the case of a boundary hit, or a boundary from extras, or under Laws 30, Note 1 and 46, Note 4 (vii). This rule applies even should a short run have been called, or should no run be reckoned as in the case of a catch.

2 A run is 'short' if either or both, batsmen fail to make good their ground in turning for a further run. Although such a 'short' run shortens the succeeding one, the latter, if completed, counts. Similarly a batsman taking stance in front of his popping crease may run from that point without penalty.

3 (i) One run only is deducted if both batsmen are short in one and the same run.

(ii) Only if three or more runs are attempted can more than one run be 'short' and then, subject to (i) above, all runs so called shall be disallowed.

(iii) If either or both batsmen deliberately run short, the umpire is justified in calling 'Dead Ball' and disallowing any runs attempted or scored as soon as he sees that the fielding side have no chance of dismissing either batsman under the Laws.

4 An umpire signals 'short' runs when the ball becomes 'dead' by bending his arm upwards to touch the shoulder with the tips of his fingers. If there has been more than one 'short' run the umpires must instruct the scorers as to the number of runs disallowed. (*See* Note 1 to Law 4.)

19 If a batsman is caught out, no runs are scored, *irrespective of the number of runs completed before the catch is made.*
If a batsman is run out, the run in progress when the dismissal is made is not recorded, *but preceding runs are.* In neither instance does the batsman return to the crease which he has left, if the batsmen have crossed, at the instant of dismissal.
If a batsman fails to complete any one run by not grounding any part of his bat or body behind the batting crease, the run is short and disallowed. If both batsmen fail to complete the *same* run, only one is disallowed. If *any* number of runs are deliberately run short, all runs, including those completed are disallowed.

One short

Boundaries

20 Before the toss for innings the Umpires shall agree with both sides on the Boundaries for play, and on the allowances to be made for them. An Umpire shall call or signal 'Boundary' whenever, in his opinion, a ball in play hits, crosses or is carried over the Boundary. The runs completed at the instant the ball reaches the Boundary shall count only should they exceed the allowance, but if the 'Boundary' result from an overthrow or from the wilful act of a fieldsman, any runs already made and the allowance shall be added to the score.

Notes

1 If flags or posts are used to mark a boundary, the real or imaginary line joining such points shall be regarded as the boundary, which should be marked by a white line if possible.

2 In deciding on the allowances to be made for boundaries the umpires will be guided by the prevailing custom of the ground.

3 It is a 'Boundary' if the ball touches any boundary line or if a fieldsman with ball in hand grounds any part of his person on or over that line. A fieldsman, however, standing within the playing area may lean against or touch a boundary fence in fielding a ball (*See also* Law 35, Note 5).

4 An obstacle, or person, within the playing area is not regarded as a boundary unless so arranged by the umpires. The umpire is not a boundary, but sight screens within the playing area shall be so regarded.

5 The customary allowance for a boundary is 4 runs, but it is usual to allow 6 runs for all hits pitching over and clear of the boundary line or fence (even though the ball has been previously touched by a fieldsman). It is not usual to allow 6 runs when a ball hits a sight screen full pitch, if the latter is on or inside the boundary.

20 Whilst it is customary according to Note 5 to allow 4 runs for a ball which reaches the boundary or is carried over by a fieldsman and 6 runs for a hit over the boundary on the full, there is provision within the Law for a greater or lesser number of runs to be allowed if the boundaries are shorter or longer than the average.

When the batsmen have run more than the number of runs allowed for a boundary hit before the ball crosses the boundary, the greater number of runs shall be counted and the boundary disallowed.

If a fieldsman causes the ball to cross the boundary from an overthrow or deliberate act, the boundary allowance shall be added to the number of runs completed by the batsmen at the time of the action of the fieldsman, which caused the ball to reach the boundary.

Provided the batsmen have crossed, a run in progress at the time of the fieldsman's action, is deemed completed.

In determining boundaries, the umpires shall fix any obstacles within the playing area as boundaries. These obstacles include the curators' equipment and sightscreens and the area under the sightscreens.

Four

Six

6 In the case of a boundary resulting from either an overthrow or the wilful act of a fieldsman, the run in progress counts provided that the batsmen have crossed at the instant of the throw or act.
7 The umpire signals 'Boundary' by waving an arm from side to side, or a boundary '6' by raising both arms above the head.

Note 3 provides for any fieldsman to lean against or touch the boundary fence, provided he does not ground any part of his body on or outside the boundary line or the ball in hand does not touch or pass over the boundary line. In grounds which have a boundary guttering, the inside edge of that guttering is deemed to be the boundary.

Lost Ball

21 If a ball in play cannot be found or recovered any Fieldsman may call 'Lost Ball', when 6 runs shall be added to the score; but if more than 6 have been run before 'Lost Ball' be called, as many runs as have been run shall be scored.

21 A ball may be deemed 'lost' though visible, within the boundary, and not recoverable within a reasonable time, for example, a dog with the ball in its mouth trotting around the outfield.
Any fieldsman may call 'lost ball'.

The Result

22 A match is won by the side which shall have scored a total of runs in excess of that scored by the opposing side in its two completed innings; one-day matches, unless thus played out, shall be decided by the first innings. A match may also be determined by being given up as lost by one of the sides, or in the case governed by Law 17. A match not determined in any of these ways shall count as a 'Draw'.

Notes
1 It is the responsibility of the captains to satisfy themselves on the correctness of the scores on the conclusion of play.
2 Neither side can be compelled to continue after a match is finished; a one-day match shall not be regarded as finished on the result of the first innings if the umpires consider there is a prospect of carrying the game to a further issue in the time remaining.
3 The result of a finished match is stated as a win by runs, except in the case of a win by the side batting last, when it is by the number of wickets still then to fall. In a one-day match which is not played out on the second innings, this rule applies to the position at the time when a result on the first innings was reached.
4 A 'Draw' is regarded as a 'Tie' when the scores are equal at the conclusion of play but only if the match has been played out. If the scores of the completed first innings of a one-day match are equal, it is a 'Tie', but only if the match has not been played out to a further conclusion.

22 The captains and the umpires should check the correctness of the scores *before* leaving the field.

The Over

23 The ball shall be bowled from each wicket alternately in Overs of either 8 or 6 balls according to the agreed conditions of play.

23 and **24** In Australia the number of deliveries in each over shall be 8 not including no balls and wides.

When the agreed number have been bowled and it has become clear to the Umpire at the Bowler's wicket that both sides have ceased to regard the ball as in play, the Umpire shall call 'Over' in a distinct manner before leaving the wicket. Neither a 'No Ball' nor a 'Wide Ball' shall be reckoned as one of the 'Over'.

Note
1 In the United Kingdom the 'over' shall be 6 balls, unless an agreement to the contrary has been made.

24 A Bowler shall finish an 'Over' in progress unless he be incapacitated or be suspended for unfair play. He shall be allowed to change ends as often as desired, provided only that he shall not bowl two 'Overs' consecutively in one innings. A Bowler may require the Batsman at the wicket from which he is bowling to stand on whichever side of it he may direct.

Dead Ball
25 The ball shall be held to be 'Dead'—on being in the opinion of the Umpire finally settled in the hands of the Wicket-keeper or of the Bowler; or on reaching or pitching over the boundary; or, whether played or not, on lodging in the dress of either a Batsman or Umpire; or on the call of 'Over' or 'Time' by the Umpire; or on a Batsman being out from any cause: or on any penalty being awarded under Laws 21 or 44. The Umpire shall call 'Dead Ball' should he decide to intervene under Law 46 in a case of unfair play or in the event of a serious injury to a player; or should he require to suspend play prior to the Striker receiving a delivery. The ball shall cease to be 'Dead' on the Bowler starting his run or bowling action.

Notes
1 Whether the ball is 'finally settled' is a question of fact for the umpire alone to decide.
2 An umpire is justified in suspending play prior to the striker receiving a delivery in any of the following circumstances:
(i) If satisfied that, for an *adequate* reason, the striker is not ready to receive the ball, and makes no attempt to play it.
(ii) If the bowler drops the ball accidentally before delivery, or if the ball does not leave his hand for any reason.
(iii) If one or both bails fall from the striker's wicket before he receives the delivery.
In such cases the ball is regarded as 'Dead' from the time it last came into play.
3 A ball does not become 'Dead' when it strikes an umpire (unless it lodges in his dress), when the wicket is broken or struck down (unless a batsman is out

25 Only the umpire determines when the ball has *finally* settled. The ball shall not be regarded as finally settled while either batsman is out of his ground and capable of being put out under any relevant law of cricket. If for any reason the umpire deems the ball to be dead before the striker receives the ball it is dead from the time that the bowler began his preceding run or delivery action. The umpire may, for instance, call 'dead ball' if a fieldsman alters his position advantageously without notifying the batsman whilst the bowler is running up. 'Dead ball' shall be called in the event of a serious injury to a player or umpire. A ball is deemed 'dead' when the ball does not leave the bowler's hand even if 'no ball' has been called.

Dead ball

thereby), or when an unsuccessful appeal is made.
4 For the purpose of this and other Laws, the term 'dress' includes the equipment and clothing of players and umpires as normally worn.

No Ball

26 For a delivery to be fair, the ball must be bowled not thrown. If either Umpire be not entirely satisfied of the absolute fairness of a delivery in this respect he shall call and signal 'No Ball' instantly upon delivery. The Umpire at the Bowler's wicket shall call and signal 'No Ball' if, in the delivery stride, no part of the bowler's front foot is grounded behind the popping crease, or if he is not satisfied that the bowler's back foot has landed within and not touching the return crease or its forward extension.

Notes

1 A ball shall be deemed to have been thrown if, in the opinion of either umpire, the process of straightening the bowling arm, whether it be partial or complete, takes place during that part of the delivery swing which directly precedes the ball leaving the hand. This definition shall not debar a bowler from the use of the wrist in the delivery swing.
2 The striker is entitled to know whether the bowler intends to bowl over or round the wicket, overarm or underarm, right or left handed. An umpire may regard any failure to notify a change in the mode of delivery as 'unfair', if so, he should call 'No ball'.
3 It is a 'No Ball' if the bowler before delivering a ball throws it at the striker's wicket even in an attempt to run him out (*See* Law 46, Note 4 (vii)).
4 If a bowler break the near wicket with any part of his person during the delivery, such act in itself does not constitute 'No Ball'.
5 The umpire signals 'No Ball' by extending one arm horizontally.
6 An umpire should revoke the call 'No Ball' if the ball does not leave the bowler's hand for any reason.

No ball

26 *Throwing*
The ball is a 'no ball' if either umpire is not satisfied beyond doubt that the ball is bowled. If *any* doubt arises in the umpire's mind that the ball is not bowled he must call 'no ball'. He does not have to say specifically that the ball is thrown. He merely states that he believes that it is not bowled.

The front foot
It is 'a no ball' if the bowler in the delivery stride has no part of the front foot behind the back edge of the line which marks the batting crease. The front foot need not be grounded.

The back foot
It is also a 'no ball' if the bowler's back foot touches or lands outside the return crease.

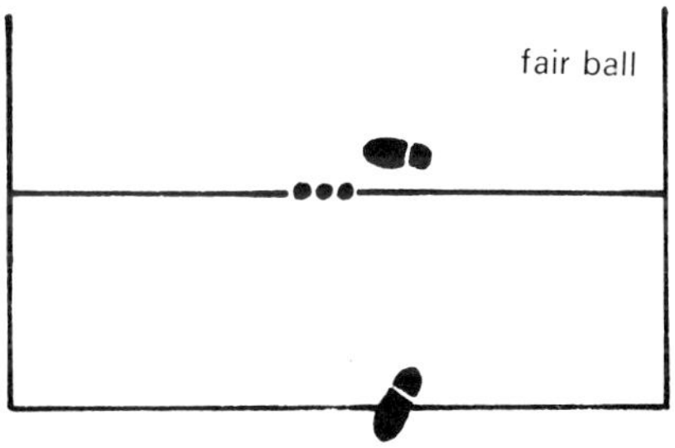

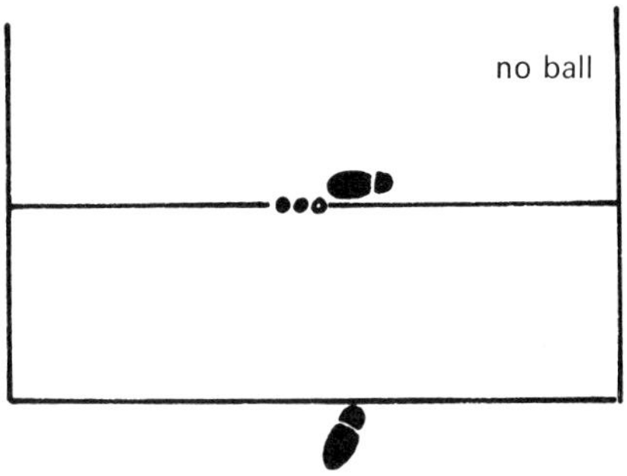

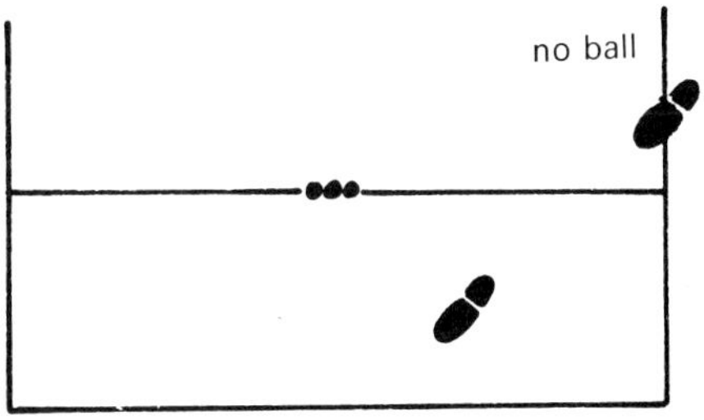

27 The ball does not become 'Dead' on the call of 'No Ball'. The Striker may hit a 'No Ball' and whatever runs result shall be added to his score, but runs made otherwise from a 'No Ball' shall be scored 'No Balls', and if no runs be made one run shall be so scored. The Striker shall be out from a 'No Ball' if he break Law 37, and either Batsman may be run out, or given out if he break Laws 36 or 40.

Notes
1 The penalty for a 'No Ball' is only scored if no runs result otherwise.
2 Law 46, Note 4 (vii) covers attempts to run before the ball is delivered, but should the non-striker unfairly leave his ground too soon, the fielding side may run out the batsman at the bowler's end by any recognised method. If the bowler throws at the near wicket, the umpire does not call 'No Ball', though any runs resulting are so scored. The throw does not count in the 'Over'.

27 A batsman can only be out from a 'no ball' by:
Hitting the ball deliberately twice when not defending his wicket
Being run out
Obstructing the field
Handling the ball.
The penalty for a 'no ball' is one run. If the ball hits the striker's bat and one or more runs are obtained, these runs are added to the striker's score and the penalty for the no ball is ignored. If the ball does not hit the striker's bat and the batsmen complete one or more runs or the ball crosses the boundary, those runs are recorded as 'no balls'—even if the ball strikes the batsman's body—and the penalty of one run is ignored.
If the batsmen do not complete the first run and either batsman is out, the penalty run *is* added.

Wide Ball

28 If the Bowler shall bowl the ball so high over or so wide of the wicket that in the opinion of the Umpire it passes out of reach of the Striker, and would not have been within his reach when taking guard in the normal position, the Umpire shall call and signal 'Wide Ball' as soon as it shall have passed the Striker.

Notes
1 If a ball which the umpire considers to have been delivered comes to rest in front of the striker 'Wide' should not be called, and no runs should be added to the score unless they result from the striker hitting the ball which he has a right to do without interference by the fielding side. Should the fielding side interfere, the umpire is justified in replacing the ball

28 This law is to ensure that the ball is delivered so that the striker may have a reasonable chance of hitting it with the bat. It also operates to prevent the batsman turning a fair delivery into a wide by moving away from or refusing to attempt to play at a ball which he could reach if he played at it in a normal way from the normal batting position.
It is *not* a wide if a ball which the umpire considers to have been *delivered* comes to rest forward of the striker's position, even if it is out of his reach. In this circumstance, the striker can move forward to hit the stationary ball without interference from any player on the

Wide ball

where it came to rest and ordering the fieldsmen to resume the places they occupied in the field before. the ball was delivered.
2 The umpire signals 'Wide' by extending both arms horizontally.
3 An umpire should revoke the call if the striker hits a ball which has been called 'Wide'.

fielding side. Each fieldsman must remain in the position which he was occupying at the time that the bowler delivered the ball. He cannot move until the striker has hit it.

29 The ball does not become 'Dead' on the call of 'Wide Ball'. All runs that are run from a 'Wide Ball' shall be scored 'Wide Balls', or if no runs be made one run shall be so scored. The Striker may be out from a 'Wide Ball' if he break Laws 38 or 42, and either Batsman may be run out, or given out if he break Laws 36 or 40.

29 A batsman can be out from a wide in the following ways:
  hit wicket
  stumped
Either batsman can be out:
  run out
  handled ball
  obstructing the field.
The penalty for a wide ball is one run but this is not added to the score, if the batsmen in running score one or more runs or the ball reaches the boundary.

Bye and Leg Bye
30 If the ball, not having been called 'Wide' or 'No Ball', pass the Striker without touching his bat or person, and any runs be obtained, the Umpire shall call or signal 'Bye'; but if the ball touch any part of the Striker's dress or person except his hand holding the bat, and any run be obtained, the Umpire shall call or signal 'Leg Bye'; such runs to be scored 'Byes' and 'Leg Byes' respectively.

Notes
1 'Leg Byes' shall be scored only if, in the opinion of the umpire, the striker has
(a) attempted to play the ball with his bat, or
(b) tried to avoid being hit by the ball.
In the case of deflection by the Striker's person, other than in (a) or (b) above, the umpire shall call and signal 'Dead Ball' as soon as one run has been

30 If the ball deflects from the striker's body and he has made no attempt to play it with his bat or has not tried to avoid being struck by the ball 'leg byes' are *not* allowed.
Since the batsman can be dismissed from an attempted though not allowed 'leg bye', in a few ways, for example, the run-out decision, dead ball is not called unless and until the batsmen have completed one run or the ball reaches the boundary.

Bye

Leg bye

completed, or the ball has reached the boundary and such runs shall be disallowed.
2 The umpire signals 'Bye' by raising an open hand above the head, and 'Leg Bye' by touching a raised knee with the hand.

The Wicket is Down

31 The wicket shall be held to be 'Down' if either the ball or the Striker's bat or person completely removes either bail from the top of the stumps or, if both bails be off, strikes a stump out of the ground. Any player may use his hand or arm to put the wicket down or, even should the bails be previously off, may pull up a stump, provided always that the ball is held in the hand or hands so used.

Notes
1 A wicket is not 'down' merely on account of the disturbance of a bail, but it is 'down' if a bail in falling from the wicket lodges between two of the stumps.
2 If one bail is off, it is sufficient for the purpose of this Law to dislodge the remaining one in any of the ways stated, or to strike any of the three stumps out of the ground.
3 If, owing to the strength of the wind, the captains have agreed to dispense with the use of bails (*see* Law 8, Note 2), the decision as to when the wicket is 'down' is one for the umpires to decide on the facts before them. In such circumstances the wicket would be held to be 'down' even though a stump has not been struck out of the ground.
4 If the wicket is broken while the ball is in play, it is not the umpire's duty to remake the wicket until the ball has become 'dead'. A fieldsman, however, may remake the wicket in such circumstances.
5 For the purpose of this and other Laws the term 'person' includes a player's dress as defined in Law 25, Note 4.

31 For a wicket to be down it is only necessary for one bail to be completely removed from the top of the stumps. If both bails have previously been removed and a wicket cannot be remade in sufficient time by replacing the bails, it is necessary to strike a stump *completely* out of the ground.
A fieldsman can put a wicket down by throwing the ball at the stumps or by having the ball in his hand and using that hand or arm to remove the bails or strike the stump(s) completely out of the ground.
If all the stumps have been removed from the ground, it is enough to replace one stump only and strike or pull it out of the ground with the hand or hands holding the ball.
It is not necessary for the ball to contact the stumps and the arm may be used, providing that the ball is in the same hand of the arm breaking the wicket.

Wicket down

Wicket not down

Out of his Ground
32 A Batsman shall be held to be 'Out of his ground' unless some part of his bat in hand or of his person be grounded behind the line of the Popping Crease.

32 When a batsman makes good his ground he must be holding the bat which is grounded behind the back edge of the batting crease in his hand—or some part of the body must be grounded behind the back edge of the batting crease.

Batsman Retiring
33 A Batsman may retire at any time, but may not resume his innings without the consent of the opposing Captain, and then only on the fall of a wicket.

Note
1 When a batsman has retired owing to illness, injury, or some other unavoidable cause, his innings is recorded as 'Retired, Not out', but otherwise as a completed innings to be recorded as 'Retired, Out'.

33 A batsman does not need the consent of the opposing captain to retire, but *must* have that consent to resume his innings irrespective of the reason for his retirement.
It is an accepted custom of the game to obtain that consent before retiring.
A retired batsman cannot resume his innings unless he is replacing a batsman who is *out*. He cannot replace a batsman who is retiring. Thus if a number 10 batsman retires, a previously retired batsman cannot resume and the whole side is out.

Bowled
34 The Striker is out 'Bowled'—If the wicket be bowled down, even if the ball first touch his bat or person.

Notes
1 The striker, after playing the ball is out 'Bowled' if he then kicks or hits it on to his wicket before the completion of his stroke.
2 The striker is out 'Bowled' under this Law when the ball is deflected on to his wicket off his person, even though a decision against him might be justified under Law 39 L.B.W.

34 A striker can be out 'bowled' if he attempts to keep the ball out of his wicket and in so doing hits it on to his wicket. He cannot be out 'bowled' if he hits the ball on to his wicket in attempting to run.
The decision 'bowled' takes precedence over the lbw decision if both are applicable.

Caught
35 The Striker is out 'Caught'—If the ball, from a stroke of the bat or of the hand holding the bat, but not the wrist, be held by a Fieldsman before it touch the ground, although it be hugged to the body of the catcher, or be accidentally lodged in his dress. The Fieldsman must have both his feet entirely within the playing area at the instant the catch is completed.

Notes
1 Provided the ball does not touch the ground, the hand holding it may do so in effecting a catch.
2 The umpire is justified in disregarding the fact that the ball has touched the ground, or has been carried over the boundary provided that a catch has in fact been completed prior to such occurrence.

Not out

3 The fact that a ball has touched the striker's person before or after touching his bat does not invalidate a catch.
4 The striker may be 'Caught' even if the fieldsman has not touched the ball with his hands, including the case of a ball lodging in the wicket-keeper's pads.
5 A fieldsman standing within the playing area may lean against a boundary to catch a ball, and this may be done even if the ball has passed over the boundary.
6 If the striker lawfully plays the ball a second time he may be out under this Law, but only if the ball has not touched the ground since being first struck.
7 The striker may be caught off any obstruction within the playing area provided it has not previously been decided on as a boundary.

35 A striker is not out 'caught' if the ball strikes the batsman on or above the wrist of the hand(s) holding the bat. A catch can be completed before the ball touches the ground even though it does not lodge in the fieldsman's hands. It can be held between the wicketkeeper's legs or lodged in a fieldsman's clothing, etc. A catch may be completed by a fieldsman leaning against a fence even though the ball is outside the fence. The fieldsman's feet, however, *must be entirely* within the boundary.

Handled the Ball

36 Either Batsman is out 'Handled the Ball'—If he touch it while in play with his hands, unless it be done at the request of the opposite side.

Notes
1 A hand holding the bat is regarded as part of it for the purposes of Laws 36, 37 and 39.
2 The correct entry in the score book when a batsman is given out under this Law is 'Handled the Ball', and the bowler does not get credit for the wicket.

36 Neither the striker nor the other batsman may handle the ball whilst it is in play—not even to return it to the bowler—unless they are requested to do so by the fielding side.

Hit the Ball Twice

37 The Striker is out 'Hit the ball twice'—If the ball be struck or be stopped by any part of his person, and he wilfully strike it again, except for the sole purpose of guarding his wicket, which he may do with his bat or any part of his person, other than his hands. No runs except those which result from an overthrow shall be scored from a ball lawfully struck twice.

Notes
1 It is for the umpire to decide whether the ball has been so struck a second time legitimately or not. The umpire may regard the fact that a run is attempted as evidence of the batsmen's intention to take advantage of the second stroke, but it is not conclusive.
2 A batsman may not attempt to hit the ball twice, if in so doing he baulks the wicket-keeper or any fieldsman attempting to make a catch.
3 This Law is infringed if the striker, after playing the ball and without any request from the opposite side, uses his bat to return the ball to a fieldsman.
4 The correct entry in the score book when the striker is given out under this Law is 'Hit the ball twice', and the bowler does not get credit for the wicket.

37 This law means that if the ball hits the bat or the body of the striker and he then deliberately hits the ball with the bat or a part of the body (e.g. his leg or arm), he has hit the ball twice. He may only hit the ball a second time to keep it out of his wicket. If a batsman tries to hit the ball a second time even whilst defending his wicket, he can be out 'obstructing the field', if in so doing he prevents a catch being taken.

Hit Wicket

38 The Striker is out 'Hit wicket'—If in playing at the ball he hit down his wicket with his bat or any part of his person.

Notes

1 The striker is 'Out' under this Law if:
- (i) In making a second stroke to keep the ball out of his wicket he hits it down.
- (ii) While playing at the ball, but not otherwise, his wicket is broken by his cap or hat falling, or by part of his bat.

2 A batsman is not out for breaking the wicket with his bat or person while in the act of running.

38 'Playing at the ball' does not mean that the batsman has to be playing at the ball with the bat to be given out 'hit wicket'. He may be trying to avoid the ball or just allowing it to pass.
Under the experimental Law 38, a batsman may be deemed out 'hit wicket' if he strikes down his wicket either in playing at the ball or in trying to run *immediately* after playing the ball. The term 'immediately' means that point of time at which the end of the batsman's stroke is barely distinguishable from the beginning of the attempt to run.

L.B.W.

39 The Striker is out 'Leg before wicket'—If with any part of his person except his hand, which is in a straight line between wicket and wicket, even though the point of impact be above the level of the bails, he intercept a ball which has not first touched his bat or hand, and which, in the opinion of the Umpire, shall have, or would have, pitched on a straight line from the Bowler's wicket to the Striker's wicket, or shall have pitched on the off-side of the Striker's wicket, provided always that the ball would have hit the wicket.

Notes

1 The word 'hand' used in this Law should be interpreted as the hand holding the bat.

2 A batsman is only 'Out' under this Law if *all* the four following questions are answered in the affirmative:
- (i) Would the ball have hit the wicket?
- (ii) Did the ball pitch on a straight line between wicket and wicket (and this case includes a ball intercepted full pitch by the striker), or did it pitch on the offside of the striker's wicket?
- (iii) Was it part of the striker's person other than the hand which first intercepted the ball?
- (iv) Was that part of the striker's person in a straight line between wicket and wicket in the moment of impact, irrespective of the height of the point of impact?

39 A batsman is out 'lbw' if the following conditions are fulfilled:
1 The ball lands in line with the stumps or outside the line of the off-stump.
2 The actual part of the striker's body which first intercepts the ball is in line with the stumps from end to end.
3 The batsman would have been bowled had the ball not been intercepted by some part of his body.
Under the experimental Law 39 a batsman may also be out 'lbw' if the following conditions are fulfilled:
1 The ball lands on the pitch outside the off-stump.
2 The batsman intercepts the ball with some part of his body which is also outside the line of the off-stump at the point of contact.
3 The batsman makes no genuine attempt to play the ball with the bat.
4 The ball would have bowled the wicket down if not intercepted by the batsman's body.

Leg before wicket
1 Not out.
2 Probably out but the umpire may rule not out if he feels the ball was turning sharply enough to have missed the stumps altogether.
3 Probably out but the umpire may rule not out if he feels the ball was still rising sharply.
4 Probably out but the umpire may rule not out if he feels the ball was turning so sharply that it would have missed off stump.
5 Not out.

Obstructing the Field

40 Either Batsman is out 'Obstructing the field'—If he wilfully obstruct the opposite side; should such wilful obstruction by either Batsman prevent a ball from being caught it is the Striker who is out.

Notes

1 The umpire must decide whether the obstruction was 'wilful' or not. The involuntary interception by a batsman while running of a throw in is not in itself an offence.

2 The correct entry in the score book when a batsman is given out under this Law is 'Obstructing the field', and the bowler does not get credit for the wicket.

40 This law means that neither batsman shall interfere with the fielding side by unfairly hindering or distracting them by means of physical contact with bat or body or by noise or exaggerated movement. The fielding side must be free to stop, catch and throw the ball.

Run Out

41 Either Batsman is out 'Run out'—If in running or at any time, while the ball is in play, he be out of his ground, and his wicket be put down by the opposite side. If the batsmen have crossed each other, he that runs for the wicket which is put down is out; if they have not crossed, he that has left the wicket which is put down is out. But unless he attempt to run, the Striker shall not be given 'Run out' in the circumstances stated in Law 42, even should 'No Ball' have been called.

Note

1 If the ball is played on to the opposite wicket, neither batsman is liable to be 'Run Out' unless the ball has been touched by a fieldsman before the wicket is put down.

41 If one or both batsmen are out of their ground, then the one nearer to the wicket which is put down, is out. If both batsmen are within the same ground or crease when the wicket is put down at the opposite end, and the batsmen had not crossed in running, the batsman leaving the wicket which is put down is out.
If both batsmen are within the same ground or crease when the wicket is put down at the opposite end, the one who last reached the crease is out.
When a substitute runner is used for an injured batsman, and that batsman is out of his ground when he is the striker, he can be run out only at the striker's end, even though the runner might be safe within his ground at either end.

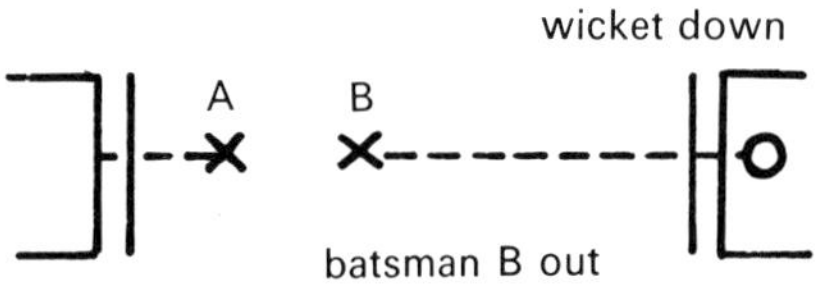

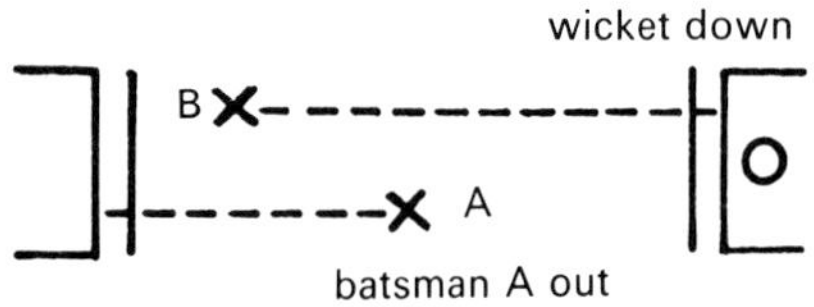

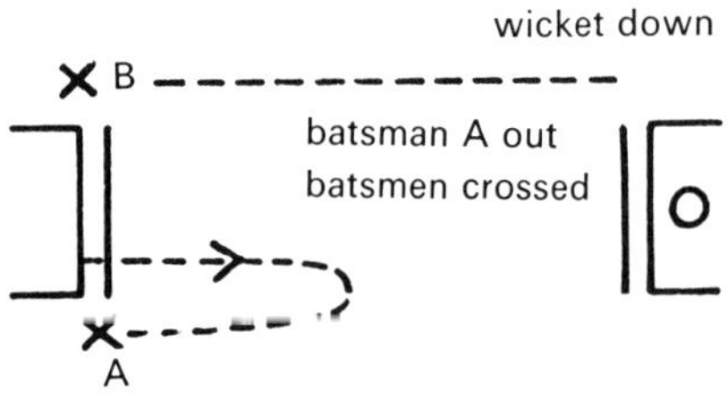

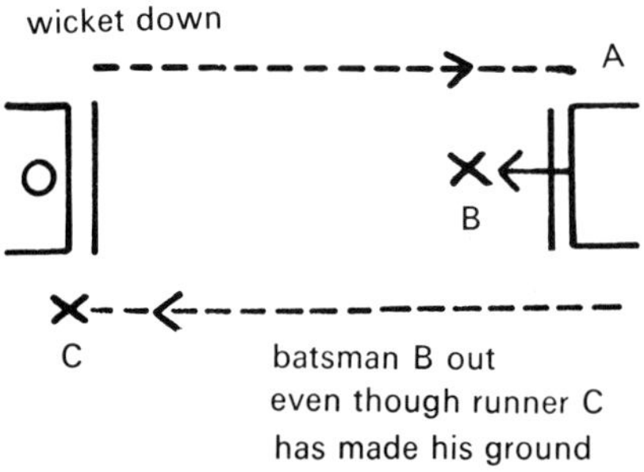

Stumped

42 A Striker is out 'Stumped'—If, in receiving a ball, not being a 'No Ball', delivered by the Bowler, he be out of his ground otherwise than in attempting a run, and the wicket be put down by the Wicket-keeper without the intervention of another fieldsman. Only when the ball has touched the bat or person of the Striker may the Wicket-keeper take it in front of the wicket for this purpose.

Note

1 The striker may be 'Stumped' if the wicket is broken by a ball rebounding from the wicket-keeper's person.

42 The striker cannot be run out by the direct action of the wicketkeeper at the striker's end unless he attempts to run. If he is not attempting to run and is out of his ground when the wicket is put down by the 'keeper, he is out 'stumped'.

The Wicket-keeper

43 The Wicket-keeper shall remain wholly behind the wicket until a ball delivered by the Bowler touches the bat or person of the Striker, or passes the wicket, or until the Striker attempts a run. Should the Wicket-keeper contravene this Law, the Striker shall not be out except under Laws 36, 37, 40 and 41, and then only subject to Law 46.

Notes

1 This Law is provided to secure to the striker his right to play the ball and to guard his wicket without interference from the wicket-keeper. The striker may not be penalised if in the legitimate defence of his wicket he interferes with the wicket-keeper, except as provided for in Law 37, Note 2.

2 If, in the opinion of the umpire, the encroachment by the wicket-keeper has not gained any advantage for the fielding side, nor in any way has interfered with the right of the striker to play the ball with complete freedom, nor has had any effect whatsoever on the dismissal of the striker, he shall disregard the infringement.

43 Whilst the umpire may disregard any encroachment of the wicketkeeper into the area in front of the stumps, even though the striker may be out (e.g., to a catch in the outfield in which the 'keeper has not impeded the batsman), this discretion on the part of the umpire does not extend to a stumping decision.
The wicketkeeper may only effect a stumping by coming in front of the wicket after the ball has touched the striker's bat or person.

The Fieldsman

44 The Fieldsman may stop the ball with any part of his person, but if he wilfully stop it otherwise five runs shall be added to the run or runs already made; if no run has been made five shall be scored. The penalty shall be added to the score of the Striker if the ball has been struck, but otherwise to the score of Byes, Leg Byes, No Balls or Wides as the case may be.

Notes

1 A fieldsman must not use his cap, etc., for the purpose of fielding a ball.

2 The five runs are a penalty and the batsmen do not change ends.

44 No fieldsman shall detach any part of his dress for the purpose of stopping the ball.
No more than two fieldsmen may field behind the batting crease on the leg side.
The experimental Law 44 restricts the maximum number of fieldsmen on the leg side to five.

3 The number of on-side fielders behind the popping crease at the instant of the bowler's delivery shall not exceed two. In the event of infringement by the fielding side, the square-leg umpire shall call 'No Ball'.
NOTE: The umpire may elect to stand on the off-side, provided he informs the captain of the fielding side and the striker of his intention to do so.

Duties of the Umpires

45 Before the toss for innings, the Umpires shall acquaint themselves with any 'Special Regulations', and shall agree with both Captains on any other conditions affecting the conduct of the match; shall satisfy themselves that the wickets are properly pitched; and shall agree, between themselves on the watch or clock to be followed during play.

Notes
1 Apart from 'Special Regulations' other conditions of play within the framework of the Laws are frequently necessary, e.g. Hours of play, Intervals, etc.
2 The captains are entitled to know which clock or watch will be followed during play.

45 Experimental and domestic laws vary the conditions relating to decisions about weather, light and fitness of the ground. These local regulations should be studied carefully by captains and umpires. The umpires are the final judges.

46 Before and during a match the Umpires shall ensure that the conduct of the game and the implements used are strictly in accordance with the Laws; they are the sole judges of fair and unfair play, and the final judges of the fitness of the ground, the weather and the light for play in the event of the decision being left to them; all disputes shall be determined by them, and if they disagree the actual state of things shall continue. The Umpires shall change ends after each side has had one innings.

Notes
1 An umpire should stand where he can best see any act upon which his decision may be required. Subject to this over-riding consideration the umpire at the bowler's end should stand where he does not interfere with either the bowler's run up or the striker's view. The other umpire may elect to stand on the off instead of the leg side of the pitch, provided he informs the captain of the fielding side and the striker of his intention to do so.
2 The umpires must not allow the attitude of the players or spectators to influence their decisions under the Laws.
3 A code of signals for umpires is laid down in Notes to the relevant Laws; but an umpire must call as well as signal, if necessary, to inform the players and scorers.

46 The umpires are the sole judges of fair and unfair play. Their duties include:
1 Preventing unfair interference with the condition of the ball, e.g. raising the seam.
2 Preventing fieldsmen from distracting the striker whilst he is receiving the ball.
3 Preventing the players from damaging the pitch, e.g. a bowler making marks on the pitch to assist other bowlers.
4 Preventing the bowlers from intimidating the batsmen with fast short-pitched balls.
5 Preventing the waste of time by batsmen or fieldsmen, e.g. a bowler taking an unduly long time to bowl an over.
6 Preventing a player from unfairly and without justification leaving the field for the purpose of having a rub down or a shower whilst play is actually in progress.

Experimental laws not currently included in the coded Laws of Cricket are being used on a trial basis by various national cricketing associations. They deal with bowlers damaging the pitch (46, Note 4, (v)), intimidating batsmen (46, Note 4, (vi)) and wasting time (46, Note 4).
1 At the first offence the umpire warns the bowler, and informs the fielding captain and the other umpire.

4 FAIR AND UNFAIR PLAY

(i) The umpires are entitled to intervene without appeal in the case of unfair play, but should not otherwise interfere with the progress of the game, except as required to do so by the Laws.

(ii) In the event of a player failing to comply with the instructions of an umpire or criticising his decisions, the umpires should in the first place request the captains to take action, and if this proves ineffective, report the incident forthwith to the executives of the teams taking part in the match.

(iii) It is illegal for a player to lift the seam of the ball in order to obtain a better hold. In such a case the umpire will if necessary change the ball for one which has had similar wear, and will warn the captain that the practice is unfair. The use of resin, wax, etc., by bowlers is also unfair, but a bowler may dry the ball when wet on a towel or with sawdust.

(iv) An umpire is justified in intervening under this Law should any player of the fielding side incommode the striker by any noise or motion while he is receiving a ball.

(v) It is the duty of umpires to intervene and prevent players from causing damage to the pitch which may assist the bowlers.

(vi) The persistent bowling of fast short-pitched balls at the batsman is unfair if, in the opinion of the umpire at the bowler's end, it constitutes a systematic attempt at intimidation. In such event he must adopt the following procedure:

(*a*) When he decides that such bowling is becoming persistent he forthwith 'cautions' the bowler.

(*b*) If this 'caution' is ineffective, he informs the captain of the fielding side and the other umpire of what has occurred.

(*c*) Should the above prove ineffective, the umpire at the bowler's end must:

(i) At the first repetition call 'Dead Ball', when the over is regarded as completed.

(ii) Direct the captain of the fielding side to take the bowler off forthwith. The captain shall take the bowler off as directed.

(iii) Report the occurrence to the captain of the batting side as soon as an interval of play takes place.

A bowler who has been 'taken off' as above may not bowl again during the same innings.

(vii) Any attempt by the batsmen to *steal a run* during the bowler's run up is unfair. Unless the bowler throws the ball at either wicket (*see* Laws 26,

2 At the second offence, the umpire gives the bowler a final caution, informing the fielding captain and the other umpire of his action.
3 At the re-occurrence of the offence, the umpire calls 'dead ball', at which stage the over is regarded as completed. He then directs the captain of the fielding side that the bowler shall not bowl again in that innings. The umpire then reports the occurrence to the captain of the batting side at the next interval.
When a bowler takes an unnecessarily long time to bowl an over, the umpire at the bowler's end, after consulting with the other umpire, warns the bowler of the consequences if he continues to take too long; he informs the fielding captain and the other umpire of the warning. If the time wasting continues, he directs the fielding captain to remove the bowler from the crease at the end of the over in progress. He is not allowed to bowl again in the same innings. At the next opportunity the umpire informs the captain of the batting side and the controlling authority of the occurrence.

Note 2, and 27, Note 2), the umpire should call 'Dead Ball' as soon as the batsmen cross in any such attempt to run, after which they return to their original wickets.

(viii) No player shall leave the field for the purpose of having a rub down or shower while play is actually in progress.

5 GROUND, WEATHER AND LIGHT

(i) Unless agreement to the contrary is made before the start of a match, the captains (during actual play the batsmen at the wickets may deputise for their captain) may elect to decide in regard to the fitness of the ground, weather or light for play; otherwise or in the event of disagreement, the umpires are required to decide.

(ii) Play should only be suspended when the conditions are so bad that it is unreasonable or dangerous for it to continue. The ground is unfit for play when water stands on the surface or when it is so wet or slippery as to deprive the batsmen or bowlers of a reasonable foothold, or the fieldsmen of the power of free movement. Play should *not* be suspended merely because the grass is wet and the ball slippery.

(iii) After any suspension of play, the captains, or, if the decision has been left to them, the umpires, unaccompanied by any of the players, will without further instructions carry out an inspection immediately the conditions improve, and will continue to inspect at intervals. Immediately the responsible parties decide that play is possible, they must call upon the players to resume the game.

Appeals

47 The Umpires shall not order a Batsman out unless appealed to by the other side which shall be done prior to the delivery of the next ball, and before 'Time' is called under Law 18. The Umpire at the Bowler's wicket shall answer appeals before the other Umpire in all cases except those arising out of Laws 38 or 42 and out of Law 41 for run out at the Striker's wicket. In any case in which an umpire is unable to give a decision, he shall appeal to the other Umpire whose decision shall be final.

Notes

1 An appeal, 'How's that?' covers all ways of being out (within the jurisdiction of the umpire appealed to), unless a specific way of getting out is stated by the person asking. When either umpire has given a batsman 'Not out' the other umpire may answer any appeal within his jurisdiction, provided it is made in time.

47 All appeals for 'hit wicket', 'stumped' and 'run out' at the striker's wicket must be directed to the square leg umpire. All other appeals are made to the umpire at the bowler's end. The correct appeal is: 'How's that?' and this covers all circumstances. If an appeal specifies a particular method of dismissal, such as 'How's that for lbw?', the umpire can only rule on that specific way of dismissal. An appeal may be made up to the time that the ball is next delivered, even though that might be in the next over, or before the call of 'Time'.

Out

Cancel previous signal

2 The umpire signals 'Out' by raising the index finger above the head. If the batsman is not out, the umpire calls 'Not out'.
3 An umpire may alter his decision provided that such alteration is made promptly.
4 Nothing in this Law prevents an umpire before giving a decision from consulting the other umpire on a point of fact which the latter may have been in a better position to observe. An umpire should not appeal to the other umpire in cases on which he could give a decision, merely because he is unwilling to give that decision. If after consultation he is still in any doubt, the principle laid down in Law 46 applies and the decision will be in favour of the batsman.
5 The umpires should intervene if satisfied that a batsman, not having been given out, has left his wicket under a misapprehension.
6 Under Law 25 the ball is 'Dead' on 'Over' being called; this does not invalidate an appeal made prior to the first ball of the following 'Over', provided the bails have not been removed by both umpires after 'Time' has been called.

In theory the Laws of Cricket are exact. In print they are specific. They have to be interpreted, however, and since their interpreters, the umpires, are subject to human error, it is important that players, captains, managers and coaches co-operate to play the game according to both the letter and the spirit of the Law. In the early days of cricket the players were so fair minded that umpires were unnecessary.

The administrators of the game should make it clear to the players that cricket should be played in the best and most sporting manner. Participants should not try to take unfair advantage of indecision, weakness, lack of knowledge or ability in an umpire or an opponent.

It is not in the spirit of cricket to attempt to coerce or influence the umpire and spoil a game by:

Frivolous, repeated and antagonistic appeals when the appealer himself knows that the appeal is unwarranted.

Appeals from positions in the field where the appealer cannot make a fair judgement; for example, a square leg fieldsman cannot judge the worth of an lbw appeal.

Mass, pre-planned and intimidating team appeals.

Glaring at the umpire when an appeal is rejected.

Appealing for a specific method of dismissal after the general appeal of 'how's that' has covered all eventualities.

Continually 'niggling' or distracting the umpire by talking so that he will see decisions one way only or be flustered into giving a wrong decision.

Questioning the umpire's decision. A player is entitled to ask factual questions about the decision itself but he should never question it. It is generally accepted that the player leaves his factual questioning until he is off the field.

Making frivolous appeals against the light.

Wasting time unnecessarily.

Players should also try to help the umpire make decisions. They should:

Indicate when a disputed catch has not been taken cleanly but has hit the ground first.

Indicate when the ball has crossed the boundary and the umpire is unsighted.

If they have edged the ball finely and been caught behind the wicket, walk from the wicket to indicate that they have hit the ball. Opinions differ widely and strongly on this matter of 'walking'. Some batsmen believe that it reflects adversely on the ability of the umpire to make a decision. Others think that 'walking' is dangerous since the player who does not 'walk' has an advantage in disputed decisions over the player who does. Therefore, they ask, why should anyone walk and give the advantage to the opposition?

Indicate when they have crossed the boundary in making a catch.

It is also not in the spirit of cricket to try to coerce or distract the opposing players by:

Continually chatting to them or 'niggling' them whilst batting.

Moving in the field or making noises such as clapping or shouting whilst the ball is in play.

Threatening them with injury.

Deprecating their ability.

Index